CW01335250

Motorsport Going Global

MOTORSPORT GOING GLOBAL

The challenges facing the world's motorsport industry

Nick Henry, Tim Angus, Mark Jenkins
and Chris Aylett

palgrave
macmillan

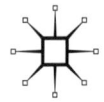

© Nick Henry, Tim Angus, Mark Jenkins and Chris Aylett 2007

Foreword © Max Mosley 2007

All rights reserved. No reproduction, copy or transmission of this publication may be made without written permission.

No paragraph of this publication may be reproduced, copied or transmitted save with written permission or in accordance with the provisions of the Copyright, Designs and Patents Act 1988, or under the terms of any licence permitting limited copying issued by the Copyright Licensing Agency, 90 Tottenham Court Road, London W1T 4LP.

Any person who does any unauthorized act in relation to this publication may be liable to criminal prosecution and civil claims for damages.

The authors have asserted their rights to be identified as the authors of this work in accordance with the Copyright, Designs and Patents Act 1988.

First published 2007 by
PALGRAVE MACMILLAN
Houndmills, Basingstoke, Hampshire RG21 6XS and
175 Fifth Avenue, New York, N.Y. 10010
Companies and representatives throughout the world

PALGRAVE MACMILLAN is the global academic imprint of the Palgrave Macmillan division of St. Martin's Press, LLC and of Palgrave Macmillan Ltd. Macmillan® is a registered trademark in the United States, United Kingdom and other countries. Palgrave is a registered trademark in the European Union and other countries.

ISBN-13: 978–1–4039–4289–0
ISBN-10: 1–4039–4289–7

This book is printed on paper suitable for recycling and made from fully managed and sustained forest sources. Logging, pulping and manufacturing processes are expected to conform to the environmental regulations of the country of origin.

A catalogue record for this book is available from the British Library.

A catalog record for this book is available from the Library of Congress.

10 9 8 7 6 5 4 3 2 1
16 15 14 13 12 11 10 09 08 07

Printed and bound in Great Britain by
Cromwell Press Ltd, Trowbridge, Wiltshire

Contents

Preface	vii
Foreword by Max Mosley	ix
Executive Summary: The Global Motorsport Industry	x
Motorsport 2035	xii
The Structure of *Motorsport Going Global*	xv

Part One	**The Global Motorsport Business**	**1**
	Defining the Business of Motorsport	1
	The Motorsport Value Chain	2
	Key Relationships	6
	Key Drivers	7
	Summary	9
	Mapping the Global Motorsport Industry	10
	Metrics for the Global Motorsport Industry	10
	Benchmarking the Global Motorsport Industry	13
	The Global Motorsport Value Chain	20
	Thinking About the Global Motorsport Industry	31
Part Two	**Frontrunners on the Global Starting Grid**	**33**
	Introduction: The Frontrunners	33
	The USA Motorsport Industry	34
	The UK Motorsport Industry	45
	The Japanese Motorsport Industry	56
	The German Motorsport Industry	63
	The Italian Motorsport Industry	73
	The French Motorsport Industry	83
	Conclusion: The Frontrunners	93
Part Three	**The Midfield**	**96**
	Introduction: The Midfield	96
	The Australian Motorsport Industry	96
	The Spanish Motorsport Industry	101
	The South American (Brazil and Argentina) Motorsport Industry	104
	The Mexican Motorsport Industry	108
	The South African Motorsport Industry	111
	Conclusion: The Midfield	115

Contents

Part Four	**Coming Through the Field**		117
	Introduction: Coming Through the Field		117
	The Malaysian Motorsport Industry		117
	The Gulf Region (Bahrain, Qatar, Dubai) Motorsport Industry		120
	The Turkish Motorsport Industry		122
	The Chinese Motorsport Industry		124
	The Czech Motorsport Industry		127
	Conclusion: Coming Through the Field		130
Part Five	**Motorsport Going Global**		132
	Globalization in Motorsport: A Driving Force for Change		134
	Consumption		137
	Supply		140
	Technology		143
	Motorsport Management		146
	Visions of the Future: *Motorsport Going Global*		148
	Motorsport Going Global: The Opportunity		155
	Summary		156
Appendix	*Global Motorsport Disciplines and Series*		157
Bibliography			159
Index			163

Preface

Motorsport Going Global reflects over a decade of research by ourselves on the motorsport industry and, for some of us, a lifetime of engagement in the sport. It deliberately seeks to blend the academic, business and consultancy knowledge that sits at the core of the service offer of Motorsport Research Associates (MRA), one of the world's leading consultancies on the business of motorsport, and of which we are members.

This book is avowedly "global" in its outlook; this is our start and end point. Nevertheless, the origin of any nuanced understanding of the global picture is to recognize your place in the world. Our place—and the place from which we view and write about global motorsport—is in the heart of the UK's Motorsport Valley®, one of the key production centers of world motorsport. We are proud of our small contribution to this world-beating location for the "business of winning" but recognize that our global search for material, data and information on the nascent motorsport industries of the world has inevitably been influenced by the origin from which we look outwards.

A critical part of the global analysis of motorsport provided in *Motorsport Going Global* has been derived from a set of key informant interviews within the industry. We owe a debt of gratitude to Gian Paolo Dallara, Peter Digby, Herb Fishel, David Richards, Sir Jackie Stewart and Pat Symonds for providing both their time and insightful commentary. Equally, Nigel Geach of Sports Marketing Surveys and Tim Bamford of the Australian Grand Prix Corporation have been invaluable in assisting our quest for data on the industry. Our most sincere thanks to all of you.

Finally, beyond those in the industry who have willingly given their time to us over the course of our many years of research, we thank Max Mosley at the FIA, the Motorsport Industry Association (MIA) for hosting our "book meetings" and Stephen Rutt and his colleagues at Palgrave Macmillan for, among other things, their patience.

"Ladies and Gentlemen, start your engines."

Birmingham, UK, October 2006   NICK HENRY
TIM ANGUS
MARK JENKINS
CHRIS AYLETT

Foreword

Ever since I first became involved in motor sport in the early 1960s the industry has been growing at an incredible rate. It has developed from something of a niche sport to the all-encompassing set of global championships that we see today.

The FIA Formula One World Championship has become the biggest annual sporting series in the world. In 2007, it featured 11 teams, running 22 drivers from 13 different countries participating in 17 races across 5 continents. It is also watched by hundreds of millions of viewers across the world and has certainly proved itself to be one of the few truly global sporting championships.

But with this global exposure comes a great amount of responsibility. This is why I am delighted that, with the introduction of new regulations and new technology, Formula One is set to contribute to the future development of the automotive industry.

Unlike other sports, the global power of Formula One is not just in entertainment but also in the way it can benefit everyday life. For instance, one future change will be to limit power not by the size of the engine but by the amount of energy the engine uses. This means that if teams want a power advantage they will have to get more out of a given quantity of energy or fuel. As such, research in the sport will go into fuel efficiency or getting the most from the least. If this is done well—which it will be in Formula One—it will make a huge contribution to the transport industry and the environment.

Other championship have also been progressing at an incredible rate. I have been delighted by the reaction to the FIA World Touring Car Championship since the FIA launched it as a global series in 2005. With races broadcast all over the world and a growing international fan-base, it demonstrates the huge reach of global motor sport and the industry that surrounds it.

Even in karting—the entry-level for motor racing—we have witnessed unexpected commercial growth. As many as five karting events, including the annual CIK-FIA World Championship, are now broadcast live across Europe. For an event that many see as the amateur level of the sport this is an impressive achievement and demonstrates that motor sport, in whatever form, can garner a strong following.

It all bodes well for an industry that I believe still has room to develop and reach its potential. And in order to do that it must overcome the many challenges that have been so succinctly examined throughout this book.

Max Mosley
President, Fédération Internationale de l'Automobile (FIA)

Executive Summary: The Global Motorsport Industry

This book defines the global motorsport business (Part One) and provides an overview of the 16 most significant national motorsport nations and regions of the world—the Global Starting Grid (Parts Two to Four). *Motorsport Going Global* ends with alternative visions of the future (Part Five) drawn from the insight of six international industry experts.

In 2005:

- we estimate the global motorsport industry to be worth some £50 billion, representing some 0.23 percent of global GDP;

- excluding kart tracks, the global stock of permanent paved circuits is estimated at approximately 600 circuits;

- official racing license holders number some 1 million around the globe;

- only four racing series can be argued to be truly global and these involved 22 constructors;

- there were 56 global motorsport events;

- on average, over 52 million viewers watched each Formula One Grand Prix; the equivalent figure for a World Rally Championship (WRC) event was 50 million viewers.

The Global Starting Grid can be segmented into the:

- **Frontrunners:** the six global frontrunners are the USA, UK, Japan, Germany, Italy and France. These nations dominate the economic development and racing history of motorsport. The frontrunners account for 75 percent of the world market, 91 percent of the global chassis constructors, virtually all of the supply chain of the vehicles racing in the global series and 41 percent of global racing events.

- **Midfield:** the five members (Australia, Spain, South America, Mexico, South Africa) have limited purchase on the global motorsport industry. The midfield accounts for less than 10 percent of the world market, 5 percent of global chassis constructors and 21 percent of global racing events.

- **Coming Through the Field:** these countries (Malaysia, the Gulf Region, China, Turkey and the Czech Republic) are in the process of building motorsport industries. With minimal global market share and 5 percent of global chassis constructors, a 25 percent share of global racing events provides a critical access point into global motorsport.

Visions of the Future: The experts strongly agree on the trend toward globalization and the opportunities it presents. Marked differences remain as to where the motorsport industry currently sits on the road to globalization. These center on whether the industry will develop in a way that is production or consumer led.

In the consumer-led model motorsport is seen as a mechanism by which a wide array of products is presented to particular consumer segments. In this model, motorsport is a brand development mechanism that allows products and services to develop their brand awareness and associations by utilizing the particular connotations associated with, and provided by, motorsport.

The production-led business model is driven by those seeking to develop the motorsport industry through the creation of racing vehicles that promote and develop particular aims. In this model, the process is initiated by the creation of particular motorsport technologies or a series (production), which then leads to participation and subsequent consumption of the ensuing events. Two different mechanisms can commence this process—original equipment manufacturer (OEM)/regulation driven (for example, Audi R10 diesel Le Mans Prototype) and entrepreneurial/emerging-markets driven (for example, CF2000 or VW Polo Racing, both in China).

Motorsport companies are facing the greatest opportunity in their history with the development of new, fast-growing global markets, from which to buy or in which to sell. This opportunity is coupled with a global requirement for alternative, more efficient and less carbon-intensive automotive technologies to be developed.

The industry is standing on the threshold of an opportunity the like of which it has never encountered before—can it seize this or will it stumble? Who will force themselves to the front of the Global Starting Grid, and gain the checkered winner's flag of *Motorsport Going Global*.

Motorsport 2035

As Healey Zipper sat down to drink a cold juice and take his caffeine supplement, the integrated communication system in his wrist band gave a short, almost inaudible, bleep. He casually pressed one of several small buttons around the band, which energized the wall facing him into a full-width display.

"Ah," he murmured, "at last, the Hydrosport Updates."

Pressing another button, the wall became a menu of articles. Healey used the small pad on his wrist band to navigate around the different items gathered under the bold heading Hydrosport Updates—February 15th 2035.

The features were dominated by his favorite race series WHCR (World Hydrogen Car Racing). He quickly sought out any information on his favorite driver Nigella Manful; she was currently driving for the Chinese-based Hydropec team and leading the World Series. Having scanned through to see how preparations were going for the next race to be held at the Karthikeyan indoor stadium (named after the first Indian F1 champion) in Chennai, India, he decided to see what else was worth viewing. For amusement he quickly selected the "historic racing" section and chuckled as he viewed a short video clip. It featured a driver called Michael Schumacher (apparently a German from the old Euroland of 30 years ago), who was enjoying a celebratory run in an old car called a Ferrari. Fitted with an internal combustion engine, embarrassingly the car had broken down after a few laps, spraying oil on the rather fractured tarmac of the original Hockenheim circuit in Germany.

"Amazing," he mused, "to think they actually raced these vehicles. I guess they'd probably see it like people racing steam-powered cars back in their day."

Skimming through the historic racing items he also noted a new museum being built in the UK local region. It was being funded by the West Asian Commission (which covered most of the old Euroland) as part of a series of initiatives commemorating past industrial achievements. The museum was to be built on the original site of the Silverstone race circuit (now a massive housing estate for commuters to the city of Milton Keynes).

Naturally, it would have a selection of cars featuring mainly internal combustion engines, but also including some more modern hybrid cars, and the first fuel cell racer, which had been developed nearby. Apparently, the museum also planned to recreate something called a "wind tunnel". Healey had no idea what this was but the text explained that these had been the very latest thing back in the late 20th and early 21st centuries, costing hundreds of millions of renminbi and requiring teams of highly skilled individuals to make them operate effectively. Each team would spend hours and hours testing out aerodynamic designs in these technological caverns, each searching for the merest of improvements to their lap times, which could mean the difference between success and failure.

As he drifted back to imagine what these past days may have been like he was suddenly startled by another bleep and an image of his friend Yardie Madly appeared on the wall.

"Hi Healey, have you seen Hydrosport yet?"

"Yep, just going through it now."

"Did you see the bit about the new synthetic wheel compound that Hydropec are planning to use for the next race?" asked Yardie enthusiastically.

"No," replied Healey, who just didn't share Yardie's interest in the technical side of things.

Like most racing fans Healey was interested in following his driver and the spectacle of the race. WHCR events used a common hydrogen fuel cell format and a common body profile, which was aerodynamically defined to ensure all the cars would be able to race close together and pass each other without losing speed. The only differences between the cars, which were raced in large, banked, indoor stadia, was the color used to identify the teams (each team had two cars), the strategies they employed regarding recharging the fuel cells and also the compounds used on the solid wheels.

WHCR had evolved from the NASCAR racing series in the USA. Originally, this had been a rather parochial race series, gradually expanding from the southern states of the USA into Mexico, Canada, South America and, eventually, parts of Asia and Europe. The growth of this format had been helped by the merging of the global automotive makers into three large conglomerates: China Auto (which included Toyota, DaimlerChrysler and BMW); Tata (which included Renault, Honda and Ford); and Shanghai Auto (which included GM-VW-Fiat-Ferrari). This new world order among automakers had led to the collapse of the previously dominant Formula One global race series.

In 2010, the rights to the F1 series had been sold to a Russian consortium of bankers, who packaged it for sale to a mobile communications company for exclusive use on a new range of personal communication devices. These had flopped and fatally damaged Formula One.

"Did you read about this museum they're going to build near Milton Keynes?" asked Yardie. "My dad says this area was once known as Motorsport Valley and was the center of race car design and manufacture, before it all went to China."

All WHCR cars use a common format of a fuel cell platform that surrounds the driver. This advanced structure, created from moulded carbon and plastic composite using the latest mass-production manufacturing techniques, made them very light and strong, as well as highly cost-effective.

China is the global center for this cutting-edge technology. They also developed fuel cell expertise and dominance, cleverly gaining their knowledge from technical alliances with the American and European carmakers that once led the world.

Their composite expertise for racing was gained from working closely with firms in the original UK-based motorsport cluster. Unsurprisingly, many of these businesses had been too preoccupied trying to out-compete their neighbor down the road to recognize the significance of what was then known as the "Far East." It seemed so far away and lacking in advanced technical or engineering skills at the time.

Healey found this all very hard to believe but decided not to challenge his friend on his father's clearly mistaken memories. He was more interested in checking out the digital feeds for the next WHCR race, which would allow him to pit his own driving skills against those of his hero, Nigella, in real time. What could be more exciting than that?

So what does the future hold for the global motorsport industry?

In this book we present a framework that helps to define and understand the distinctive nature of this emerging and highly specialized global industry. We break it down into a series of nine core elements and consider how these exist currently on a region by region basis across the globe. We go on to consider how they may evolve in the future. Each element is connected to other parts of the system but, fundamentally, for the whole sector to continue to work there has to be an audience, an end customer. People must want to watch or participate in motorsport for the system to operate. Perhaps it is this simple fact that is sometimes forgotten in the politics and glamor that epitomize global motorsport.

The imaginary scenario involving Healey, depicted above, presents a vision of a global motorsport industry that is more centralized than the fragmented structure we see today. Its center of gravity has moved to Asia, particularly China, whereas today the industry gravitates around Europe and North America. The scenario implies the technological base will shift to hydrogen fuel cells, which mirrors longer-term expectations in the automotive industry. Technology becomes standardized in the form of global 'one-make' series, which deliver identical cars racing for different teams and drivers (and suggesting that technological differentiation and the role of the auto manufacturers is reduced).

Of course, the one certainty of any such scenario is that it will be wrong. There are many highly credible views of the future that create a very different picture to the one we outline. Such debates are invaluable in informing future decisions. It is important, however, to recognize that, no matter what may happen, the industry *will* change. It will change in a way that will advantage some businesses, regions and technologies and seriously disadvantage others.

Our point, in putting this picture forward, is to recognize the very inevitability of change and to stress that, while change is inevitable, the basic principles that underpin the current motorsport industry model will remain.

First, there will continue to be a demand to view as a spectator or participate in all sports, including motorsports. Second, there will always be a supply of technology that allows the spectacle to be created, enjoyed and also distributed. While all the other elements of event creation and management, sponsorship, car construction, regulation and supply are critically important, they are nothing without these first two principles. This provides our basis for considering how the global motorsport business operates and, more importantly, how these principles of supply and demand (production, participation and consumption) are currently defined and how they may develop in the future.

This leads us to consider a number of potential hypotheses for the industry and the conditions necessary to bring them about. For example, many of the trends in information technology and digital media suggest that sport-based entertainment may become far less regional than in the past. While there is undoubtedly a global demand for motorsport, this materializes in many different forms in different geographic regions. With the spread of formats such as NASCAR beyond North America and the development of global series such as WTCC and GP2 it is possible that motorsport will become more standardized on a global platform.

In contrast, with perhaps a few exceptions, the supply side of car construction and event management is currently a very localized activity. With regional clusters in the UK, USA and Italy (among others), one view is that this knowledge will inevitably disseminate and leak geographically and allow the motorsport manufacturing industry to spread anywhere in the world. The alternative view suggests that this specialized technical knowledge and expertise is "sticky" and does not move or spread easily. Such logic implies we may see the development of new competing regional clusters, which excel in new emergent technologies (for example, fuel cells), and which replace the established motorsport business centers of today.

The Structure of *Motorsport Going Global*

The scenario of Motorsport 2035 and its inherent drivers of change is, of course, conjecture; but it is well-informed conjecture. It starts from a detailed analysis of the nature and scope of the global motorsport industry as it is today, and this forms the first four parts of the book.

Part One—The Global Motorsport Business—provides the conceptual and analytical framework, the Motorsport Value Chain, through which the book subsequently analyzes the motorsport industries of the world's nations. Part One ends with an overview of what we mean, as of today, when we talk of a "global motorsport industry." The overview includes a benchmarking of the scale of motorsport industries around the world (the "Global Starting Grid") and this acts as the key organizational framework for the remainder of the book.

Parts Two, Three and Four run through the Global Starting Grid, which comprises these motorsport industries. The analytical framework of the Motorsport Value Chain is used to provide quantitative and qualitative description of each national or regional industry. These are segmented into the Frontrunners (Part Two), Midfield (Part Three) and Coming Through the Field (Part Four).

In Part Five—Motorsport Going Global—we pull together our conclusions. We draw on our conceptual model, our previous empirical analysis of the global industry and the substantive interviews and opinions gleaned from industry commentators and leaders, to consider in what directions the global motorsport industry might be heading by 2035.

PART ONE

The Global Motorsport Business

Part One introduces our understanding of the global motorsport business: what it is comprised of, how to analyze it and how to measure it. We outline motorsport as an economic sector comprising both an engineering industry and the business of sport. The dynamic complexity of the sector and its economic relationships are captured within the concept of the Motorsport Value Chain. Part One ends with a current overview of the global motorsport industry. The value chain heuristic is then applied throughout the remainder of the book to benchmark the Global Starting Grid of national motorsport industries.

Defining the Business of Motorsport

We define motorsport broadly as competitive racing by equivalent machines on a frequent basis, on designated tracks and circuits. These machines include, for example, motorcycles, moto-cross, karts, historic cars, drag, open-wheel, single-seat, sports, GT, Formula Ford, touring cars, rallying, sports compact, CART, IRL and Formula One. Racing is organized around series, championships, events and meetings arranged by promoters, circuits and racing clubs at all levels (professional race and amateur sport).

The industry comprises:

- "motor": meaning the provision (construction and preparation) of cars and bikes;

- "sport": meaning the infrastructure including clubs, circuits, promotion, insurance and so on that is needed to participate in, spectate, or view the sport;

- a sport that is part of the leisure and entertainment industry; and
- a marketing opportunity for sponsors.

Within this book, we concentrate on *four-wheeled* motorsport.

The Motorsport Value Chain

The motorsport business involves a complex system, which comprises a shifting network of relationships between all of the elements described above. These elements and business relationships can be conceptualized within a value chain framework.

Figure 1.1 depicts the Motorsport Value Chain. This framework:

- provides a classification scheme for all firms within the motorsport sector; and
- illustrates the interrelationships between the firms as a motorsport supply chain, which culminates in the delivery of a motorsport event to an audience.

The typology used in Figure 1.1 provides an overview of the typically diverse series of organizations and activities that form the motorsport industry. While some larger firms may have a portfolio of activities that place them in more than one category, within each cell of the value chain, examples are provided of specific types of firm that fit into the following categories.

Constructors

A constructor is a firm that creates a motorsport vehicle of some sort. In this sense it is the "OEM" of the motorsport sector. This would be typified by the Formula One and World Rally Championship (WRC) constructors, such as Ferrari, Honda, Prodrive and Mitsubishi Ralliart. In the USA, examples of constructors would be Panoz in Champcar and Roush in NASCAR. In South America, Berta is a constructor of touring cars, while in Italy, both Tatuus and Dallara are well-known single-seat constructors. In the UK, Lola typifies this group.

Constructor Suppliers

These represent the specialized suppliers to the constructors, which allow them to create the final vehicle (in automotive terms the Tier 1 and Tier 2 companies).

Figure 1.1 **Motorsport Value Chain**

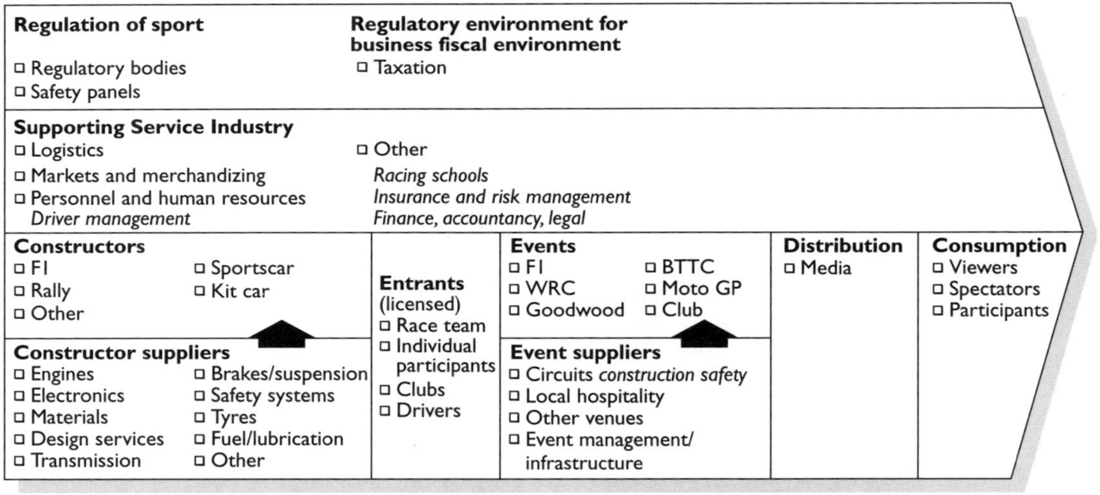

Regulation of sport
- Regulatory bodies
- Safety panels

Regulatory environment for business fiscal environment
- Taxation

Supporting Service Industry
- Logistics
- Markets and merchandizing
- Personnel and human resources
- Driver management
- Other
- Racing schools
- Insurance and risk management
- Finance, accountancy, legal

Constructors
- F1
- Rally
- Other
- Sportscar
- Kit car

Constructor suppliers
- Engines
- Electronics
- Materials
- Design services
- Transmission
- Brakes/suspension
- Safety systems
- Tyres
- Fuel/lubrication
- Other

Entrants (licensed)
- Race team
- Individual participants
- Clubs
- Drivers

Events
- F1
- WRC
- Goodwood
- BTTC
- Moto GP
- Club

Event suppliers
- Circuits construction safety
- Local hospitality
- Other venues
- Event management/infrastructure

Distribution
- Media

Consumption
- Viewers
- Spectators
- Participants

Source: MRA 2005

They include suppliers of engines (Cosworth, Hendrick Motorsports); aerodynamic components (Fondmetal Technologies, B3 Technologies); gearboxes (Xtrac, SADEV); tires (Goodyear, Pirelli) and fuel and lubricants (Shell, BP and Castrol). Similarly, there are the specialist services, for example, the technical consultancy provided by organizations such as MIRA, Ricardo and ORECA.

Entrants

An entrant is the organization that enters and is responsible for racing or rallying the vehicle. It includes individuals and racing teams. In some cases, the entrant is the same organization as the constructor, but this allows for the identification of this distinct area of activity with examples of firms that are purely entrants, including Manor Motorsport of the UK, DAMS of France and Andretti Green in the USA.

Events

This category covers those organizations that manage and operate racing events, either as a series or individually. It includes racing clubs, such as the BRSCC in the UK; operations within manufacturers, such as Renault UK motorsport; and specialists such as Formula Palmer Audi. Commercial promoters include NASCAR in the USA or companies such as BMP or SRO, which may promote many series.

Event Suppliers

These include all the components necessary for an event to take place, including circuits (for example, Silverstone or Goodwood in the UK, Hockenheim in Germany and Daytona and Indianapolis in the USA) and specialist suppliers in, for example, construction, catering and related hospitality.

Distribution

These include all media, specialist and general, concerned with dissemination of events, through radio, TV, Internet and press coverage more generally. In the UK Haymarket is a leading print media specialist, while in the USA Fox and

NBC/Turner televise NASCAR. RTL in Germany is the leading TV distributor of F1 on TV, while RAI and TF1 perform the same role in Italy and France respectively.

Consumption

This identifies the groups involved in consumption of the events, either as spectators, participants, viewers, listeners or readers of the various media.

All of the above groups represent a simplified yet relevant supply chain, which extends from car components to the motorsport event itself. Additionally, there are a number of other groups that influence and provide input to all of the aforementioned organizations.

Supporting Service Industries

These firms provide critical services across the industry in specialized areas such as insurance (THB Clowes, UK), personnel management (IMG, USA, or CSS Stellar, UK), market research (MRA and Sports Marketing Surveys), freight, logistics, legal, marketing, finance, sponsorship recruitment and other areas, like racing schools (Henry Morogh Racing School, Italy; Richard Petty Driving Experience, USA).

Regulation

Regulatory and sanctioning bodies such as the FIA, CIK, CSAI, ACCUS, SCCA, FIM or ACO are influential at all levels in the sport and thereby the industry. They define the "manufacturing" specification of the vehicles and also influence the nature of the delivery and format of events. Similarly, their safety regulations influence manufacturers, component suppliers and circuits.

Regulatory and Fiscal Environment for Business

In addition to the specific regulatory environment of motorsport, organizations operate within the broader regulatory environment that affects all businesses. An obvious example from Formula One would be the differing legal framework for tobacco sponsorship across different nations.

Key Relationships

Preliminary analysis of the Motorsport Value Chain highlights a complex *system of interdependence* in which each category is dependent on the others for its continued development. The simple schematic in Figure 1.1 highlights that:

- events need to attract coverage and spectators through the quality of the motorsport spectacle;
- this requires consumer interest in the sport, which needs to be generated (and includes amateur participation);
- events need to attract teams and racers and vice versa;
- entrants need events to showcase their (and their sponsors') products (and to participate);
- constructors need suppliers in order to access the highly specialized and diverse technologies needed to create a motorsport vehicle.

Nevertheless, the linkages and relationships within Figure 1.1 are *highly variant upon the nature of the motorsport event.* For example, compare a NASCAR event to a World Championship F1 Grand Prix, or a one-make Formula Nippon event to a club-racing day.

We have concluded that there are two essential primary categories that are core to the sustainability of the business system of motorsport:

- *constructors*, who effectively bring together the diverse range of technologies, products and services to create a vehicle. Constructors build vehicles with which to compete. As businesses, they act as "system integrators", drawing on a components and performance engineering supply chain, which crosses into other economic sectors. Entrants purchase these vehicles to compete in motorsport events, and their ability to do so allows them to raise sponsorship as a revenue source.
- *events*, which provide a marketable spectacle of vehicles and drivers competing. Motorsport events are part of the global sports-event industry that relies, primarily, on revenues generated by TV coverage and spectators. Event promoters act as integrators, relying on specialist service companies—circuits, driver management, insurance, media, etc.—to deliver the event product, in a similar way to constructors who deliver vehicles.

Both *constructors* and *events* are, therefore, jointly responsible in delivering the end points in two distinct, yet complementary, parts of the system. Simply put, this is the unique relationship between "motor" and "sport" within the term "motorsport", as depicted in Figure 1.1.

Key Drivers

Following the Motorsport Value Chain outlined above, we can then identify a specific series of inputs and outputs that represent the *main drivers of the industry* (see Figure 1.2). It is the ability to sustain and maintain a balanced flow between input and output that provides the dynamic for the ongoing development of the industry.

It can be seen that a wide and diverse range of funding sources currently underpins the industry. An outcome of this diversity is potential for conflicting objectives, such as the need for short-term returns required by equity finance and the longer-term, sustained brand development of automotive manufacturers.

Figure 1.2, importantly, identifies the key drivers of the industry and where potential vulnerabilities exist. If any one part of the system breaks down, it will negatively affect the other elements. Similarly, any change in the balance of flows will, in turn, shift the balance of outputs expected or required.

For example, we can reflect on the *historical* development of motorsport from wealthy gentleman drivers to the Gold Leaf Team Lotus of 1968, the venture capital investments of the 1990s, the new non-tobacco global sponsors and the constant "ins and outs" of the OEMs over time. From such reflection, a richer understanding of the dynamics of the sport and its position within global business strategy becomes apparent.

Moreover, a particular flow of investments can be demonstrated through further market *segmentation* of the value chain. In different contexts the flow of funds and outcomes become radically different.

If context is defined, for example, in terms of the potential *audience* for events (see Figure 1.3), then we can see that those events that deliver a global audience will secure funding from sources that reflect global brand strategies and international media rights. In contrast, events delivering a predominantly *national* audience have funding reflecting national or regional marketing strategies, perhaps even from local agencies delivering very localized benefits. At the grass roots tier, *club*-level funding is more likely to be from private memberships and localized interest groups. The benefits are located more in the enjoyment of participants than any significant viewing audience.

Critically, while these three layers have distinctly different characteristics, they are also *interdependent* in that they are reliant on the movement of individuals through what has been referred to as the "staircase of talent." Here, drivers, co-drivers, mechanics and engineers progress through the various levels. While each involves quite distinct types of funding and benefits, they are integrated as a basis for progression through to the premier levels of motorsport. In Figure 1.3 these linkages are illustrated as a *flow of knowledge and skills between levels*.

This framework emphasizes the critical importance of national motorsport events and the vital, yet often distant, linkage between the local amateur clubs

Figure 1.2 Motorsport Value Chain: Key Drivers

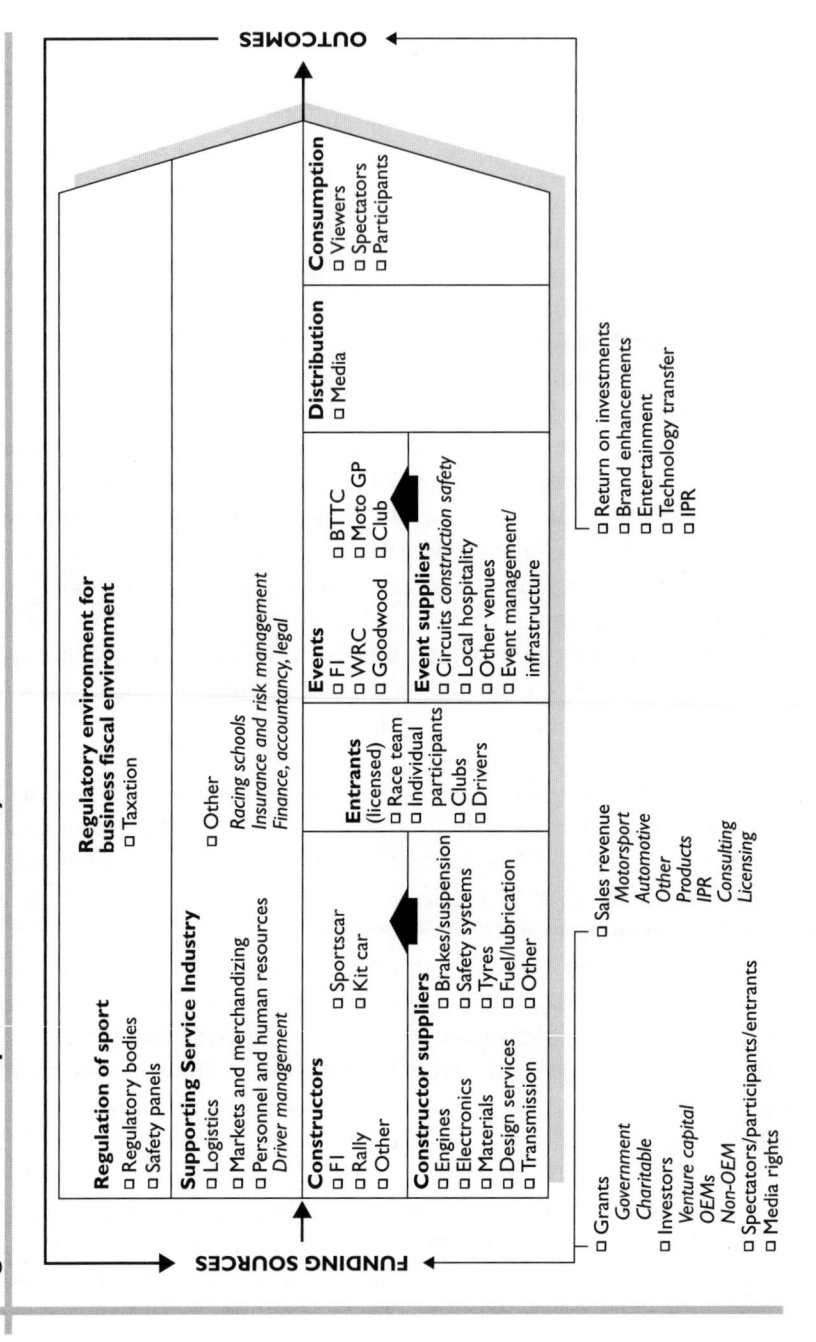

FUNDING SOURCES →

- Grants
  - Government
  - Charitable
- Investors
  - Venture capital
  - OEMs
  - Non-OEM
- Spectators/participants/entrants
- Media rights

Regulation of sport
- Regulatory bodies
- Safety panels

Regulatory environment for business fiscal environment
- Taxation

Supporting Service Industry
- Logistics
- Markets and merchandizing
- Personnel and human resources
- Driver management
- Other
  - Racing schools
  - Insurance and risk management
  - Finance, accountancy, legal

Constructors
- F1
- Rally
- Other
- Sportscar
- Kit car

Constructor suppliers
- Engines
- Electronics
- Materials
- Design services
- Transmission
- Brakes/suspension
- Safety systems
- Tyres
- Fuel/lubrication
- Other

Entrants (licensed)
- Race team
- Individual participants
- Clubs
- Drivers

Events
- F1
- WRC
- Goodwood
- BTTC
- Moto GP
- Club

Event suppliers
- Circuits construction safety
- Local hospitality
- Other venues
- Event management/infrastructure

Distribution
- Media

Consumption
- Viewers
- Spectators
- Participants

- Sales revenue
  - Motorsport
  - Automotive
  - Other Products
  - IPR
  - Consulting
  - Licensing

- Return on investments
- Brand enhancements
- Entertainment
- Technology transfer
- IPR

→ OUTCOMES

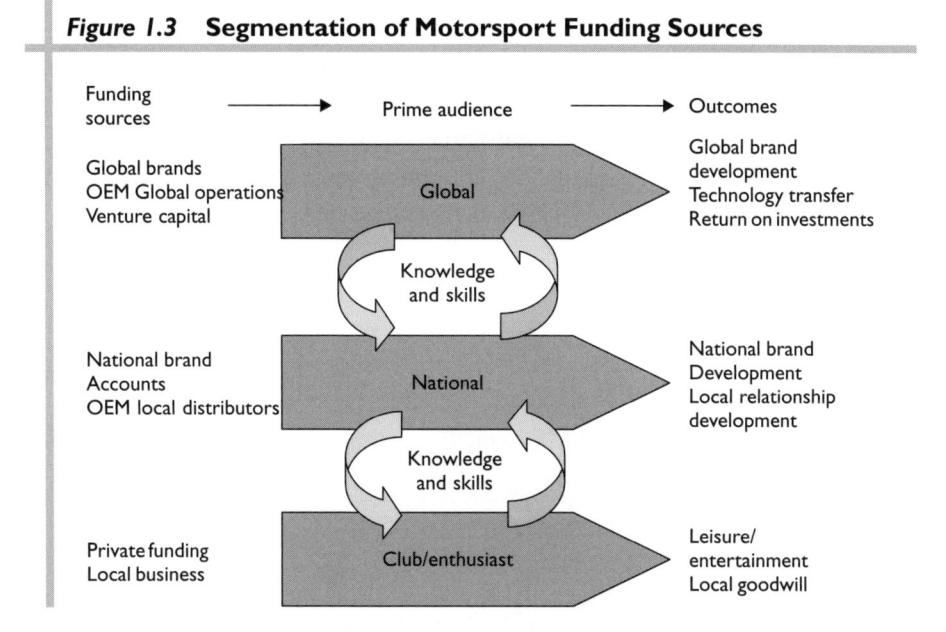

Figure 1.3 **Segmentation of Motorsport Funding Sources**

Funding sources	Prime audience	Outcomes
Global brands OEM Global operations Venture capital	Global	Global brand development Technology transfer Return on investments
	Knowledge and skills	
National brand Accounts OEM local distributors	National	National brand Development Local relationship development
	Knowledge and skills	
Private funding Local business	Club/enthusiast	Leisure/entertainment Local goodwill

and global series such as F1 and WRC. These national events provide a proving ground for talent, where drivers or technicians, marketing or PR specialists can hone and develop their skills. Similarly, those who leave global series can stay in the industry within the national series, thereby sharing their knowledge and experience with the new talent emerging through the system and continuing the process of value creation.

Figure 1.3 highlights the point that funds, in the main, move through each individual tier and not between them. Virtually *no funds trickle down* to the grass roots from the better-financed and -resourced tiers above, suggesting a real weakness in the sustainability of the current model over a given period of time.

Summary

In summary, the global motorsport business comprises:

- a motorsport value chain combining both motor and sport, with vital interdependence between the two;
- key elements of the value chain—the constructors and events;
- the range of funding that drives the industry and its business outcomes, which has changed over time and can be segmented;
- participation in the sport, which remains a critical component of any growth in the motorsport industry.

Mapping the Global Motorsport Industry

The following section provides a unique overview of the Global Starting Grid of the motorsport industry. Using the Motorsport Value Chain framework, a series of both quantitative and qualitative measures have been devised that allows the scale and scope of the global industry to be outlined systematically. We apply these measures throughout the remainder of the book to analyze national motorsport industries. The following overview of the global motorsport industry comprises three parts:

- Metrics for the Global Motorsport Industry;
- Benchmarking the Global Motorsport Industry; and
- The Global Motorsport Value Chain.

Metrics for the Global Motorsport Industry

To devise a series of measures of the global motorsport industry required a prior definition of the industry. Earlier in Part One we have outlined the major elements of the industry—motor and sport—against which indicators of activity may be aligned. So, for example, for any standard analysis of an economic sector or industry, measurements such as value of turnover, percent of gross domestic product (GDP) or numbers of firms or people employed can be utilized.

Similarly, in terms of analysis of sporting activity, standard indicators such as numbers of participants and/or events (and/or spectators) can be used, as can the level and quality of facilities (for example, number and size of pitches and number of sporting clubs).

Standard indicators of industry and sport, then, can be created for motorsport (see Table 1.1). For example, in Table 1.1, we use turnover value and percent of GDP as an indicator of the size of the motorsport industry, estimating that the global motorsport industry was worth some £50 billion in 2005 and 0.23 percent of global GDP. Nevertheless, even simple indicators such as these are hard to collate for the motorsport industry. Worldwide, only a handful of studies of national industries have ever been undertaken using rigorous research methods—see the Bibliography.

International indicators need to be suitable across nations. In terms of measurement of the sport of motor racing, participation, for example, can be measured through numbers of official competition license holders registered with their national associations. Nevertheless, the effectiveness of this licensing process can vary considerably from country to country. Our studies have shown that there may be as many as three times the number of unlicenced motorsport participants as licenced at any one time. Similarly, within international motorsport, the numerous types of racing and other activities means that facilities vary considerably.

Table 1.1 **Estimated Metrics for the Global Motorsport Industry, 2005**

Indicators	Global measure in 2005
Total value of annual motorsport turnover for engineering and services	£50b
Motorsport turnover as % GDP	0.23
Permanent paved circuits (including ovals over ¼ mile but not kart)	600
Competition license holders	1,000,000
Global chassis constructors (F1, WRC, WTCC and A1GP)	22
Number of racing series	
— Global	4 (F1, WRC, WTCC, A1GP)
— Regional	10 (Champcar, IRL, NASCAR, GP2, FIA GT, LMS, 4 FIA Regional Rally)
Global motorsport events (F1, WRC, WTCC and A1GP)	56 across 29 countries
Average F1 viewing figures per race event (Sports Marketing Surveys)	52.5 m
Average WRC viewing figures per event (wrc.com)	50.1 m

In Table 1.1 we have chosen to use the indicator of permanent paved circuits, including ovals, over ¼ mile in length. This does not include short tarmac ovals under ¼ mile in length, any non-tarmac circuit (shale oval), any type of kart track, drag strip, hillclimb or sprint venue but it does provide virtually the only reliable and available (through research work) international circuit indicator, and one which implies a certain level of economic investment. Globally, of course, the number of circuits of all types, all surfaces, permanent or temporary and for all types of motorsport, undoubtedly numbers many thousands.

Contrary to most data requirements in motorsport research, data available on spectatorship or, more precisely, viewing is more readily available. Clearly, in global motorsport, the financial relationship between levels of sponsorship and viewing audiences is a key business driver. This has necessitated the collection of viewing figures for the global championships as evidence of sponsorship value. Table 1.1 uses the official figures available for Formula One and the World Rally Championship.

In outlining our choice of indicators of the global motorsport industry, we have not articulated thus far our understanding of "global" as applied to this particular industry. For example, in the sporting regulations for motorsport, the world regulating body, the FIA, is very clear on when it will define a championship as a "world" championship or series in contrast to a national set of races. The FIA states that a series or championship may not use the word "world" in its title unless it "include(s) events taking place on at least three *continents* during the same season" (International Sporting Code, S24, Part d, Section i).

On this basis, we argue that there are only four truly global racing championships (Formula One, World Rally, World Touring Car and A1GP) with the latter two only coming in to existence in 2005. This will prove to be an important statement.

While it is clear that there is growing internationalization of motorsport taking place (increasing numbers of countries involved in motorsport; increasing numbers of championships and participants crossing national borders; increased broadcasting of national championships to overseas audiences), our argument is that the world of the truly global motorsport industry (where motorsport is practiced, supplied and broadcast across at least three continents) is still rarefied and highly selective. So, for example, NASCAR may have a financial worth on a similar scale to that of Formula One but we must define it as a regional, rather than global, championship as it is practiced across several nations but only within one continent (see Table 1.1).

Furthermore, within our definition of global—utilizing the value chain analysis discussed earlier to identify the qualitative significance of constructors and events—current global chassis constructors comprise a mere 22 firms and global events number 56 in total (see Table 1.1).

In summary, data is very hard to collate on the global motorsport industry but a number of simple indicators—utilizing the value chain to adapt standard indicators—can be created to measure the size, scale and scope of the industry. In turn, these indicators reflect the three critical domains of the sector, which are: supply of cars, participation in the sport of racing and consumption of the racing spectacle.

Table 1.1 shows that:

- in 2005, we estimated the global motorsport industry to be worth some £50 billion, representing some 0.23 percent of global GDP;

- excluding kart tracks, the global stock of permanent *paved* circuits is estimated at approximately 600 circuits;

- official racing license holders number some 1 million around the globe;

- only four racing series can be argued to be truly global and these, in 2005, involved 22 constructors;

- there were 56 global motorsport events in 2005;

- on average, over 52 million viewers watched each Formula One Grand Prix in 2005; the equivalent figure for a WRC event was 50 million viewers.

Benchmarking the Global Motorsport Industry

Following our measurement of the global motorsport industry in its entirety, the global metrics template can be applied to benchmark the comparative size and significance of what we have estimated to be the largest 16 national or regional motorsport industries—the Global Starting Grid (see Figures 1.4–1.11).

Figure 1.4 provides estimates of motorsport turnover value for 16 countries or world regions from the largest, the USA, through to the smallest, the Czech Republic.

First, not surprisingly, Figure 1.4 identifies a group of *frontrunner* countries for the global motorsport industry. These are led by the USA, which, at £13 billion annual turnover, is twice the size of that of any of its competitors. UK, at £6 billion annual turnover, lies second, followed by Japan, then Germany and Italy.

While both France and Australia have industries of similar size (£1.5 billion), we would view France as the last of the frontrunner countries. Its industry has a history of success in global motorsport (for example, Formula One and WRC), whereas the scale of Australia's industry is mostly directly related to its domestic and regional market.

We are, then, adding a further dimension to our understanding of "global" related to success in global motorsport markets (first and foremost the global championships identified in Table 1.1) and evidence of the associated processes of economic globalization (for example, levels of export and overseas investment in motorsport). Detailed analysis of the frontrunners comprises Part Two of the book.

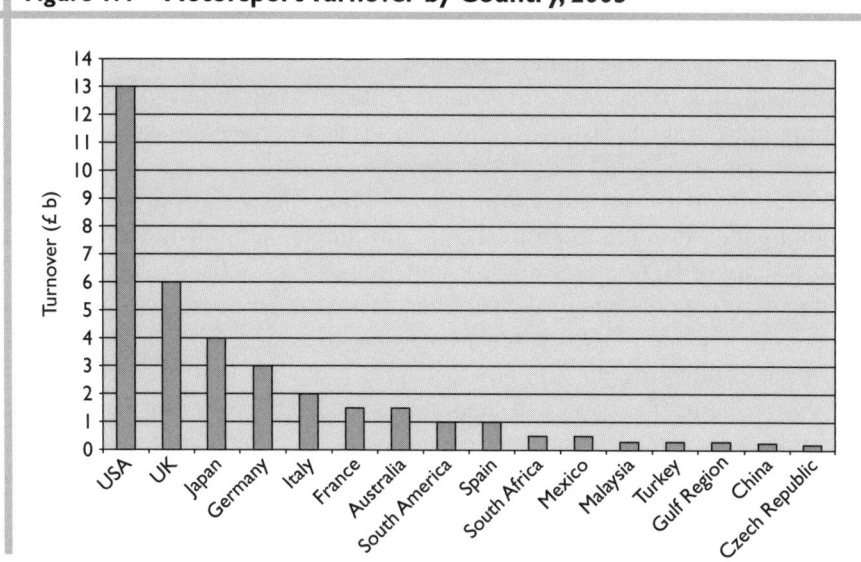

Figure 1.4 **Motorsport Turnover by Country, 2005**

Australia heads up the *midfield* tier, which includes regional markets (South America, £1 billion) as well as countries (Spain, £1 billion; Mexico, £0.5 billion and South Africa, £0.5 billion). A number of these are identifiable as having a long national heritage of motorsport, which has been translated into moderate size sectors. Detailed analysis of the midfield, using that material and data that does exist, comprises Part Three of the book.

The remaining countries and regions comprise what we have termed as the *coming through the field* tier of the global starting grid. Malaysia, Turkey and the Gulf Region achieve turnover values of £0.3 billion, China £0.25 billion and the last entrant on our grid of 16 is the Czech Republic. Analysis of this latter group—notwithstanding the parsimony of data—comprises Part Four of the book.

Overall, an initial glance at the Global Starting Grid reveals a stable set of six Frontrunner countries, which have—between them—dominated the history of international motorsport. The boundary between the Midfield and Coming Through the Field is rather more porous, with great potential for considerable swapping of places. For example, in the last decade the potential for Malaysia and South Africa to move up the grid through their inclusion within the international supply chains of motorsport has been argued in various forums. As yet, they have made limited headway and, arguably, are looking nervously in their mirrors at the "new kids on the grid" from the Gulf Region and China.

Several further conclusions about the global industry may also be drawn through closer inspection of Figure 1.4. First, taking the figure for the global motorsport market given in the table above, £50 billion, this highlights that almost half of world turnover is currently accounted for by three countries alone: USA, UK and Japan.

Second, on the one hand, the true global reach of the industry can begin to be discerned—each of the top three countries is placed in a different continent—with national representation in Africa, Australasia, the Gulf Region and China. On the other hand, the limited extent of the claim to "globalness" might be argued with our 16 nations representing almost 75 percent of global turnover. An important strategic issue for future plans is that neither Russia nor India, for example, has yet entered the grid of 16.

While Figure 1.4 provides a picture of scale, Figure 1.5 provides further insight by measuring the significance of any single nation's motorsport industry as a share of GDP; the result is a shuffling of the Global Starting Grid.

Of particular note, then, is the performance of the UK, confirming the industry as not only one of global scale but, also, of national importance. Leader of the pack following the UK now becomes Malaysia (0.45 percent GDP)—possibly reflecting the concerted support provided to the sector by the Malaysian government as part of its broader economic development strategy—then followed by Australia and South Africa. While the overall average figure for turnover expressed as a percentage of GDP is in the order of 0.17 percent, the UK figure is almost triple (0.5 percent). China is ranked last but, clearly, with

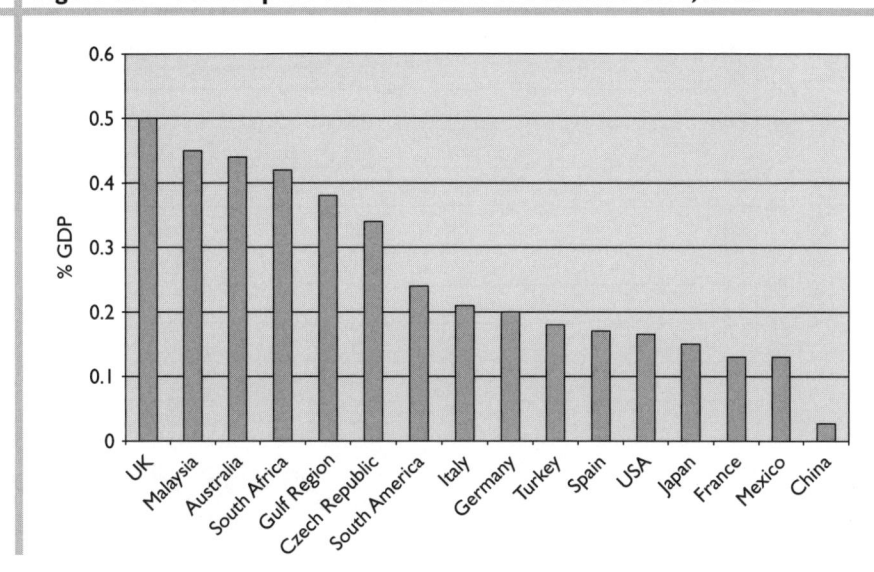

Figure 1.5 Motorsport Turnover as % of National GDP, 2005

[Bar chart showing % GDP for: UK (~0.50), Malaysia (~0.45), Australia (~0.44), South Africa (~0.42), Gulf Region (~0.38), Czech Republic (~0.34), South America (~0.24), Italy (~0.21), Germany (~0.20), Turkey (~0.18), Spain (~0.17), USA (~0.17), Japan (~0.15), France (~0.13), Mexico (~0.13), China (~0.02)]

substantial potential if its industry raised its share of GDP to the international average of 0.17 percent.

A further simple indicator of the penetration of motorsport is racing infrastructure—in this case meaning the number of permanent paved racing circuits (see Figure 1.6). The first point to note is the overall low *average* number of such circuits across nations. Globally, the number hovers around the 600 mark (see Table 1.1) with the USA accounting for close to half of the global stock. While this numerical dominance by the largest market in the world is not surprising, the level of investment in circuits should be seen as a reflection of the spectator and service orientation of motor racing in the USA. Events are geared to creating a full "day out for all the family" within a clearly understood leisure market dynamic.

South America (Brazil and Argentina) and Mexico have a disproportionately large number of circuits, which may be explained by the racing history of these countries. One example is the strong government support of Argentinean motorsport in the 1950s (associated with the international emergence of the legendary driver Fangio). Similarly, the UK's high position reflects a century-old tradition of participation and success in (international) motorsport.

When the number of circuits is graphed as a proportion against population (Figure 1.7), a more nuanced description of racing culture can be seen. The USA, with its dominant oval racing culture, remains evident, as does the "home of motorsport", the UK.

Australia has a long and proud tradition of domestic racing in contrast to the relatively low rates of participation often commented upon in Germany. The newcomer China barely registers, as car ownership, let alone racing participation,

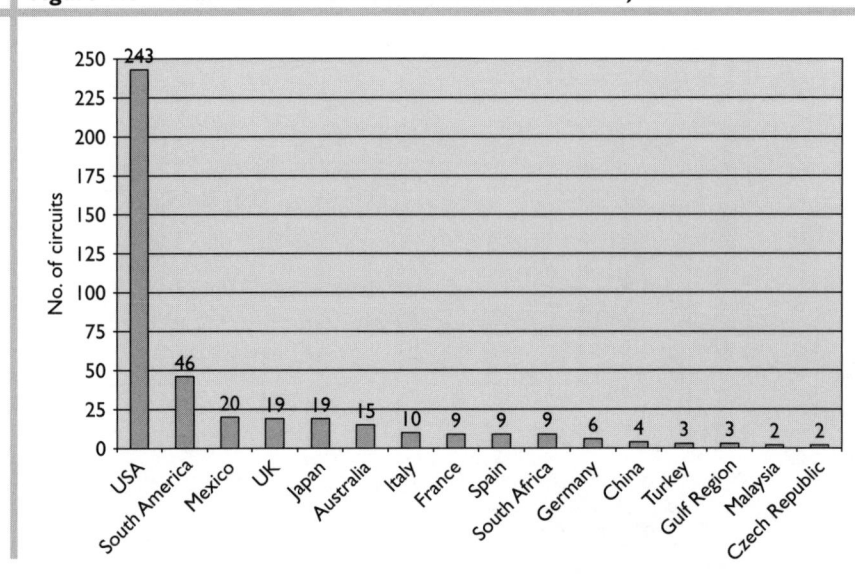

Figure 1.6 **Number of Permanent Paved Circuits, 2005***

Country	No. of circuits
USA	243
South America	46
Mexico	20
UK	19
Japan	19
Australia	15
Italy	10
France	9
Spain	9
South Africa	9
Germany	6
China	4
Turkey	3
Gulf Region	3
Malaysia	2
Czech Republic	2

* Permanent paved circuits including ovals over ¼ mile in length. This does not include short tarmac ovals under ¼ mile in length, any non-tarmac circuit (shale oval), any type of kart track, drag strip, hillclimbs or sprint venue.

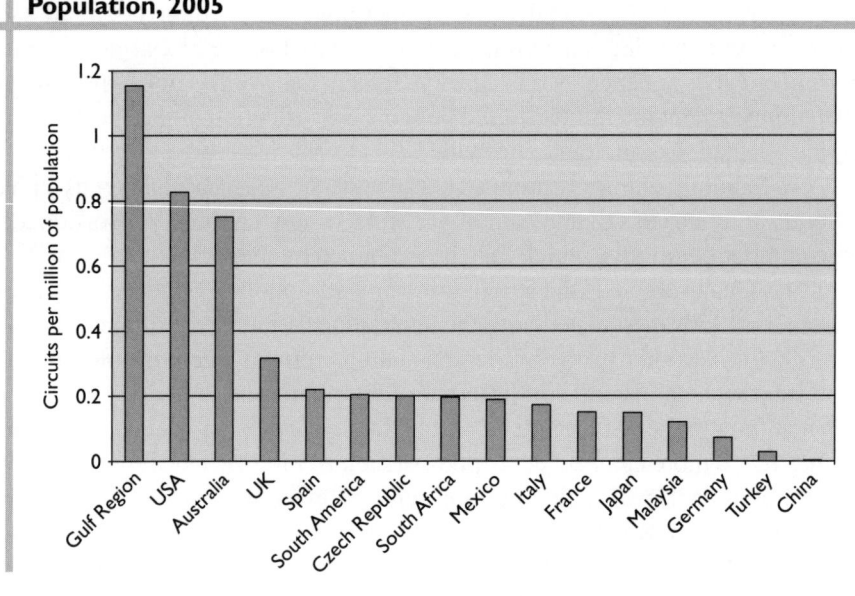

Figure 1.7 **Number of Paved Permanent Circuits per 1 Million of Population, 2005**

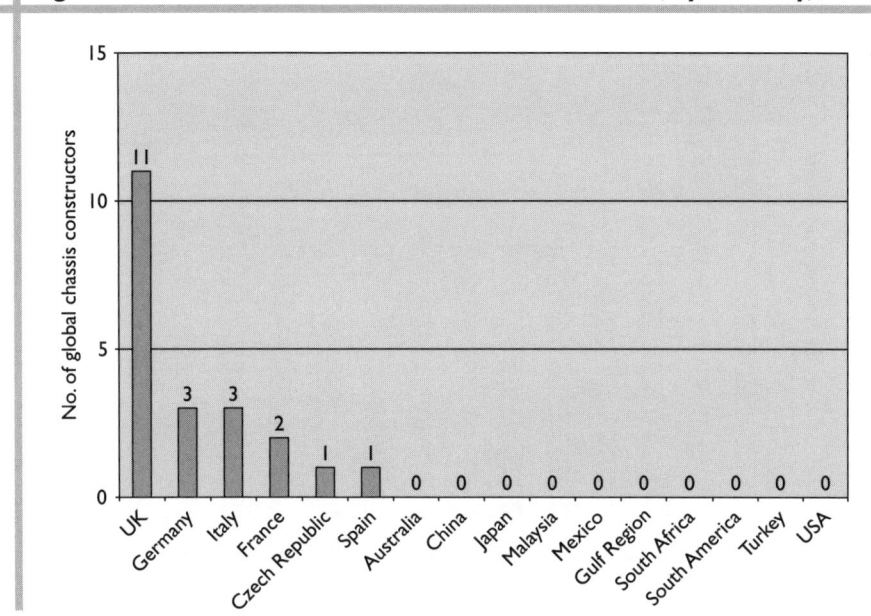

Figure 1.8 **Number of Global Chassis Constructors, by Country, 2005**

[Bar chart showing: UK 11, Germany 3, Italy 3, France 2, Czech Republic 1, Spain 1, Australia 0, China 0, Japan 0, Malaysia 0, Mexico 0, Gulf Region 0, South Africa 0, South America 0, Turkey 0, USA 0]

has still to build any significant percentage share among its immense population. This is in clear contrast to the evident enthusiasm of the oil-rich countries of the Gulf Region to build state-of-the art circuits.

Number of circuits is, of course, related to motorsport participation but international figures for participation remain very scarce. In Table 1.1 we are able to estimate numbers of official license holders worldwide at 1 million but national breakdowns are difficult to access and often reflect differing racing and licensing regimes.

Figures that have been accessed for the Frontrunner countries include, for example, over 30,000 license holders in the UK, 54,000 in France and a mere 10,000 in Germany. Additionally, we know that numbers of participants in the USA (a broader figure than license holders) measures some 443,000 individuals.

Figure 1.8 provides a striking graphic of the concentration of global chassis constructors. Of the 22 constructors who provide cars to the four global series, 11 (or 50 percent) are based within the UK. Germany and Italy each have three global constructors and, in total, four Frontrunner countries account for 19 of the 22 constructors (or 86 percent).

Midfield countries Spain and the Czech Republic are notable in hosting a global constructor in 2005 with the remaining constructor, Sauber, based in Switzerland.

In contrast to the supply of cars, hosting of global series events is a more global pattern (see Figure 1.9). Of the 56 events that took place in 2005, Frontrunner

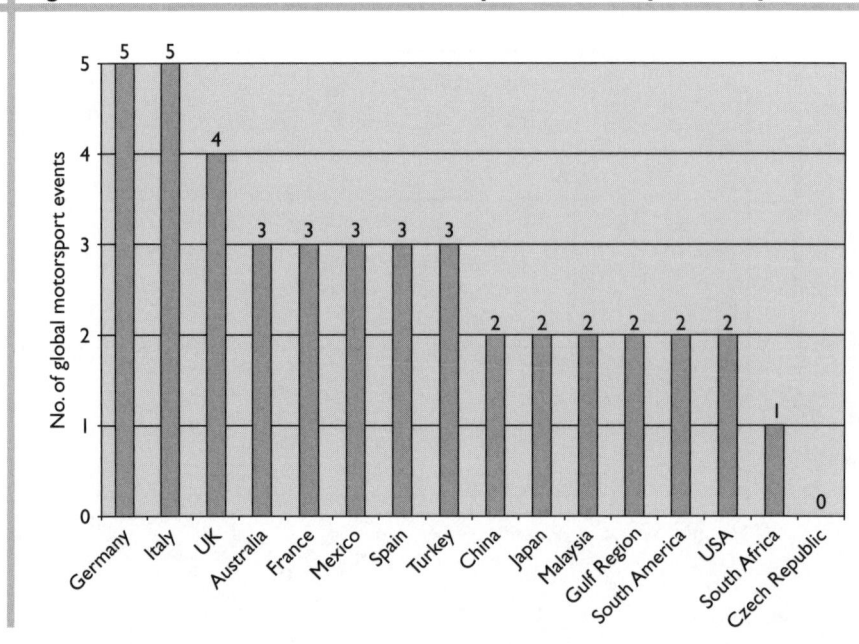

Figure 1.9 Number of Global Motorsport Events, by Country, 2005

Germany 5, Italy 5, UK 4, Australia 3, France 3, Mexico 3, Spain 3, Turkey 3, China 2, Japan 2, Malaysia 2, Gulf Region 2, South America 2, USA 2, South Africa 1, Czech Republic 0

countries accounted for 21 (38 percent) of global events. Headed by Germany and Italy, who each hosted five events in 2005, the domestic orientation of the world's largest industry, USA, is reflected in its hosting only two global events.

The countries of both the Midfield (for example, Australia and Spain) and Coming Through the Field (for example, Turkey and Malaysia) are comparatively well represented. Overall, it is also the case that our Global Starting Grid accounted for only 71 percent of global events.

A final comparator indicator to assist in mapping the global industry is that of "viewing" figures. Figures 1.10 and 1.11 map the (incomplete) viewing figures publicly available for the global championships by nation in 2005. Only the two global championships of WRC and Formula One publish their figures and, in 2005, only those figures for the countries shown were available through public sources of data.

For Formula One, Figure 1.10 confirms what we might reasonably expect. Italy, with possibly the strongest brand in world motorsport (Ferrari), shows its passion for Formula 1 while German viewing figures remain high relative to low participation rates (see Figure 1.7). As a group, the Frontrunner countries dominate viewing but with some notable exceptions. Spanish viewing figures for F1 are third largest in the world but there remains a glaring gap in Formula 1's global presence—extremely low viewing figures in the world's largest motorsport market, the USA. In contrast, China is now the fifth largest viewing market

Figure 1.10 Average Viewing Figures, for Global Grid, for F1 Race Event, 2005

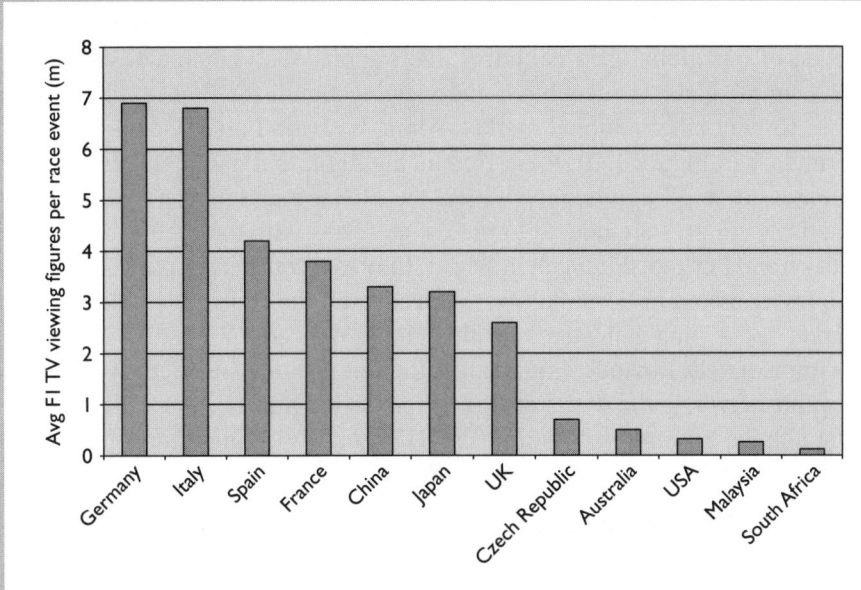

Source: Sports Marketing Surveys

Figure 1.11 Average Viewing Figures, for Global Grid, World Rally Championship, 2005

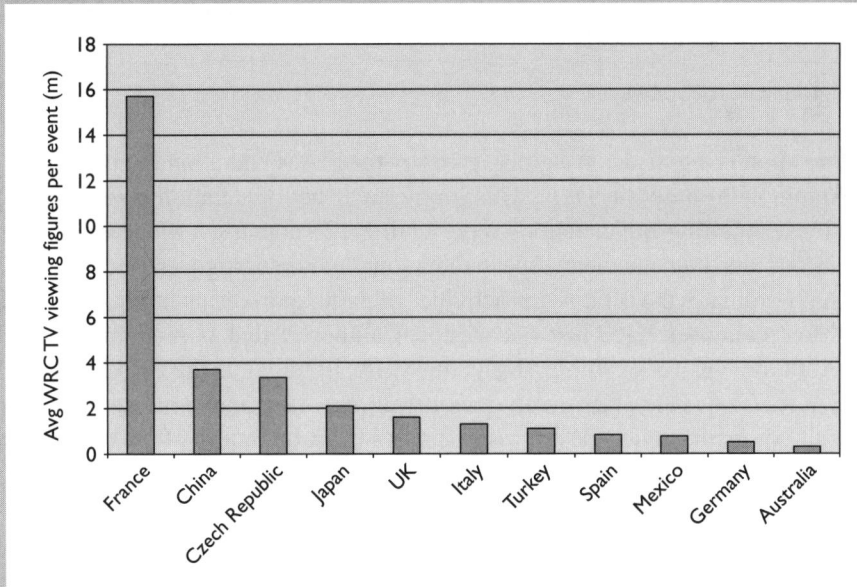

Source: www.wrc.com

despite its lack of global car production or racing culture. (This figure, in absolute terms, is of course distorted by the sheer magnitude of the potential Chinese market in comparison to other nations.)

For the World Rally Championship, figures for 2005 are only available for eleven of our global grid countries and regions. One notable absentee is the USA. Immediately noticeable is the viewing figure for France which dwarfs those for any other national market. Along with the Italian viewing figure for Formula 1 in Figure 1.10, these figures highlight that national racing cultures continue to be of significance within the global marketplace: and, of course, that these cultures are related to racing success—with the French constructors Citroen and Peugeot dominant in World Rally in recent years (and as with Ferrari to a lesser extent in Formula One). Once again, the sheer potential size of the market sees China gain status for this global indicator although there remains no immediately obvious explanation for the position attained by the Czech Republic. Overall, the segmentation of the Global Starting Grid is less clear cut although the Frontrunner countries still dominate viewing figures to an extent.

The Global Motorsport Value Chain

Use of the Motorsport Value Chain (see Figure 1.1) allows further analysis and description of the motorsport industry on a global scale. In this section, each element is studied in turn and applied to the industry on the global scale. The result is a comprehensive description of the scope and geography of the global motorsport industry that complements the benchmarking undertaken above.

Regulation of Sport

Motorsport is regulated on a global basis by the FIA (Fédération Internationale de l'Automobile) based in Paris. This long-established Federation consists of 213 national motoring organizations representing 125 countries. Member organizations or clubs manage their respective national motorsport governance, while the FIA co-ordinates the actions and activities of motorsport on an international basis.

Most countries have just one national authority that is recognized by the FIA. In the UK, for example, this is the MSA, in Italy it is the CSAI and, in the USA, ACCUS. One of the main demonstrations of such governance is the issuing of competition licenses to residents and track operators of the country that the authority represents.

Supporting Service Industry

The supporting service industry for motorsport comprises logistics, marketing, driver management, insurance, racing schools, media, legal, sponsorship, hospitality, etc. Clearly, those supporting service industries that serve global motorsport series like F1 and WRC have a greater global footprint. Examples of these include marketing firms like WWP and KHP, and driver management companies like IMG and CSS Stellar. It remains the case, however, that the majority of these services are national in nature.

Constructors

Our definition of global motorsport identifies four "global" motorsport series (F1, WRC, WTTC and A1GP). In total, in 2005, 22 chassis constructors built cars for these series; all were European-based, with 20 located within our Frontrunner countries and, of those, 11 (50 percent of the total) were located in the UK (see Table 1.2).

During 2005 only four countries hosted a Formula One chassis constructor. Of the ten F1 constructors, six (60 percent) were based in the UK with a further two located in Italy. In 2006 an 11th constructor joined the series, the UK-based, but Honda-backed, Super Aguri.

From 2008, a 12th constructor, the UK-based Prodrive, will join the F1 grid. As an independent franchise, Prodrive will buck the ten-year trend of OEM-owned constructors and join Williams as the only independent constructor still owned by the original founders.

In 2005 there were six constructors involved in the World Rally Championship. Two of these (Citroën and Peugeot) were French-based, three (50 percent) were UK-based (Ford, Mitsubishi and Subaru) and one was based in the Czech Republic (Skoda). Due to the OEM-related nature of the cars used in WRC, there are no non-OEM-related constructors involved in the WRC. Some OEMs, however, use independent motorsport specialists to prepare their cars. In 2005, Skoda, Peugeot, Mitsubishi and Citroën maintained OEM-owned (though in the case of Mitsubishi, geographically separate) constructors, while Ford and Subaru utilized independent UK-based motorsport specialists to construct their cars.

In 2007, Peugeot, Skoda and Mitsubishi will no longer be involved in WRC as constructors, leaving Ford, Subaru and Citroën (with Suzuki, Mitsubishi and Hyundai rumoured to be set to join the series in 2008).

The other two series we term as "global" are the World Touring Car Championship (WTCC) and A1GP. In 2005, the WTCC became a global series by visiting three continents, with five OEM-backed constructors supplying saloon cars to the field. All these constructors were Europe-based. Two of the five were run from OEM-led facilities (SEAT in Spain and BMW in Germany), with the remainder utilizing outsourced specialists such as the use of the UK-based RML by Chevrolet.

The A1GP series began in late 2005 as a Nations Cup of one-make single-seat chassis constructed by UK-based Lola and engines from Zytek of the UK.

Table 1.2 **The Global Motorsport Chassis Constructors, 2005**

Chassis constructor	Racing series	Location
Ferrari	F1	Italy
Minardi	F1	Italy
Renault	F1	UK
Sauber	F1	Switzerland
Midland	F1	UK
Williams	F1	UK
McLaren	F1	UK
Toyota	F1	Germany
BAR Honda	F1	UK
Red Bull Racing	F1	UK
Subaru	WRC	UK
Mitsubishi	WRC	UK
Citroën	WRC	France
Peugeot	WRC	France
Skoda	WRC	Czech Republic
Ford	WRC	UK
BMW	WTCC	Germany
SEAT	WTCC	Spain
Ford	WTCC	Germany
Chevrolet	WTCC	UK
Alfa Romeo	WTCC	Italy
Lola	A1GP	UK

While we classify USA-based NASCAR as a *regional* series, it has a turnover and income close to that generated by Formula One. All the chassis constructors for NASCAR are USA-based, even for the Japanese-owned Toyota. In the main, the steel spaceframe cars with composite bodies are built by the USA-based teams that have the franchise to run them, supported by an intricate infrastructure of domestic suppliers. Engine and transmissions have been developed over many years and are particular to the USA. Constructors/teams like Roush, Hendricks, Dale Earnhardt, Evernham and RCR predominate.

Arguably the most important single-seat regional series are the USA-based CART Champcar and IRL championships. In 2005, UK-based Lola constructed all CART chassis but, from 2007, all chassis will be supplied by USA-based Panoz, to a one-make chassis specification.

From 2005 to 2007, constructors supplying the IRL are the Italian company Dallara, and the USA-based Panoz. In 1999, after the CART-IRL championship split, CART and IRL still had a strong European constructor presence (Italy's Dallara, UK's G-Force, Reynard and Lola) and a small American presence from Riley and Scott. In summary, the last decade has seen a substantial shift in chassis construction within the frontrunner countries away from the UK, to Italy and then the USA.

Within lower-ranking regionally based single-seat racing, from 2005, the F1 supporting F3000 series was replaced by GP2. GP2 is a one-make chassis/engine formula with chassis being constructed by the Italian constructor Dallara.

Other regional single-seat categories highlight the increasing move to OEM-controlled one-make formula, where OEMs award a large run of racing car production to one race car specialist. For example, Renault has invested heavily in their "World Series by Renault" and Formula Renault 2000. The Italian company Tatuus constructs all the chassis for the various national Renault 2000 championships, while Dallara constructs all World Series by Renault chassis. Another example of an OEM-supported one-make single-seat championship is Formula BMW. BMW awarded its Formula BMW Junior single-seat control formula chassis contract to Mygale in France. Formula BMW started in Germany but is currently expanding into championships in other nations, including a championship in Asia.

In the USA both IRL and CART have supporting championships closely resembling the concept of the F1-supporting GP2. The IRL has the Infiniti Pro series, a controlled formula with chassis constructed by Dallara in Italy. Champcar's GP2 equivalent in the USA is the Formula Atlantic series that utilizes Swift chassis constructed in the USA.

Other single-seat series feeding in to Infiniti Pro and Atlantic include the Formula 2000 series, which has UK-based (but USA-owned) Van Diemen International as the key player. Formula Mazda is another control formula that utilizes Van Diemen chassis, which are built in the USA by its parent company Elan Motorsport Technologies.

Formula 3 (F3) is a key regional and national single-seat series with strong bases in Europe, Japan and South America. In F3, the Italian manufacturer Dallara has been dominant for over a decade in most championships around the world, with some competition from other Europe-based constructors like Lola, SLC, Martini and the Japanese-based Dome. Below F3, in nationally based single-seat championships such as Formula Ford, the USA-owned, but UK-based, Van Diemen International faces a challenge from British compatriots Ray, and French manufacturer, Mygale. Overall, within lower-ranking regionally based single-seat racing, the competitive strength of Italian constructors sits to the fore with UK, USA and French constructors in the mix.

Across the globe, there are a number of regional and national saloon championships. The most significant is the German-based DTM championship, catering for highly powered saloon "silhouettes" with major German-based OEM support. Opel (until 2005), Mercedes and Audi compete in the DTM, utilizing various German-based, and OEM-related (sometimes owned), constructors.

Below the DTM are nationally based saloon car championships including the UK's BTCC, French Supertourisme, Argentinean TC2000, Australian V8 Supercar and many USA-based stock car championships. The majority of the constructors for these series are domestically based. For example, the British-based BTCC at one stage involved nearly all the major manufacturers in the market—Alfa Romeo, Audi, Peugeot, Volvo, Ford, Honda, Renault, Toyota, Nissan and Vauxhall. Most cars were designed and built in the UK. In the late 1990s, the BTCC slumped as its competitiveness and changing regulations priced manufacturers out of the market. Since 2005 the series saw increasing OEM involvement from Vauxhall and SEAT, with successful privateer entries from MG-Rover and Honda, the majority utilizing UK-based constructors.

Another strong domestic saloon car series is Australia's V8 Supercar series. Just two OEM brands race in this series, Ford and Holden, and UK specialists like Prodrive and Triple 8 build chassis in Australia for the series alongside domestic manufacturers. It is worth noting the continuing reach of UK companies, with Ford Performance Vehicles (FPV) owned jointly by Prodrive and Ford, and Holden Special Vehicles (HSV) by UK-based Tom Walkinshaw.

In terms of the regionally and nationally significant sportscar series like Grand-Am, FIA GT and ALMS/LMS, most constructors are European or USA-based. In the USA-based Grand-Am, most constructors are domestic, with the occasional international interloper, such as Italy's Picchio. The USA-based ALMS has constructors principally from Europe (Audi, Lola, Zytek), while its European equivalent, LMS, and the Le Mans race itself, also has a European-based set of constructors (Lola, Zytek, Audi, Courage, Dallara, Pescarolo).

The FIA GT series is for production-based sportscars and the constructors tend to reflect the country of origin of the original road-going vehicle. There are exceptions to this, and where non-domestic constructors are utilized in GTs the UK has a strong reputation (Prodrive, RML).

Other than these high-profile national saloon and single-seat series (like F3, the BTCC or Australian V8 Supercar) there is a plethora of national series in countries around the world catering for the club racer or enthusiast competitor. Where these are based on production road cars then constructors are likely to be locally based. When there are club-based series for single-seat cars like FF1600, or stock cars like those that predominate in the USA, then a slightly more global supply chain can be discerned.

The global presence of a series like FF1600 operating at club level in many countries tends to reflect the location of those constructors where the series first originated. For example, the British-based Van Diemen chassis is popular in many club FF1600 series throughout the world but there are also many examples of local chassis in this formula in domestic markets (for example,

Swift in the USA). In addition, the presence in many countries of series modeled on the USA oval-based stock car series (for example, the UK-based SCSA) tends to reflect the location of some of the chassis constructors for that market, though again with local variations.

Constructor Suppliers

The main valued component under the constructor supplier part of the global value chain is the engine. Table 1.3 records engine supply to the F1 constructors in 2005, with all suppliers based in the Frontrunner countries.

One striking aspect of Table 1.3 is that, while the history of independent engine specialists has been weakened substantially by the OEMs, the relationship between parent country and country of engine build is not clear-cut.

F1 engine building has increasingly been brought in-house by the OEMs either setting up specialist engine-building facilities from scratch (Toyota in Germany) or expanding on existing OEM competition engine-building facilities (Renault, Honda, BMW) based in the OEM parent country. A third solution is to buy an existing engine specialist, as did Ford with Cosworth and Mercedes Benz with the Ilmor engine-building specialist, now renamed Mercedes Benz High Performance Engines—both operations are based in the UK.

At the time of writing, substantial changes are occurring in the F1 engine supply chain following legislation changes from the FIA. Cosworth have ceased to supply any F1 teams for the first time in over 30 years. There are now no independent F1 engine suppliers, as all teams are now supplied by OEMs.

In the WRC, engine building is undertaken mostly by the OEMs supporting the series, sometimes with the support of domestic engine specialists. For example, in 2005, Peugeot and Citroën engines were built in France by the OEM competition departments, with the help of domestic specialists (for example, Pipo Moteur). Mitsubishi engines were built by the OEM in Japan, Subaru's engines by UK-based Prodrive and Ford's by UK-based MSport.

Turning to the international single-seat series below F1, from 2003 onwards, all engines in CART Champcar are supplied by the UK-based Cosworth. In 2005, all engines for the Champcar-supporting Formula Atlantic were supplied by TRD but, from 2006, Cosworth supplied these.

In IRL, Honda utilize the UK-based Ilmor Engineering in co-ordination with USA-based Honda-owned race engine specialist HPD. Until GM pulled out of IRL in 2005, UK-based Cosworth built their engines and Toyota (who also pulled out of IRL in 2005) used engines built by the USA-based and OEM-owned TRD. The IRL supporting Infiniti Pro Series has engines built by the UK-based MEL concern.

Looking at the European-based regional single-seat series, many of these series are one-make chassis and therefore have the same engine in all chassis

Table 1.3 **Formula One Engine Suppliers, 2005**

Constructor	Engine supplier	Engine supplier location
Ferrari	Ferrari	Italy
Minardi	Cosworth	UK
Renault	Renault	France
Sauber	Ferrari	Italy
Midland	Toyota	Germany
Williams	BMW	Germany
McLaren	Mercedes High Performance Engines	UK
Toyota	Toyota	Germany
BAR	Honda	Japan
Red Bull Racing	Cosworth	UK

from the same engine builder, usually designated by the OEM involved in the series. For example, the F1-supporting GP2 series has engines built by the French Mecachrome-owned, but Swiss-based, Mader engine builders.

In lower one-spec single-seat formulae like Formula BMW, the OEM again stipulates an engine builder, in this case the German-based Schnitzer organization. Outside one-spec single-seat formulae like F3 and Formula Ford, domestic engine builders fulfill the market. For example, in F3 two of the best-known suppliers are the British-based Neil Brown and the German-based Spiess, and in Formula Ford, the UK's Minister concern.

In international sportscar racing there are many suppliers. UK engine builders like Prodrive, Zytek, Cosworth, AER and EDL have a strong presence alongside Italian companies such as ORAL Engineering, the French Mecachrome firm, German companies like Audi Sport and the Japanese firm Mugen. In 2005, for international saloon series like the DTM, engine supply was provided by the German-based AMG (Mercedes) and Spiess (Opel), and British-based Neil Brown (Audi).

The American stock car championships, like NASCAR, utilize a mainly USA-based engine supply chain. Engine builders like TRD, Evernham, Hendrick, Arrington Manufacturing and Penske-Jaspar predominate, although latterly NASCAR has been accessing UK engine-building expertise (MEL, Ilmor Engineering and Cosworth) in order to gain a competitive edge and access F1 engine-building expertise. The vast majority of USA engine builders are domestic only and concentrate on the generic American V8 engine, for which there is a very large home market.

In regional or national saloon car series utilizing USA-type V8 engines (UK's SCSA, Argentina's Stock Car, Australia's V8 Supercar), competitors also use the USA engine supply chain in these respective countries.

One area of constructor supply where it is possible to spot a very strong area of supplier strength is drivetrain components, particularly gearboxes. Here the UK enjoys a strong lead, though it is facing increasing competition below F1 from firms like the French-based SADEV. Many F1 teams make their own gearboxes, but they rely on gearbox components and design from UK firms like Xtrac.

In WRC, all gearboxes come from the UK-based gearbox specialists, Xtrac, Ricardo and Hewland. In fact, most of the international motorsport series, right down to F3, will be supplied by one of these three UK companies. The main exception is the USA market, where domestic manufacturers like Tex and Jericho predominate (although Xtrac is making inroads) and some European formulae, particularly one-make series like GP2 (currently supplied by Mecachrome).

The supply of brakes is another very important part of the supply chain where European suppliers are strong in most markets, except the USA, where domestic manufacturers predominate. The main three European suppliers are Italian-based Brembo, UK-based (but Brembo-owned) AP Racing and the independent UK-based Alcon.

Overall, internationalization of the supply chain is increasing. Competitors inexorably spend more to stay competitive so they seek out the best supplier from an international market. F1 sits at the pinnacle of this international process, closely followed by the WRC. Even a regionally based series like NASCAR, in spite of tight technical regulations, has slowly increased its internationalization of the supply chain. As sponsorship income in NASCAR has increased over the last decade, so teams have sought European-based, and F1-linked, technical expertise in the engine, drivetrain, electronics, brakes and aerodynamics supply chain.

Entrants (Licenced)

An entrant is the organization that enters and is responsible for racing and rallying the vehicle. It includes individuals and racing teams. In some cases, the entrant is the same organization as the constructor (as is the current case in Formula One and the top WRC teams). International and large regional series are likely to have more entrants who are also constructors. At the level of national events, particularly at club level, the entrant is likely to be an individual competitor who buys their vehicle separately.

There are approximately 1 million licensed individual motorsport competitors in the world. By "licenced competitors" we mean individuals holding competition licenses to participate in motorsport issued by the appropriate national governing body or a similar organization, recognized by the FIA. Of these 1 million competitors, we estimate that 10,000 are "professional" entrants, or those who make all or part of their living from driving competition vehicles.

We estimate that, of these 1 million competitors, approximately 40 percent, are based within the USA and it is likely that fully 50 percent of all professional entrants are also resident in the USA.

Events

This category covers those organizations that manage and operate racing events, either as a series or individually.

Table 1.1 outlines our definition of the global racing series—F1, WRC, WTCC and A1GP—and, across these four series, a total of 56 events took place in 2005. These are spread across 29 countries—headed by Germany and Italy with five events each, followed by the UK with four events (see Table 1.4). A number of countries follow these three Frontrunner countries, hosting three global racing events each—Australia, Spain, France, Turkey and Mexico.

NASCAR is a prime example of what we term a *regional* series (see Table 1.1). As a series it is most certainly of significant value, with a total number of 35 events in its premier Nextel Cup series alone, but it operates exclusively within the regional boundaries of NAFTA (Canada, USA and Mexico). All Nextel Cup events are held in the USA, and it is only in recent years that NASCAR's secondary series, Craftsman Truck and Busch Series, have started to hold events in Canada and Mexico.

There may be a case for identifying those world motorsport events that have individual global standing and reputation outside of any series of which they may be part. We must, for example, recognize the importance and significance of the 24-hours of Le Mans in France, the Monaco GP, the Indianapolis 500 and the Daytona 500. All of these "marquee events" have a combination of history, "brand", global impact and audience second to none within the motorsport world. Other but lesser contenders include the Paris-Dakar off-road event, the Bathurst 1000 for V8 Supercar and the Long Beach Champcar event.

Event Suppliers

The major financial activity in this category is in the supply of venues for motorsport events, and the most frequent venue used for motorsport is the racing circuit. In Table 1.1, for comparative purposes, we delineated a circuit as being *a paved facility over ¼ mile in length (not including kart tracks)*. World

Table 1.4 **Global Motorsport Events in 2005**

Country	Event	Circuit (F1, WTCC, A1GP)
Germany	F1(2), WRC, WTCC, A1GP	Hockenheim, Nurburgring, Oschersleben, Lausitz
Italy	F1(2), WRC, WTCC(2)	Imola, Monza
UK	F1, WRC, WTCC, A1GP	Silverstone, Brands Hatch
Australia	F1, WRC, A1GP	Melbourne, Eastern Creek
France	F1, WRC, WTCC	Magny Cours
Mexico	WRC, WTCC, A1GP	Puebla, Monterrey
Spain	F1, WRC, WTCC	Catalunya, Valencia
Turkey	F1, WRC, WTCC	Istanbul
Belgium	F1, WTCC	Spa
China	F1, A1GP	Shanghai
Japan	F1, WRC	Suzuka
Malaysia	F1, A1GP	Sepang
Monaco	F1, WRC	Monaco
USA	F1, A1GP	Indianapolis, Laguna Seca
Argentina	WRC	—
Bahrain	F1	Bahrain
Brazil	F1	Interlagos
Canada	F1	Montreal
Cyprus	WRC	—
Dubai	A1GP	Dubai
Finland	WRC	—
Greece	WRC	—
Hungary	F1	Hungaroring
Indonesia	A1GP	Sentul
Macau	WTCC	Macau
New Zealand	WRC	—
Portugal	A1GP	Estoril
South Africa	A1GP	Durban
Sweden	WRC	—

motorsport has approximately 600 such facilities; the USA has the largest number, around 240 in 2005, of which approximately 75 percent are ovals.

There are many other types of facility for motorsport, which we have not included in our above figure, including drag strips, kart tracks, hillclimb and sprint venues, unpaved ovals and paved ovals of ¼ mile or less. For example, the USA has approximately 1,400 tracks of all types (excluding kart tracks) and, additionally, many other events are held away from any sort of formal venues, such as rallying, desert raids and off-roading. Overall, very little is known about the full stock of racing venues across the motorsport world.

Other major event suppliers include, for example, catering and hospitality, which has grown to meet the apparently insatiable demand from corporate activity in recent years. In addition, PA systems and other myriad goods and services support any spectator event but these vary substantially depending on the type of racing event and activity.

Distribution

The media distribution of motorsport on television is achieved by TV companies buying TV rights from the commercial rights holders. For example, in every country where F1 is screened, a national TV network will negotiate with Formula One for the rights to show the events. This system applies to all other global motorsport series.

The vast majority of broadcasters are terrestrial channels with a national broadcasting range, as a satellite, or limited terrestrial broadcast, would be unlikely to recoup the advertising fees needed to pay for the TV rights to F1. In general terms, the higher the domestic TV audience figure for F1, the higher the fee paid to the F1 commercial rights holder. The domestic TV network then holds the sole rights to screen F1 within its borders and a similar structure applies to WRC.

On a regional level, the same TV rights structure generally holds. In NASCAR, however, this is slightly different for its domestic USA market. Three TV companies currently hold the domestic broadcasting rights for NASCAR, splitting the season between them for broadcasting purposes.

At a national level generally the same structure holds true. Within the UK in 2005, for example, the terrestrial ITV network held the sole terrestrial broadcast rights to F1, WRC and the BTCC.

In the print media there is really only one specialist international player, the UK-based Haymarket Publishing. Haymarket publishes *Autosport*, *F1 Racing* and *Racer* on a global basis, together with UK-based titles like *Motorsport News* for a UK-based audience. Haymarket's position as the only international motorsport publisher should not overlook the myriad of national motorsport publications against which even Haymarket plays only a small part in numerical terms. Each country has many of its own specialist motorsport publications, with the larger markets like the USA having a range of specialist magazines and newspapers covering the entire spectrum of motorsport activity.

Consumption

The main *global* motorsport series is F1. In 2005, 52.5 million viewers watched each F1 race event on television (Sports Marketing Surveys); by comparison 50.1 million viewers watched each round of the WRC on television (wrc.com).

On the ground, at the actual events, spectator figures for WRC are not known, but are likely to be higher than F1 due to the wider geographical spread of the event, compared to the one stadium-based venue of F1. Spectator attendance claimed for the total three/four days of an F1 event varies from 370,000 for the Australian Grand Prix in 2005 to 86,000 for the Bahrain Grand Prix. Overall, the average attendance for the 19 Grand Prix held in 2005 was 201,000, spread over the three/four day events (all attendance figures courtesy of the Australian Grand Prix Corporation).

NASCAR is, by far, the leading *regional* motorsport series in the world. It holds 38 races (including invitational events), twice as many events per year than F1, and in 2005 attracted 6.9 million race-day attendance spectators to its 38 events, compared to 2.2 million race-day attendance spectators for just 19 events in F1 in that year (Australian Grand Prix Corporation). This averages out to 182,000 attendees to each NASCAR race and 116,000 to an F1 race.

While global event TV viewing figures are not known for NASCAR, event viewing figures for the USA are approximately 14 million per NASCAR event (NASCAR).

By comparison, a leading national-level motorsport series like the UK-based BTCC attracts approximately 1 million UK-based TV viewers for each of the ten events. Spectator attendance on race day at a BTCC event varies between 10,000 and 30,000.

Thinking About the Global Motorsport Industry

In Part One we have outlined our definition of the *global motorsport industry*. Comprising motor and sport—and the three domains of production, participation and consumption—we have provided a set of metrics that take global to imply not only international but intercontinental, with global reach across at least three continents. As we explained earlier, there exist only four truly global racing series, 56 events and 22 global chassis constructors.

Of course, the global segment of the industry is the pinnacle. Sitting below this are the feeder and regional series with supply chains all the way down to the grass roots of the individual club participant. In total, we estimate the global industry to be worth something in the order of £50 billion worldwide. A simple mapping of the Global Starting Grid has highlighted both the surprisingly still limited geographical extent of the global sport and its currently limited penetration within (potentially extremely large) national and regional markets.

Benchmarking the global industry by nation and region highlights what is well known—there exists a set of Frontrunner national industries (USA, UK, Japan, Germany, Italy and France), which continue to dominate international and global motorsport. Europe remains dominant in the spectacle and consumption of global motorsport but, reflecting globalization processes, its dominance is slowly decreasing with the rise of new regions and nations.

In production, while the Frontrunner countries remain totally dominant, application of the Motorsport Value Chain reveals significant shifts within this group. There is a clear rise of a newly internationally focused US industry and the expansion of an independent Italian capacity—both at the expense of the still-dominant UK industry. This dominance is beginning to wane and is under threat.

Behind the Frontrunners on the Global Starting Grid reside a large number of hopefuls. While some of the longer-term members of the Midfield should not be ignored (for example, Australia, South Africa, South America), one conclusion would be that, on a global scale, they provide limited further market (even if potential niche) opportunities and are unlikely to improve their grid positions. Indeed, their challenge will be to hold their position in the face of those countries Coming Through the Field.

If countries and regions such as China and the Gulf Region are to move up the Global Starting Grid, one interesting question to ask is on what basis—whether within the sphere of production, participation or consumption?

For example, a recent trend has been the creation of a global motorsport presence for a country through the winning of a F1 Grand Prix contract, invariably linked to the building of a highly expensive state-of-the-art circuit. No evidence exists, at present, that success in the production of motorsport vehicles, or the industry associated with the sport, has followed nor that substantial participation—or even spectating—has been stimulated. How long this investment model continues must be open to question in the light of this situation. In contrast, purely on the basis of consumption potential, global commentators await the inevitable arrival on the Global Starting Grid of countries such as India and Russia.

Part One—and the analytical tools of the Motorsport Value Chain and the global motorsport metrics it introduces—sets the strategic framework for asking such questions on the future development of the global industry. We have explained, and exemplified at the *global* scale, how we might understand the motorsport industry and its dynamics. The context is now set for a detailed description and analysis of the Global Starting Grid, nation by nation, in Parts Two to Four. After all, if you are going to win the race, you need to know the starting point—and who is on the grid and in the race with you.

PART TWO

Frontrunners on the Global Starting Grid

Introduction: The Frontrunners

Part One outlined the Global Starting Grid of international motorsport and identified the six global frontrunners as the USA, UK, Japan, Germany, Italy and France. These nations have dominated the economic development and racing history of motorsport. The frontrunners account for 75 percent of the world market, 91 percent (20) of the global chassis constructors, virtually all of the supply chain of the vehicles racing in the global series and 41 percent (23) of the global racing events.

The largest motorsport industry in the world is in the USA (see Figure 1.4). Historically, the national industry has focused upon producing vehicles for its huge, and in the main technologically distinctive, domestic championships (for example, NASCAR)—with a strong bias toward oval or drag competition venues. Market penetration by overseas suppliers into this vast domestic market is limited—especially outside of single-seat racing. In those championships where the use of technology is similar to European racing series, such as CART and IRL, it has been the European manufacturers (especially UK and Italy) that have dominated. Most recently, the growth of an internationally focused US industry can be discerned with companies such as Panoz, Menard, Roush, PMI and PFC producing for global series and investing overseas.

Since the late 1950s, the UK can be described as having been the "home of motorsport." In 2005, 50 percent of the global constructors were based in the UK (see Table 1.2) including six F1 chassis constructors and three WRC teams. It has the highest industry sales turnover as a percentage of national GDP of any country in the world (see Figure 1.5). The UK high-performance industry is a world leader in motorsport aerodynamics, engines, electronics, transmissions and logistics and, despite significant recent inroads by competitor nations, remains the dominant force in global motorsport supply chains.

Japan's involvement in global motorsport is headed by the OEMs. Honda first competed in F1 in the 1960s and has global expertise in engine supply. Toyota, Subaru and Mitsubishi are all involved in global racing series but reflect a long tradition of delivering vehicles through outsourcing specialists located throughout the other frontrunner countries.

Germany has a distinguished history in international motorsport led by its OEMs (for example, Mercedes, Audi, BMW and Porsche). Germany's international presence stretches across a range of racing (especially sportscar and saloon), a world-class set of international suppliers, and includes significant overseas investment (especially within the UK).

The Italian motorsport industry once dominated the sport through marques such as Alfa Romeo, Lancia, Ferrari and Maserati. The city of Modena in Emilia Romagna was the Motorsport Valley® of the 1950s. Today, Ferrari still represents the strongest brand in global motorsport and new constructors such as Dallara and Tatuus have had sustained success in single-seat competition. Italy remains the center of the world karting industry.

Finally, France's industry, led by Peugeot, Citroën and Renault, has a more checkered career of success in international motorsport. Global involvement is closely related to the fortunes of these domestic OEMs, who have had recent success in F1 and WRC. Beyond these giants, the domestic industry has always struggled in the face of international competition.

The following Part Two provides a detailed description and benchmarking of each of these frontrunner nations, in order of size of national industry, and by using the analytical framework of the global metrics and motorsport value chain. We begin each country review with its own global metric table before a short history of the national motorsport industry and a description of its current position. Thereafter, the motorsport value chain is applied for each national industry and a case study provided before the completion of a SWOT (strengths, weaknesses, opportunities and threats) analysis and final summary.

The USA Motorsport Industry

Table 2.1 provides the global metrics for the USA motorsport industry. As the largest industry player in the world, it is estimated to comprise 26 percent of the world industry turnover and 40 percent of the world's permanent paved circuits. Despite this size, the domestic character of the industry is confirmed by its lack of global chassis constructors and its hosting of just two global racing events.

Table 2.1 **The USA Motorsport Industry in 2005**

Indicators	USA 2005	% of world total
Total value of annual motorsport turnover for engineering and services	£13b	26.0
Motorsport turnover as % GDP	0.17 percent	—
Permanent paved circuits (including ovals over ¼ mile but not kart)	243 (182 ovals and 61 road)	40.0
Competition license holders	443,000 (*participants not license holders—figures from* PRI)	—
Global chassis constructors (F1, WRC, WTCC and A1GP)	0	0
Number of racing series		
— Global	F1; A1GP	—
— Regional	CART Champcar, IRL Indycar, NASCAR, Grand-Am, ALMS	—
Global motorsport events (F1, WRC, WTCC and A1GP)	2	3.6
Average F1 viewing figures per race event (*Source*: Sports Marketing Surveys)	0.32 m	0.6
Average WRC viewing figures per event (*Source*: wrc.com)	Not Known	—

A History of the USA Motorsport Industry

The early history of motorsport in the USA was similar to that of Europe, based around long-distance open-road races. In fact, the earliest international series of road races—the Gordon Bennett Cup—was organized in the USA. These series of races were hosted in the country of the previous year's victorious manufacturer and were designed to pull USA car manufacturers into international competition by competing with the leading European motorsport manufacturers of the day. The Gordon Bennett series of races inspired the purely USA-based competition called the Vanderbilt Cup. This was, again, an open-road racing series, which attracted the cream of international entrants to the USA.

Alongside open-road racing in the USA, early oval-racing venues were developed based on the existing layout of horse-racing tracks and provided a great spectacle, attracting vast audiences. In the pre-World War I era, these two forms of racing developed alongside each other.

Crowd-control problems began to arise on the open-road races in the USA, as they did in Europe, with many accidents and fatalities occurring among competitors and spectators. As these incidents began to escalate, motorsport in the USA began to swing toward closed oval racing. These closed circuits had the advantage of being far safer to police, and also the possibility of charging admission, something that was very hard to do when the competition arena was the open road. The opening of the Indianapolis Motor Speedway in 1909 foretold the future development of USA motorsport. By 1917 all races in the USA's national racing championship, organized by the AAA, would take place on oval tracks.

In the pre-World War I era, European manufacturers dominated USA motorsport. At this stage, although firms like Ford and Buick were involved, they preferred to concentrate on perfecting their production lines for the fast-growing home consumption of road-going vehicles. A striking factor of the early stages of motorsport in the USA was the emergence of commercial sponsorship of race vehicles. Even from the mid-1890s, USA firms that were not in automobile manufacturing or supply still became involved in commercial arrangements with motorsport teams and organizations in order to publicize their goods and services. European motorsport at this stage was a far more genteel and gentlemanly affair, which refused to be sullied by the indignity of outside commercial involvement.

Throughout the 1920s, the USA motorsport industry specialized more and more in oval racing as road racing suffered a severe decline in popularity. In this era, USA motorsport specialist firms like Miller and Duesenberg began to rise in single-seat oval racing categories. These firms offered specialized forms of race car to cater for the different demands of racing on ovals as opposed to the road courses now prevalent in European motorsport. One famous name from this era was the Offenhauser Indycar engine, first seen in 1935. This was developed from the engine of the Miller race car of the 1920s and became the dominant Indycar engine from the 1930s through to the 1970s. Its reign was ended by the construction of a Ford-sponsored Cosworth engine designed for the USA market by the UK firm.

In the 1930s the Great Depression put an end to the reign of highly specialist USA motorsport firms, as costs were reduced to meet changing economic conditions. For example, the Indianapolis 500 race moved toward a production-based form of competition using modified OEM equipment rather than very specialist race cars. In this pre-war era the European motorsport industry drew ahead as its technological development was part-funded by governments. Miller and Duesenberg had proved very competitive in the 1920s, when competing in the occasional European Grand Prix, but lost this competitive edge as the Depression hit the USA.

The move toward production-based racing on the grounds of cost affected more than just the Indianapolis style of single-seat race car. Production-based road cars had always been a secondary but popular form of competition in the USA, with racing mainly on the many ovals that had been built all over the country.

Daytona Beach in Florida held a very successful series of races for production-based road cars in the 1930s, using a course cut partly on the beach itself. Post-war, production car-based oval racing remained relatively disorganized at a national level until the Daytona Beach race organizer, Bill France, united the various factions under the NASCAR banner in 1947. In 1959 France also opened the Daytona International Speedway, now the spiritual home of the NASCAR organization.

Road racing in the USA was very much a secondary motorsport category through the 1920s and 1930s. This was revived slightly in the 1930s with the introduction of the Vanderbilt Trophy, modeled on the earlier Vanderbilt Cup, and based at a closed circuit on Long Island. The meeting attracted international Grand Prix teams and was organized by ARCA. The races were stopped by World War II but, post-war, the road-racing movement began to flourish under the organization of the SCCA. This was partly due to the availability of unused military airfields that could be easily and cheaply converted for use as closed-circuit racing venues—just as in the UK. Road racing, however, never regained its early popularity in comparison to oval racing and drag racing.

Alongside road racing, single-seat Indycar racing and NASCAR, the fourth element of USA motorsport to arise was drag racing. Drag racing developed from outright straight-line speed record attempts on the Bonneville Salt Flats and Daytona Beach. Initially these involved illegal street racing on any quiet, straight road away from the police. These activities began to be legitimized in the late 1930s by organizations such as the NHRA. Drag racing really took off with the post-war manufacturing boom in the USA and the availability of cheap, fast, easily modified road cars to a newly affluent teenage market.

These various disciplines of USA motorsport have always remained relatively discreet from one another. One of the main theories as to why this should be so is that drivers are not allowed to compete in rival series (or disciplines) as the loss of a major "name" can lead to a loss of spectator interest in that particular series. Hence, series fight very hard to maintain their star names, in order to maintain market share. It is a comment that highlights the marketing- and service-led focus of USA motorsport, compared to the more engineering-led form of motorsport in Europe.

Post-World War II, the USA motorsport industry was dominated by USA firms (for example, Kurtis and Watson) in those categories where specialist disciplines like oval racing were common. In European-style road racing in the USA, European firms like Lola and Porsche remained very competitive with the best that USA motorsport firms could offer.

In Europe, UK firms had begun to dominate the world of motorsport with their post-war lightweight aircraft-influenced designs and rear-engine chassis. In the 1960s firms like Cooper, Lotus, Lola and Brabham exported this technology successfully to the USA single-seat oval-racing categories epitomized by the Indianapolis 500 race. These firms revolutionized the technological paradigm of Indycar racing in the same way that they had revolutionized Grand Prix. It presaged an era of dominance in Indycar racing for UK chassis manufacturers that lasted to 2006, when Italian and USA manufacturers became dominant and opened the door to many other UK specialist motorsport component suppliers to enter the USA market. For example, by the mid-1970s, a development of the F1 Ford Cosworth DFV had replaced the USA-built Offenhauser engine as the dominant engine in Indycar racing.

Current Industry Position

The USA specialized motorsport market is the world's largest—we estimate £13 billion in 2005. In 2002, its worth was estimated as £11 billion, with over 400,000 competitors, dwarfing any other country for domestic participation and value (MRA, 2002). Where technical regulations are of a similar type to European-style racing, then UK-based firms have a very strong presence (for example, Lola, Van Diemen, Cosworth, Ilmor, Alcon, Xtrac and Pi Research) but with growing international competition (Dallara, Toyota, Honda).

Most USA competitors, and the industry that supports them, participate in low-tech, high participant and spectator value series like the oval-based stock cars series and in drag racing. The key series here are the oval-based NASCAR series (equivalent in value to Formula One), with high domestic USA OEM participation, and the NHRA Drag Race Championships.

USA motorsport services, in terms of spectator value for money, sponsorship and marketing, are world leaders—significantly ahead of much of the European industry. Its participant- and spectator-centered approach involves current best practice in sophisticated marketing and sponsorship techniques.

USA Motorsport Value Chain Analysis

Table 2.2 below summarizes the motorsport value chain applied to the current USA motorsport industry. Each cell of the table is discussed to complete a comprehensive empirical description of the USA industry.

Regulation of Sport

The FIA's official sporting authority in the USA is the Automobile Competition Commission for the United States (ACCUS). The USA does, however, have many motorsport authorities, split on a sporting and regional basis. Each type of motorsport tends to have a governing body of its own, and while there

Table 2.2   **The USA Motorsport Value Chain**

Value chain position	Companies/organizations involved in supply chain
1. Regulation of sport	
Regulatory bodies	Numerous and includes: NASCAR, SCCA, IRL, USAC, NHRA
Safety panels	NASCAR, SCCA, IRL, USAC
2. Supporting service industry	
Logistics	Domestic
Markets and merchandizing	Domestic
Personnel and human resources (driver management)	IMG
Other (racing school, insurance and risk management, finance, accountancy, legal)	Racing school—Richard Petty, Skip Barber, Bob Bondurant; Trade association—SEMA, North Carolina Motorsport Association, Indianapolis Motorsport Association, MIA
3. Constructors	
F1	None
Rally	None
Sportscar	Panoz, Riley Technologies, Pratt and Miller, Chase Competition, Crawford, Doran, FABCAR
Kit car	—
Other	*Stock car*—numerous including Roush, Hendrick, LRP, Hess, Chas Howe; *Sprint car*—numerous including Maxim, Eagle, J&J, Avenger, Twister; *Single seat*—Panoz, Swift
4. Constructor suppliers	
Engines	TRD, Evernham, Hendrick, Arrington Manufacturing, Penske-Jaspar
Electronics	—
Materials	—
Design services	Pratt and Miller, Riley Technologies
Transmission	Jericho, Tex, Weismann
Brakes/suspension	Willwood, Performance Friction
Safety systems	Simpson, Impact Racing
Tyres	Goodyear, Cooper, Hoosier
Fuel/lubrication	Chevron, Conoco, Valvoline
Other	—
5. Entrants (licensed)	
Race team	NASCAR, SCCA, USAC, IRL
Individual participants	443,000 participants
Clubs	Track, local and regional
Drivers	Internationally low

(*Continued*)

Table 2.2 **(Continued)**

Value chain position	Companies/organizations involved in supply chain
6. Events	
F1	Indianapolis
WRC	None
Historic	Monterey Historics, HSR, SVRA, VARA
Saloon	NASCAR
Club	At each of 1,400 circuits
Other	NHRA
7. Event suppliers	
Circuits (construction, safety)	Daktronics, A1 Bleacher Brokers, Musco Lighting
Event management/ infrastructure	ISC, SMI, Dover Downs, IMS
8. Distribution	
Media	NASCAR TV—Fox/SPEED Channel, ABC/ESPN, and TNT, F1 TV—Speed Channel; Magazine—*National Speed Sport News*, *PRI* (industry) among many
9. Consumption	
Viewers	F1 viewing figures per race event 2005: 0.32 m (*Source*: Sports Marketing Surveys)
Spectators	Very high
Participants	Very high

are some national sporting authorities for certain types of car, there are a plethora of regional sporting authorities beneath those national bodies. Some of the national bodies are NASCAR (stock car), SCCA (road racing), NHRA (drag racing), IRL (single-seat ovals) and USAC (sprint cars), and below these national governing bodies are approximately 200 regional and local governing bodies.

Supporting Service Industry

The USA has a more service sector-oriented motorsport industry than that prevalent in Europe. The *National Survey of Motorsport Engineering and Services Survey* (MIA, 2000) estimated that the split between engineering and services in the UK motorsport industry was approximately 60 : 40. The *USA Motorsport Market Research Report* (MRA, 2002) estimated that the engineering/services split in the USA was approximately 50 : 50 due to more complex distribution channels in the USA and a spectator-oriented motorsport culture concentrating on lower levels of car sophistication.

The motorsport service sector, particularly in marketing and sponsorship, is considerably more sophisticated than that prevalent in Europe. This reflects a historic USA approach to sports marketing and sponsorship more widely. Consequently, USA motorsport has a substantial amount of home-grown service-sector support industry to support it. Overseas penetration of this market is low. IMG, a sports marketing, promotion and management company, is but one example of an agency with a high impact in USA motorsport and across the globe, particularly in F1.

Racing schools and driver experiences are common in the USA. Due to the very high number of racing tracks, and the high media profile of NASCAR, many local tracks offer this sort of experience. NASCAR drivers will often lend their name to a driver training/experience facility in return for a share of the income generated.

Constructors

There are no WRC or F1 constructors in the USA. In single-seat road-racing/oval-racing categories with similar regulations to Europe, like CART and IRL, European (Dallara) and USA companies (Panoz) dominate. At the highest levels of sportscar road racing (ALMS and Grand-Am) USA companies are also involved, though European influence is present. For example, in the more technically restrictive Grand-Am sportscar category, domestic manufacturers like Riley Technologies, Pratt & Miller, Chase Competition, Crawford, Doran and FABCAR predominate. In ALMS, European names like Audi and Lola are joined by USA constructors like Panoz and Pratt & Miller.

Road racing remains a very small percentage of USA motorsport action. Most is geared toward saloon car, sprint car, oval racing or drag racing.

Drag racing encapsulates specialist-built machinery but the vast majority are modified production cars. Oval racing of the saloon or sprint car variety mainly entails purpose-built spaceframe chassis. There is a vast domestic industry supplying this sector of USA motorsport with very little overseas market penetration, except at the very highest levels of NASCAR. Some of the domestic constructors for saloon car oval racing are Roush, Hendrick, LRP, Hess and Chas Howe. In sprint car some well-known constructors are Maxim, Eagle, J&J, Avenger and Twister.

Constructor Suppliers

In the sorts of motorsport categories where European-style technical regulations occur, then European constructor suppliers have a significant presence.

In motorsport categories like CART and IRL, the main engine suppliers are the UK-based Cosworth and Ilmor Engineering, USA-based and Honda-owned HPD, and the USA-based Toyota Racing Developments (TRD). TRD is a California-based, but parent company-owned, organization that builds engines for Toyota's NASCAR Nextel and Craftsman Truck entries, together with a smaller-scale off-road engine-building involvement.

In the main, the engines used for the vast majority of USA motorsport are US-manufactured V8s produced and developed by a domestic supply chain. Examples of NASCAR-supplying engine makers would include Evernham, Hendrick, Arrington Manufacturing and Penske-Jaspar. One important subsector where this is not the case is in the area of four-cylinder turbocharged Japanese Sports Compact motorsport where the engine supply chain is more international in nature.

Transmissions for much of USA motorsport are similarly domestically produced by companies such as Jericho and Tex. Braking suppliers for much of USA motorsport, European-oriented road-racing categories excepted, are domestic companies like Willwood and Performance Friction (PFC). Major tire suppliers like Goodyear, Hoosier and Cooper supply the home market, while Simpson and Impact Racing do the same for safety equipment like helmets and race suits.

Fuel and lubricant suppliers have a long history of motorsport trade support and sponsorship in the USA, where the service and engineering side of the business can be seen to combine to best advantage. Chevron, Conoco and Valvoline are some of the best-known USA-based fuel and lubricant suppliers.

Entrants (Licensed)

The sheer size of the USA motorsport market is matched by a large number of professional and semi-professional teams. To give some idea of the size of the market the *USA Motorsport Market Research Report* (MRA, 2002) categorized USA motorsport as forming eight discrete subsectors based on type of motorsport competed. The subsectors were: Oval Racing—Stock Car; Oval Racing—Open Wheel; Drag Racing, Off-Road, Rallying, Road Racing, Karting and Autocross.

In just one of these segments, Oval Racing—Stock Car, catering for NASCAR like saloon-bodied cars, the report split this subsector into three levels: professional, semi-professional and amateur. The report estimated there were 100 teams in the professional level of this sector alone, mainly racing in NASCAR's top three categories (Nextel Cup, Busch and Craftsman Truck). At the semi-professional level, it was estimated there could be as many as 5,000 teams racing in semi-professional regional series across the USA. At the amateur level the report estimated 50,000 owner/drivers competing in the category across the country.

To put these figures in context, Oval Racing—Stock Car represents no more than 15 percent of *total* entrant activity across all motorsport disciplines in the USA. The professional and semi-professional number of entrants across the country could be as many as 50,000 teams across all motorsport categories, with as many as 400,000 amateur competitors on top of that figure. Clearly, motorsport in the USA is big business.

Events

F1 originally held Grand Prix in the USA in the late 1950s. The USA event became a regular feature of the Grand Prix calendar until rising sanctioning fees and competition from domestic motorsport drove F1 out of the USA for much of the 1990s. In 1999, a Grand Prix was introduced at a purpose-built track at the famous Indianapolis Motor Speedway, and this has become an important toehold for F1 in the USA. This is in a market that has not been receptive to European-style road racing over the last 20 years, due to the growing interest in NASCAR and the downfall of single-seat racing in the USA as a result of in-fighting between the two major series (CART and IRL).

The different domestic tastes of USA motorsport can be seen in the low profile of rallying in the USA and consequently no USA WRC round. Historic motorsport is growing in popularity in the USA, as it is in many countries, with events catering for historic machinery across all the subsectors of USA motorsport. Some of the historic road-racing organizers are SVRA, VARA and HSR, who hold multi-round championships across the country, while one of the biggest road-racing meetings is the annual Monterey Historic Festival.

The service-oriented nature and entertainment-value approach of USA motorsport combines with the 1,400 tracks present in the country to promote a unique but multi-polar motorsport experience. Tracks are as much a part of USA culture as are football stadiums or baseball fields, and local promoters tend to be very proactive in putting on family-friendly, value-for-money entertainment to attract customers through their gates. For example, drag racing is probably second only in popularity in the USA to oval racing, and the main sanctioning body, the NHRA, claims to sanction 4,000 events per year at 144 tracks.

Circuit Suppliers

The *USA Motorsport Market Research Report* (MRA, 2002) established that there were 1,372 motorsport venues across the USA in 2001. Of these, 282 were drag strips, 61 road-racing facilities and 1,029 ovals. With such a large number of tracks a large domestic support industry has been built to supply the circuits with all sorts of equipment, from lighting to seating and electronics. There is even a speciality track-buying broker. The vast majority of this industry is domestically oriented only.

This large number of tracks has led to the formation of a number of organizations that own and promote events at a collection of tracks. The best known of these are ISC, SMI and Dover Downs, who, between them, owned and promoted events at 23 tracks in 2001, and in the same year had a combined turnover of $1.3 billion. Another well-known owner/promoter is IMS, which controls the Indianapolis Motor Speedway under the direction of Tony George.

Distribution

The main TV distribution channel for motorsport in the USA is Fox and NBC/Turner's broadcast of the Nextel Cup, NASCAR's top racing category. In December 2005 it announced a new eight-year $4.8 billion deal to televise the sport from 2007–14 with Fox/SPEED Channel, ABC/ESPN and TNT. As far back as 1999, it was estimated that NASCAR merchandize alone produced $1.2 billion in revenue per year. There is also a popular cable motorsport channel called Speed Channel that televises much of USA motorsport. Speed Channel also currently televises F1 in the USA but the sport attracts few viewers. The USA marketplace is F1's weakest and it faces heavy and entrenched competition from NASCAR if it is to establish itself in the country.

There is a large print media across all sectors and geographical regions of USA motorsport; perhaps one of the widest ranging and most respected is Chris Economaki's *National Speed Sport News*.

Consumption

TV viewing figures for motorsport in the USA, particularly NASCAR, are very high. NASCAR is the second most watched sport in the USA, behind American football. Drag racing is probably the second most viewed USA motorsport, but both it and other categories like CART and the IRL come a long way behind in the USA sport-viewing hierarchy.

The Indianapolis 500, now part of the IRL series, still attracts high numbers of TV viewers, and in terms of spectators remains the largest one-day sporting event in the world, attracting over 300,000 at the Indianapolis Motor Speedway. Unfortunately, spectator and viewing figures for the IRL more widely have suffered in recent years due to the in fighting between IRL and CART, which has allowed NASCAR to gain the initiative from both.

Motorsport events are numerous and well attended in the USA. For example, in 2005, 6.9 m fans attended 38 headline NASCAR events. Another 6.1 m fans paid to watch other NASCAR-sanctioned events. NASCAR sanctioned events are probably the most popular spectator events in the USA, but other oval racing series and drag racing championships also attract high numbers of spectators.

Finally, the USA has the highest number of participants in motorsport compared to any other country in the world. This was estimated at 443,000 participants across eight categories of motorsport in the USA in 2002 (MRA, 2002).

USA Motorsport Industry Case Study: NASCAR

NASCAR is a championship sanctioning body with the largest single group of motorsport competitors and the largest spectator following in the USA. In 1947 NASCAR's founder, Bill France, united various other organizers under the NASCAR banner. NASCAR sanctions 13 series across 2,200 events at 135 tracks. The top three series (Nextel Cup, Busch and Craftsman Truck) are national series. The rest are mainly regional series, utilizing similar regulations to the top series. NASCAR dominates

USA motorsport TV coverage, as it is the second most popular TV sport in the USA behind the NFL. In December 2005 it announced a new eight-year $4.8 billion deal to televise the sport from 2007–14 with Fox/SPEED Channel, ABC/ESPN and TNT. As far back as 1999, it was estimated that NASCAR merchandize alone produced $1.2 billion in revenue per year. NASCAR is very much based on a successful marketing and service-industry strategy designed to appeal to a very broad demographic. It encourages closely policed, relatively low technology, racing with a high concentration of spectator-friendly initiatives. NASCAR has produced figures suggesting that 40 million Americans, or one in seven of the entire USA population, are hardcore NASCAR enthusiasts who are passionate about the sport. NASCAR is slowly starting to expand internationally. It now has rounds of its top series in Mexico and sanctions events in Canada.

SWOT Analysis: USA Motorsport Industry

Following description of the USA motorsport value chain, a SWOT analysis summarizes some of the key aspects of the position on the global grid (see Table 2.3 overleaf).

Conclusion: The USA Motorsport Industry

The USA is the world's largest motorsport market but is dominated by domestic (less technologically intensive) forms of racing (oval and drag), with very high levels of grass roots participation. The racing packages on offer are the best in the world for delivering consumer value (whether to participants, spectators, viewers or sponsors). European-style racing formats are major markets for overseas (especially UK) suppliers. Evidence exists of a growing trend by international firms to supply new US market possibilities (performance engineering, mid-technology value products, technological niches such as safety) from a USA-base. As globalization continues apace, tentative international expansion of spectator-centered series is underway and the USA domestic industry is expanding its overseas investment—particularly in the UK and mainland Europe.

The UK Motorsport Industry

Table 2.4 provides the global metrics for the UK motorsport industry. As the second largest motorsport industry in the world, it is estimated to comprise 12 percent of the world industry turnover. Of clear global significance is the location of 50 percent of global constructors in the UK and a representative event from all of the global racing series.

Table 2.3 **SWOT of the USA Motorsport Industry**

Strengths	Weaknesses
1 World's strongest economy, with a race culture unique to USA 2 Very large home motorsport marketplace with very competitive product pricing 3 Spectator-centered motorsport culture 4 Good mid-level technology/price ratio 5 Strong sales and service ethos 6 Well-developed ladder of opportunity using similar technology 7 Financially self-sufficient 8 High levels of grass roots participation at low cost 9 Growing presence of motorsport trade associations, e.g. North Carolina Motorsport Association	1 Fragmented regulatory framework which has led to in-fighting within series (IRL vs CART) 2 Motorsport generally low tech 3 Geographically the industry is very widely spread 4 Motorsport culture can be insular 5 Safety not promoted as well as it might be 6 No global motorsport presence and limited export opportunities 7 Road racing relatively unpopular 8 Relatively undeveloped nature of indigenous technology
Opportunities	**Threats**
1 Low production costs of mid-price, mid-technology motorsport products leads some overseas firms to move production process to USA 2 State-level government aid to attract overseas firms, e.g. Hampton Motorsports Technology Alliance 3 Higher-level supply chain expertise being shipped from Europe to USA (Panoz Champcar chassis; engine technology—Nick Hayes at RCR) 4 Exporting "spectacle" expertise to emerging centers of motorsport	1 Litigious nature of USA society 2 Domestic OEM weakness compared to Japanese rivals 3 Further fragmentation of regulatory bodies

A History of the UK Motorsport Industry

The growth of a globally significant UK motorsport industry can be traced to the post-World War II era. Henry gives a comprehensive account of this in his report *In Pole Position: Motor Sport Success in Britain and its Lessons for the World's Motor Industry* (1999), from which much of the following is drawn. Before 1939, UK involvement in international motorsport had been intermittent with motorsport essentially the domestic preserve of wealthy gentlemen drivers. For example, the first Grand Prix on the oval circuit at Brooklands, held in 1928, was viewed as part of "the season," along with Ascot, Wimbledon and Henley.

Table 2.4 **The UK Motorsport Industry in 2005**

Indicators	UK 2005	% of world total
Total value of annual motorsport turnover for engineering and services	£6.0b	12.0
Motorsport turnover as % GDP	0.50 percent	—
Permanent paved circuits (including ovals over ¼ mile but not kart)	19	3.2
Competition license holders	30,000	—
Global chassis constructors (F1, WRC, WTCC and A1GP)	11	50.0
Number of Racing Series		
— Global	F1; WRC; WTCC; A1GP	—
— Regional	GP2; FIA GT; LMS	—
Global motorsport events (F1, WRC, WTCC and A1GP)	4	7.1
Average F1 viewing figures per race event (*Source*: Sports Marketing Surveys)	2.6 m	5.0
Average WRC viewing figures per race event (*Source*: wrc.com)	1.6 m	3.2

Honorable competitive exceptions on the international stage included Bentley and ERA but, overall, it was Italian and German cars that dominated between the wars.

It was during the decades after World War II that the UK laid the foundations to grow a motorsport industry that today dominates global production. The introduction of the 500 cc formula in Britain, later known internationally as Formula 3, opened up the sport to a new breed of constructor, epitomized by Cooper. Drawing on the organizational form of the "network" firm, the UK *garagistes*, as they were named by Enzo Ferrari himself, transformed the technological and organizational framework for building world-beating racing cars.

In 1946, the Cooper-JAP consisted of a frame joining together a Fiat Topolino suspension and wheels, a Triumph gearbox and a JAP motorcycle engine. In essence, the assembly of a rear-engined car constructed using extensive subcontracting and by utilizing existing components—a vertically disintegrated production system. By 1959, Cooper had sold over 1,000 of this type of car worldwide. The firm had become the world's largest manufacturer of pure-bred racing cars with a staff that barely ever exceeded 35 employees.

Similarly, in the 1950s, Lotus, Lola, Chevron and Mallock all started by building one-off specials as part of the 750 Motor Club-organized racing events. These lower formulae became the training ground for engineers to rise to the forthcoming UK challenge at the pinnacle of the sport, Grand Prix or Formula One.

Vanwall was the first British firm to win the Formula One World Championship for Constructors in 1958. They did so by the partial adoption of a process of subcontracting production and collaboration between a network of small British-based specialists. In 1959 and 1960 it was the turn of Cooper to win the World Championship and, since then, only Ferrari has won the World Championship from a base entirely located outside the UK.

Cooper was significant not only for its production process but also its reliance upon income derived solely from selling racing cars and prize money from winning races. John Cooper led a set of racing entrepreneurs who took advantage of the falling costs of racing, consequent upon increased product specialization within a vertically disintegrated production network, to design and build their own cars. Ex-racers turned team owners and constructors in their own right included, for example, Lotus (1958), Tyrrell (1960), Brabham (1962), McLaren (1963), Williams (1968), March (1970) and Surtees (1970). By the end of the 1960s, the UK had in place an industrial structure that subsequently supported the sustained development of a commercial motorsport industry, a business cluster now known as Motorsport Valley®, that had attained a position of global dominance by the end of the 20th century.

In 1999, it was estimated that 75 percent of single-seat racing cars used in more than 80 countries across the world emanated from Motorsport Valley. In Formula One, 21 of the 36 (60 percent) significant constructors involved in the World Championship since 1950 had been UK-based. In that year, seven of the 11 F1 teams were based in the UK, as was the supply of a third of their engines and three WRC teams.

In 2000, analysis of the supply chain for the winning competition cars of F1, CART Champcar, F3000 and WRC found 39 percent of components supplied from within the UK (MRA, 2003). Over the decade from 1990 to 2000, the top 50 UK motorsport engineering firms had experienced an (unadjusted) average turnover in growth rate of some 523 percent (MIA, 2001b).

Current Industry Position

Today, the global dominance of the UK's Motorsport Valley® is under threat and has diminished. Nevertheless, the UK motorsport industry remains the second largest in the world, with a turnover of £6 billion in 2005, comprises a half of the global constructors and continues to dominate the global supply chain. Motorsport Valley® continues to sit at both the heart and the apex of a global industry financed by the OEMs and commercial sponsorship, with finance, sponsorship, drivers, engineers, parts and expertise drawn to the UK from across the world. UK specialist companies provide a growing array of world-class motorsport services delivering expertise and service across the leisure, club and promoted segments of the sport and industry.

UK Motorsport Value Chain Analysis

Table 2.5 summarizes the motorsport value chain applied to the current UK motorsport industry. Following the table, each cell of the table is discussed to complete a comprehensive empirical description of the UK industry.

Regulation of Sport

Motorsport in the UK is regulated by the Motor Sports Association (MSA), the nationally designated organizing body recognized by the FIA. All UK motor clubs involved in motorsport are members of the MSA and follow MSA and FIA rules and procedures for organizing and administrating motorsport, including safety matters.

Supporting Service Industry

The supporting specialized service industry is strong in the UK. We estimate a UK motorsport service turnover of some £2.4 billion in 2005 (calculations based on MIA, 2001b). The range of motorsport specialists includes skills in areas such as HR, insurance, finance and accountancy, marketing, logistics, driver management and racing schools.

Constructors

Fully 50 percent of the chassis constructors supplying the four global motorsport series are located in the UK—at the top of this list are those constructors entered in F1. In 2005 this provided six of the ten constructors involved in F1; by 2008 this is likely to have expanded to eight of the 12 constructors. A less-dominant, though still strong, position is demonstrated in WRC; in 2005, three of the six constructors involved were based in the UK. In 2006, M-Sport of Cumbria secured for Ford the WRC manufacturers' title for the first time since 1979. In 2005, one of the five WTCC constructors was UK-based and one UK-based constructor supplied the entire field of A1GP.

Below these global series the UK holds a less-dominant position. In single-seat series below F1, Italian (Dallara, Tatuus) and USA firms (Panoz) have usurped the historical lead position of UK-based constructors. Lola remains a key player in this sector supplying Formula Nippon and F3 and, prior to 2007, the entire CART grid. In club-level single-seat racing the UK remains competitive through companies such as Van Diemen and Ray (although, again, facing growing competition from other frontrunner companies such as France's Mygale).

Outside single-seat racing, the UK holds a notable, though not dominant, position in sportscar and GT racing, with successful firms including Aston Martin, Bentley, Lister, Radical, Prodrive, RML, Zytek and Lola. The UK also has a wide variety of road-going/competition car niche vehicle specialists, with larger names like Lotus, Caterham and TVR being joined by smaller producers such as Darrian, Ginetta and Westfield.

Table 2.5 **The UK Motorsport Value Chain**

Value chain position	Companies/organizations involved in supply chain
1. Regulation of sport	
Regulatory bodies	MSA
Safety panels	FIA, MSA
2. Supporting service industry	
Logistics	Firstair, Delivered on Time, Rapid International
Markets and merchandizing	Grand Prix Legends, Monogram Group, SMS
Personnel and human resources (driver management)	2MB, Alexander Associates, Action Resources
Other (racing school, insurance and risk management, finance, accountancy, legal.	Palmersport, Rawlinson and Hunter, THB Bill Gwynne, Edwards Hospitality Services
3. Constructors	
F1	Williams, Honda, SuperAguri, Renault, Spyker/Midland, Red Bull, Honda
Rally	MSport (Ford), Prodrive (Subaru), MMSP
Sportscar	TVR, Lotus, Caterham, Morgan
Kit car	GTM, Darrian
Other	Lola, Van Diemen, Radical, RML
4. Constructor suppliers	
Engines	EDL, Cosworth, Ilmor Engineering, AER, IES, NME, LPE, Mahle
Electronics	Pi Research, TAG Electronics, Tony James Wiring
Materials	CTG, Crosby Composites, KS Composites, Retrac Composites
Design services	B3 Technologies, Ricardo, MIRA, Pilbeam
Transmission	Xtrac, Hewland, Jack Knight, Quaife, Ricardo
Brakes/suspension	Alcon, AP, Leda, Penske, Spa
Safety systems	Corbeau, Grand Prix Racewear, Willans, Lifeline
Tyres	Cooper-Avon, Dunlop, Colway
Fuel/lubrication	Shell, Millers
Other	Goldline, Goodridge, Piper
5. Entrants (licensed)	
Race team	LMS, GP2, F3, WTCC
Individual participants	30,000
Clubs	BRSCC, HSCC, 750MC, BRDC
Drivers	Colin McRae, David Coulthard, Jenson Button, Anthony Davidson, Lewis Hamilton, Gary Paffett

(*Continued*)

Table 2.5 **(Continued)**

Value chain position	Companies/organizations involved in supply chain
6. Events	
F1	Silverstone
WRC	Wales
Historic	International Historic Motorsport Show, Tour Britannia, Goodwood (Festival of Speed and Revival), Silverstone Classic
Saloon	British Touring Cars, One-make
Club	5,000 club events per year
Other	GP2, LMS, FIA GT
7. Event Suppliers	
Circuits (construction, safety)	—
Event management/infrastructure	BRDC, TOCA
8. Distribution	
Media	FOM, ISC, ITV, Haymarket
9. Consumption	
Viewers	F1 viewing figures per race event 2005: 2.6 m (*Source*: Sports Marketing Surveys)
Spectators	Medium
Participants	High

Constructor Suppliers

The UK is arguably the world center for motorsport suppliers to those countries where European-style regulations are enforced. Even in countries such as the USA, where regulations differ, the UK still holds a key supplier role.

Principal within this supply chain are engine suppliers for F1, like Cosworth and Mercedes High Performance Engines, who supplied three of the ten F1 teams on the field in 2005. Outside F1, notable international engine suppliers are EDL (Sportscar) and Ilmor Engineering (IRL, NASCAR).

The UK also holds a strong position as a leading supplier for competition transmissions. Xtrac, Ricardo and Hewland, supply F1, WRC, Sportscars and F3 on an international basis. A similar position is demonstrated in the supply of brakes, with Alcon and AP major global suppliers for F1, NASCAR, WRC and many lower-level categories.

Composites are also strong in the UK supply chain—due to linkages with aerospace and the F1 teams—with firms like CTG, Spa Composites and Advanced Composites prominent. The aerospace linkage with motorsport also shows up with aerodynamic expertise in the UK from leading universities such as Cranfield, Imperial and Southampton. Engineering consultancies like MIRA, B3 Technologies and Ricardo are also global motorsport industry players.

Entrants (Licenced)

The UK remains a center for global motorsport entrants and grass roots participation. At the pinnacle, entrants in the UK include the F1, WRC and WTTC teams. Below this level, UK teams make up a significant proportion of series like GP2 and A1GP in single-seat racing, and LMS and FIA GT in sportscar categories (for example, Arden, DPR, Prodrive, RML and Lister).

UK teams including Carlin, Raikkonen Robertson Racing and ADR contest the strong domestic F3 championship. Other teams like Carlin and Manor Motorsport are also prominent in European single-seat championships such as World Series by Renault and the European F3 Championship.

At the level of the individual competitor, the MSA issues over 30,000 competition licenses a year, and believes there could be five times this number involved in non-licenced activities. This grass roots strength is viewed as one of the key pillars for the success of the UK motorsport industry.

Events

The MSA governs the majority of sporting activity in the UK. The organization's heritage stretches as far back as 1897 and reflects the UK's history and tradition of high levels of "grass roots" participation in motorsport. There are almost 800 recognized motorsport clubs in the UK, representing around 200,000 members (MSA, 2002). The MSA regulates almost 5,000 events per annum and has around 30,000 license holders. A further 100,000 people participate annually in non-regulated motorsport activity, particularly within the growing leisure—corporate, track and driving experience—market.

The high level of grass roots participation is reflected in the highest, and most diverse, number of venues in Europe, if not the world. The UK has around 60 venues representing 22 motorsport "disciplines" (for example, karting, hillclimb, drag racing, rallycross, etc.) and including 19 circuits. The UK sport includes 2,800 licensed officials, 8,000 marshals and a world-class safety record.

Circuit operation, in terms of admissions and revenues, is dominated by four companies: Motorsport Vision, Donington Park Leisure (now a subsidiary of SFX International), the BRDC (Silverstone), BARC (Thruxton, Mallory Park, Croft, Pembrey) and Goodwood Road Racing Company. These circuit operators accounted for 80 percent of event revenues in 2000 due to their domination of the major promoted events of the motorsport calendar (Mintel, 2001).

The UK holds rounds of the F1, WRC, WTCC and A1GP championships, as well as regional series like FIA GT, LMS and GP2. National-level events are highlighted by the strong British Touring Car Championships and the British F3 Championship, the latter being one of the most well-regarded F3 championships in the world. Similarly, the UK holds a reasonably strong national British GT championship and a reviving national British Rally championship (BRC).

Historic motorsport is particularly strong in the UK, with arguably the strongest sector in the world highlighted by the two Goodwood events. Supporting historic motorsport in the UK are the grass roots championships, with one-circuit, regional and national championships for every conceivable type of car and type of event.

Event Suppliers

Event management is headlined in the UK by organizing clubs like the BRDC, who control Silverstone, but also by series producers like TOCA, who organize the BTCC. The largest circuit management group is Motorsport Vision, which manages Brands Hatch, Cadwell Park, Oulton Park, Snetterton and the Bedford Aerodrome test track.

Distribution

The UK is home to two of the world's leading motorsport promoters and rights holders. FOM (Formula One Management) is headed by Bernie Ecclestone and controls the series rights to World Championship Grand Prix. ISC (International Sportsworld Communications) is headed by David Richards and controls the rights to the World Rally Championship.

ITV screens much of the motorsport shown on UK terrestrial TV, showing F1, WRC and BTCC. Channel 5 screens series like NASCAR, Australian V8 Supercars and IRL, while Channel 4 also has a small presence in the marketplace, showing national F3 and GT events. Motors TV is a specialized satellite channel focussing on motorsports of all kinds and Sky Sports has the rights to A1GP.

The leading non-screen media distribution is by Haymarket Publishing, one of the world's largest motorsport publishers. Haymarket produces *Autosport*, the leading motorsport weekly in the world, as well as *F1 Racing*, the best-selling F1 magazine. In the USA, Haymarket produces *Racer* magazine, while also producing the weekly *Motorsport News* for the UK market. Haymarket also organizes the world's second largest motorsport show, the Autosport International Show in Birmingham (the largest in the world is the PRI show in the USA).

Consumption

TV viewing figures for F1 are high on a global scale, but they are only average within the UK when compared to other key European markets. On average, 2.6 million UK TV viewers watched each F1 event in 2005, while Italy, Germany, Spain and France all had bigger audiences.

Viewing figures for WRC are proportionately higher than for F1 in relation to the key markets just mentioned. France is ahead by a long way in terms of viewers per event (see Figure 1.11) but the UK is second highest among the major markets, with an average of 1.58 million viewers per event.

Domestic spectator consumption for the headline BTCC series averages around 10,000 per event. The numerous events at club level in UK motorsport means that some events are very well attended by spectators (for example, events held at the Castle Combe circuit), while at other events the competitors can outnumber spectators. Historic events are growing in popularity with, for example, the Goodwood

Revival meeting attracting 110,000 spectators over the three-day event in 2006 and, at club level, the events organized by the HSCC being notably well attended.

UK Motorsport Industry Case Study: Prodrive

Prodrive is one of the world's largest motorsport and vehicle technology businesses, employing almost 1,000 staff in Europe, North America, Australia and Asia Pacific. Its main base is in Oxfordshire in the UK, although it also has another main site in nearby Warwickshire, which it plans to increase in size. While the company's roots are in motorsport, half of company turnover comes from developing niche cars and automotive technologies for OEMs. Prodrive was founded in 1984 by Ian Parry and David Richards. Richards is now chairman of the group. Prodrive's first motorsport involvement was running successful rally teams for Porsche, MG and BMW. In 1987 Prodrive expanded into touring cars, running BMWs in the British Touring Car Championship. Since that time, Prodrive has been almost continuously involved in touring cars, running campaigns for Alfa Romeo, Honda and Ford. It currently runs touring cars for Ford in Australia's V8 Supercar series. In 1990, Prodrive began a long-standing and highly successful relationship with Subaru in the WRC, helping them to win three Drivers' and three Manufacturers' World Rally Championships. This relationship is ongoing and has proved highly significant in raising the profile of the Subaru brand name. In 1999, investment group Apax Partners bought 49 percent of Prodrive. From 2001, Prodrive privately developed a Ferrari sportscar for Le Mans and the FIA GT series, with great success. This private initiative led Aston Martin in 2005 to commission Prodrive to build a GT racing version of the Aston Martin DB9, the DBR9. Prodrive has long held ambitions in F1, and in 2001 Prodrive was brought in to manage Formula One constructor BAR. Richards was appointed as team principal of BAR but, after Honda increased its share in the team in late 2004, Richards was replaced in that role. This followed an earlier one-year role for David Richards as Chief Executive of the Benetton Formula F1 team in 1997–8. In 2006, Prodrive's F1 ambitions were finally realized when the company was officially granted entry to F1 as constructors in their own right for the 2008 Formula One World Championship. Also in 2006, Prodrive announced its plans for a 200-acre motorsport facility called *The Fulcrum*, which will be based in Warwickshire. This facility will be based near the current site of the Prodrive Automotive Technology Division, and could potentially become Prodrive's UK center of operations, including staffing and facilities for the F1 entry.

SWOT Analysis: UK Motorsport Industry

Following description of the UK motorsport value chain, a SWOT analysis summarizes some of the key aspects of the position on the global grid (see Table 2.6).

Table 2.6 **SWOT of the UK Motorsport Industry**

Strengths
1 Strong, integrated technical and service capability
2 Skilled labor pool (technical, design)
3 Infrastructure—circuits, wind tunnels, testing
4 Motorsport history/culture
5 Technology/R&D led
6 Entrepreneurial managerial skills
7 Grass roots sport and industry symbiosis
8 Inward investment track record
9 Industrial base of aerospace/automotive/defence

Weaknesses
1 Lack of customer focus
2 Future viability of circuits (low profits)
3 No home OEMs—i.e. OEMs tend to local appropriate knowledge in the medium/long term
4 Technological lock in—composites/aerodynamics
5 Management highly entrepreneurial and suited to smaller businesses
6 Participation rates have peaked

Opportunities
1 Development of new technological base (e.g. CFD, Energy Efficient Motorsport)
2 Development of base of SMEs toward world-class companies
3 Appropriation of enhanced knowledge created by OEM inward investment
4 Standardized value-for-money technology
5 Strengthening of grass roots structure (skilled volunteers, license holders, participation avenues)
6 Transfer of motorsport capabilities in to other sectors (e.g. performance engineering, event management)
7 Generate value from historic motorsport base

Threats
1 Substitution of existing technology (composites, rolling-ground wind tunnels)
2 Italian strength in lower formulae
3 Development of industry infrastructure in US and Far East
4 The loss of world-class events
5 Increasing cost base unsustainable
6 Growing OEM overseas ownership creates knowledge and supply leakage
7 Standardization of motorsport technological paradigm (spec parts, one-make series)
8 Weakening grass roots structure (skilled volunteers, license lapse rates, fragmented participation routes)

Conclusion: The UK Motorsport Industry

The UK's Motorsport Valley® remains the premier business cluster for world motorsport production and it sits at the center of an expanding global motorsport production system. Within the UK, there is a strong symbiotic relationship between the industry and the sport with world-class motorsport engineering complemented by an array of motorsport services.

Looked at from the vantage point of 2005, no other nation has delivered such long-term commercial success across the breadth of international motor racing championships achieved by the UK industry. Nevertheless, the growing impact of competitor nations—especially Germany, Italy and the USA—can be identified as a threat.

The Japanese Motorsport Industry

Table 2.7 provides the global metrics for the Japanese motorsport industry. As the third largest motorsport industry in the world, it is estimated to comprise 8 percent of the world industry turnover. Despite a significant level of participation

Table 2.7 **The Japanese Motorsport Industry in 2005**

Indicators	Japan 2005	% of world total
Total value of annual motorsport turnover for engineering and services	£4.0b	8.0
Motorsport turnover as % GDP	0.15 percent	—
Permanent paved circuits (including ovals over ¼ mile but not kart)	19	3.2 —
Competition license holders	60,000	
Global chassis constructors (F1, WRC, WTCC and A1GP)	0	0
Number of racing series		
— Global	F1; WRC	—
— Regional	Rally; IRL	—
Global motorsport events (F1, WRC, WTCC and A1GP)	2	3.6
Average F1 viewing figures per race event (*Source*: Sports Marketing Surveys)	3.2 m	6.1
Average WRC viewing figures per event (*Source*: wrc.com)	2.13 m	4.3

and racing infrastructure in a strong domestic market, no global chassis constructors are to be found in Japan and only two global events.

A History of the Japanese Motorsport Industry

Japan really only entered into international motorsport history in the 1960s, with its success defined by its dominant position in motorcycle racing through the global producers of Honda, Yamaha, Kawasaki and Suzuki.

In four-wheeled motorsport, Honda had a brief F1 involvement in the 1960s but could not maintain a favorable cost/performance relationship when compared with its competitors in the increasingly specialist UK-based motorsport industry. Eventually Honda co-operated with UK chassis specialist Lola, before pulling out of F1 in the late 1960s.

In the 1970s and 1980s, Japanese motorsport involvement paralleled that of other nations, as Japanese OEMs (like the German BMW and French Renault OEMs) became F1 engine suppliers. Honda was the first to return to F1 as a very successful engine supplier to UK chassis specialists such as Lotus, Williams and McLaren.

In contrast to Honda's F1 success, Toyota has a long history of successful rallying involvement, but always competed through its German subsidiary, Toyota Team Europe, based in Cologne. Also competing within rallying, Subaru and Mitsubishi entered international motorsport in the 1990s and achieved great success but through partnership with UK-based rally specialists in Motorsport Valley®. Nissan has been very careful to select certain categories from time to time and proven very successful—rallying and long-distance racing being just two.

Most notable in the last decade has been the success of Japanese manufacturers in the USA (as "domestic" OEMs as well as importers), with successful USA-based Japanese motorsport involvement through TRD (Toyota) and HPD (Honda) in series like CART, IRL and NASCAR.

Current Industry Position

Japan is a contradictory case study country in motorsport—a strong domestic racing scene but global presence delivered entirely through overseas partnerships.

An interesting point is the relative strength of Japan's national motorsport scene. National series involving saloon cars and sportscars are dominated by Japanese specialist motorsport organizations—such as Mugen, TOMS, TRD, Le Mans Co and NISMO—who have close links to the Japanese OEMs. In domestic series motorsport specialists from outside Japan are rare. One exception is the case of single-seat chassis supply from UK firms such as Lola and

Italian firm Dallara but, even then, Japanese specialists like Mugen, HKS and TOMS produce engines for these chassis.

The difference in industry approach is apparent when Japanese OEMs seek to compete on the world stage. Japanese OEMs outsource their participation, usually to European-based motorsport specialists. For example, Toyota's entry into F1 is based in Germany at Cologne, at the site of Toyota's rally department of the last 30 years. The facility makes both F1 chassis and engines and employs around 900 personnel.

In international rallying, Mitsubishi's motorsport engineering center and team has long been based in the UK's Motorsport Valley®, although engines are supplied from Japan. Similarly, in WRC, the highly successful Subaru team has long been run by Prodrive in Banbury who construct the cars and engines for the program from their base in the UK.

In F1, Honda is one of the few Japanese OEMs to build its engine in Japan. Nevertheless, the company has entrusted its chassis production to the UK-based (and formerly independent, before Honda bought it in 2006) BAR Formula One team. Furthermore, Honda's engine for the USA-based IRL series is built by the UK-based engine specialists Ilmor Engineering, in co-ordination with the USA-based and Honda-owned HPD.

HPD is one example of how Japanese OEMs like Honda and Toyota have become closely involved with motorsport in the USA. Some of this involvement has been chanelled through Japanese OEM-owned motorsport specialists like HPD and TRD. Toyota used California-based TRD to build its IRL engines (and formerly its CART engines), and is currently involved in producing engines for a USA-based domestic sportscar series. In 2007, engine production will extend to an entry into NASCAR's Nextel Cup.

One of the few independent motorsport specialists in Japan is the chassis manufacturer Dome; Dome does, however, have strong historic links to Honda. Dome produces moderately successful chassis for international sportscar racing and a single-seat chassis utilized mainly in the domestic Formula 3 series as a result of a recent partnership with Lola of the UK.

One unique aspect of Japanese industry is their interest in the Le Mans 24-hour race. Each year several Japanese teams or OEMs, including Nissan, enter the event with wide-ranging results—but from time to time they achieve outstanding results.

Japanese Motorsport Value Chain Analysis

Table 2.8 summarizes the motorsport value chain applied to the current Japanese motorsport industry. Following the table, each cell of the table is discussed to complete a comprehensive empirical description of the Japanese industry.

Table 2.8 **The Japanese Motorsport Value Chain**

Value chain position	Companies/organizations involved in supply chain
1. Regulation of sport	
Regulatory bodies	JAF
Safety panels	JAF, FIA
2. Supporting service industry	
Logistics	—
Markets and merchandizing	RACENOW
Personnel and human resources (driver management)	—
Other (racing school, insurance and risk management, finance, accountancy, legal)	Honda Racing School
3. Constructors	
F1	None
Rally	None
Sportscar	Dome, Le Mans Co, SARD
Kit car	Tokyo R@D
Other	F3, FDream—Dome; Junior Single Seat—Tokyo R&D
4. Constructor suppliers	
Engines	Mugen, TOMS, Autech, Tomei, Techno Craft, M-TEC
Electronics	Tokyo R&D
Materials	—
Design services	Dome
Transmission	Yanagawa Seiki
Brakes/suspension	Showa
Safety systems	—
Tyres	Bridgestone, Yokohama
Fuel/lubrication	—
Other	—
5. Entrants (licensed)	
Race team	F. Nippon, SuperGT, F3
Individual participants	Unknown
Clubs	—
Drivers	Takuma Sato
6. Events	
F1	Suzuka
WRC	Hokkaido
Historic	—
Saloon	—

(*Continued*)

Table 2.8 **(Continued)**

Value chain position	Companies/organizations involved in supply chain
Club	—
Other	F. Nippon and SuperGT, IRL
7. Event suppliers	
Circuits (construction, safety)	—
Event management/infrastructure	Honda, Toyota
8. Distribution	
Media	—
9. Consumption	
Viewers	F1 viewing figures per race event 2005; −3.2 m (*Source*: Sports Marketing Surveys)
Spectators	Medium
Participants	Unknown

Regulation of Sport

Motorsport in Japan is regulated by the Japanese Automobile Federation (JAF), the nationally designated organizing body recognized by the FIA. All Japanese motor clubs involved in motorsport are members of the JAF and follow FIA rules and procedures for organizing and administrating motorsport, including safety rules.

Supporting Service Industry

Some local market and sponsor agents like RACENOW exist in the Japanese motorsport market but most are oriented toward the home market only. Racing schools exist at the main circuit, the most famous being the Honda Racing School at Suzuka.

Constructors

There are two Japanese F1 constructors, although neither builds chassis in Japan. Toyota F1 is based in Germany, where it builds both engines and chassis for its F1 program and for 2007 will supply the Williams F1 team. Honda's F1 chassis construction is left to its UK-based subsidiary, formerly known as BAR, and they also supply engines to their second F1 team—Super Aguri.

Several Japanese OEMs are involved in the WRC or JWRC, namely, Mitsubishi (although on sabbatical from WRC from 2006), Subaru and Suzuki—all three currently utilize UK-based constructors or teams. Japan has one international chassis constructor, Dome, which builds F3 chassis and also builds sportscars for an international marketplace. Several sportscar manufacturers produce for the successful SuperGT sportscar series, such as SARD and the Le Mans Company, but this series is domestic only, though currently tentatively expanding internationally.

Constructor Suppliers

In F1 Honda supplies engines to its UK-based subsidiary from its Japanese facility. Toyota also helps develop F1 engines in Japan for its German-based team, although much engine work is done in Germany at its Toyota facility. In WRC both Mitsubishi and Subaru are involved in engine development work for their UK-based entrants/constructors Mitsubishi Ralliart and Prodrive. Suzuki developed much of their JWRC in Japan, although the team was also UK-based until 2006.

Historically, there have been close relationships between the Japanese OEMs and certain motorsport specialists in Japan—the most well known of these is the relationship between Honda and Mugen (see Case Study below). This relationship sees these motorsport subsidiaries working closely with the OEMs on their domestic motorsport programs. Currently the most successful motorsport series in Japan is the SuperGT and specialists including TOMS (Toyota) and NISMO (Nissan) exist alongside Mugen (Honda) in supplying specialist support for the OEM motorsport programs. This support can take the form of chassis and engine preparation in the case of the bigger motorsport specialists.

There are specialist Japanese engine builders with weaker ties to the OEMs, for example, firms such as Autech, Tomei, Techno Craft and M-TEC also supply race engines to entrants in the SuperGT.

Outside of the SuperGT much of Japanese motorsport relies on European specialists. One area where Japanese suppliers are strong is in tire manufacture, particularly Bridgestone, who currently supply 40 percent of the F1 grid. From 2007 they will supply the entire grid and supply the control tire for the GP2 single-seat category supporting F1.

Entrants (Licenced)

Japan has three top-line road-racing motorsport disciplines. The most popular is the Japan GT Championship (SuperGT) where all the main Japanese OEMs support teams running heavily modified production sportscars. The second and third most important categories in Japan are Formula Nippon, a one-make single-seat championship, and F3.

Events

Japan has held a successful F1 Grand Prix at the Honda-owned Suzuka circuit since the mid-1980s. From 2007, the Toyota-owned circuit at Fuji will host the round of the F1 championship, after extensive investment in the circuit from the OEM. The rise of WRC, and the role of Japanese OEMs such as Subaru and Mitsubishi in the championship, means that from 2004 there has been a round of the WRC based in Hokkaido. Honda's involvement in the USA IRL single-seat championship has secured a round of that series held once a year at the Honda-owned Motegi circuit in Japan.

In terms of domestic events, the SuperGT, due to its support from the OEMs, is particularly successful. This championship is expanding tentatively into mainland Asia, and in 2004 included a demonstration race in the USA at the California Speedway. This innovative event combined the synergies of the SuperGT with the burgeoning California-based sports compact market.

Event Suppliers

Many of the larger circuits are connected to the Japanese OEMs. Suzuka and Twin Ring are owned by Honda, which has, therefore, been involved in the promotion of the F1 Grand Prix and the IRL event. Toyota has bought and is redeveloping the Fuji Circuit and from 2007 has attracted the F1 Grand Prix from Suzuka.

Consumption

F1 has a large following in Japan and this is reflected in good TV-viewing figures. The race at Suzuka always attracts extremely large and enthusiastic crowds. In terms of domestic championships the OEM-supported SuperGT attracts large numbers of spectators and a good-sized domestic TV audience.

Japanese Motorsport Industry Case Study: Mugen

National racing series in Japan involving saloon cars and sportscars are dominated by Japanese specialist motorsport organizations with very close links to the Japanese OEMs. Mugen has this sort of relationship with Honda. Hirotoshi Honda, the son of the founder of the Honda motor company, set up Mugen in 1973. Mugen concentrated on the production and modification of engines for competition use, using Honda-produced original equipment. Initially the company supplied engines across the range of motorsport categories; motor racing, motorcycle racing and karting. It also produced aftermarket equipment for modified road-going Honda cars. The company gained much success at a national level and, into the 1990s, supplied the standard-setting competition engine for F3, (although this period also saw the company withdraw from the motorcycle engine market). In the early 1980s Mugen produced a standard setting F2 engine in co-operation with Honda, and this co-operation eventually carried over into F1. When Honda officially withdrew from F1 in the early 1990s, Mugen took its place as a semi-official Honda works representative in the category. On Honda's official return to F1 in 2000, Mugen stepped back again to become a

> valued Honda subcontractor in the category. Mugen has worked in close co-operation in the past with another Honda-favored firm called Dome, who concentrate on the chassis production side of motorsport. This co-operation extends today to the Japanese GT Championship (SuperGT), while Mugen also produces engines for the one-make Formula Nippon Series. Outside Japan, and alongside its Honda F1 subcontractor role, it continues to supply engines to the global F3 market.

SWOT Analysis: Japanese Motorsport Industry

Following description of the Japanese motorsport value chain, a SWOT analysis summarizes some of the key aspects of the position on the global grid (see Table 2.9).

Table 2.9 **SWOT of the Japanese Motorsport Industry**

Strengths	Weaknesses
1 Large and growing manufacturer involvement in world motorsport: Honda (F1 and IRL), Toyota (F1 and IRL, NASCAR), Subaru (WRC), Mitsubishi (WRC), Nissan (off-road and sportscars), Suzuki (WRC)	1 Sparse specialist infrastructure and, consequently, a history of continuing UK specialist links to plug the gap
2 Strong supply side, particularly tyres	2 Japanese engineering can be conservative and avoids the risks needed for more radical innovation
3 Extremely strong national motorsport scene funded by domestic OEMs and run by specialist Japanese motorsport firms with close links to OEMs	
4 Significant country-focused sponsorship available for team/drivers	
5 10 percent of Japan's workforce is employed in auto and auto-related industries	
6 Large number of motorsport participants	
Opportunities	**Threats**
1 Skills transfer from UK to Japan	1 Continued links with European specialists stop industry critical mass developing
2 Development of Asian market	2 Minimal single-seat specialists
	3 Development of Asian competition

Conclusion: The Japanese Motorsport Industry

The Japanese motorsport industry is characterized by a strong domestic series supported by OEM-linked Japanese specialists (especially engines). On the international stage, Japanese OEMs have a major and growing presence in world motorsport. Traditionally, this presence is delivered through outsourcing partnerships to specialists in the UK, Italy, Germany and USA, combined with some successful OEM provision of engines. Consequently, the country has very few internationally capable specialist motorsport companies.

The German Motorsport Industry

Table 2.10 provides the global metrics for the German motorsport industry. The fourth largest motorsport industry in the world, Germany's industry has a critical mass of global constructors, global racing series and events, and viewers backed up by the domestic OEMs. The anomaly remains participation, with a relatively low level of circuit infrastructure and license holders.

Table 2.10 **The German Motorsport Industry in 2005**

Indicators	Germany 2005	% of world total
Total value of annual motorsport turnover for engineering and services	£3.0b	6.0
Motorsport turnover as % GDP	0.2 percent	—
Permanent paved circuits (including ovals over ¼ mile but not kart)	6	1.0
Competition license holders	10,000	—
Global chassis constructors (F1, WRC, WTCC and A1GP)	3	14.0
Number of racing series		
— Global	F1, WRC, WTCC, A1GP	—
— Regional	FIA GT, GP2, LMS	—
Global motorsport events (F1, WRC, WTCC and A1GP)	5	9.0
Average F1 viewing figures per race event (*Source*: Sports Marketing Surveys)	6.9 m	13.1
Average WRC viewing figures per event (*Source*: wrc.com)	0.48 m	1.0

A History of the German Motorsport Industry

In the early part of the 20th century, Mercedes was one of the strongest names in this era of OEM-dominated motorsport. In the 1930s this presence was magnified as Mercedes, together with Auto Union (now Audi), successfully met the edict from Hitler, backed up with finance, to export Third Reich sporting success.

Post-World War II, Germany was banned from international competition until 1950. Private entrants did use pre-war BMW engines in single-seater specials in the Formula 2 category but the subsequent re-emergence of the OEMs reabsorbed many of these specialist builders.

Mercedes made a successful F1 re-entry in the mid-1950s as a manufacturer team, and also had conspicuous success in international sportscar events. The company pulled out of motorsport again due to financial pressure and the bad publicity surrounding the 1955 Le Mans disaster, when a works-run Mercedes went into the crowd, killed 80 people and injured many more.

By the 1960s, the success of the UK industry's network production system had made OEM in-house motorsport involvement an extremely expensive option. Porsche, for example, found this out to its cost in when it entered F1 as both a chassis and engine manufacturer. Estimates have put Porsche's financial commitment to an only moderately successful motorsport program at some ten times the expenditure of its successful UK motorsport rivals at the time. A few small specialist German firms did attempt success in Formula One—such as Zakspeed, ATS and Rial—but they remained generally uncompetitive, and reliant to a greater or lesser extent on UK-built components and personnel.

It is not until 2001 that Germany saw a revival of single-seat chassis manufacturing based almost entirely upon one company, the Japanese firm Toyota. Toyota Team Europe had, for 30 years, run successful world rallying, and occasional world sportscar, programs from its base in Cologne. In 2001, and with huge financial backing (estimated to be at least $1 billion over five years), Toyota expanded the former rally team into a fully fledged F1 chassis and engine-building organization.

In contrast, German OEMs had maintained a Formula One presence through the provision of engines to specialist (UK) chassis constructors. Following Renault's introduction of the turbocharged engine in the mid-1970s, BMW built engines for Brabham and Porsche for McLaren. In the early 1990s, Mercedes re-entered international motorsport, initially through a sportscar liaison with the Swiss motorsport specialist Sauber. Mercedes had long been involved in national saloon car racing with great success, and also occasionally international rallying, and had relied on a mixture of German specialists like AMG (now wholly owned by Mercedes), and UK motorsport specialists such as Cosworth, among others. When Mercedes entered F1 it entrusted the chassis building and team operation to Sauber. Engine manufacture, however, was provided by the British specialist Ilmor. Most recently, Mercedes transferred the running of the team, and the building of chassis, away from Sauber to the UK-based McLaren, which still uses the UK-based (but now Mercedes-owned) Ilmor. It is an interesting mark of globalization to note also that Mercedes chose to build their flagship supercar, the SLR, at the UK base of McLaren F1 in a new $500 million factory.

German OEMs have found great success in motorsport since the 1960s in international formulae below the specialized arena of F1. Porsche, for example, has achieved outstanding success in sportscar events, particularly Le Mans, and, likewise, BMW has won countless championships in national and international saloon car racing.

Audi, currently part of the VAG Group, is another German OEM with a strong history of motorsport success in the lower professional categories of motorsport. Its parent company was the former Auto Union, famed for pre-war sporting success in Grand Prix racing. After a long post-war gap from competition, in the 1980s the company successfully rewrote the technical rules in rallying with its four-wheel-drive rally car, the Quattro, which went on to gain much success. The four-wheel-drive aspect of this success soon became a part of the Audi "brand" that the company successfully exported to other aspects of motorsport, particularly national saloon car racing in many different countries. Audi has recently dominated long-distance sportscar racing and in 2006 won Le Mans, using a diesel engine for the first time. VAG enjoyed reflected success when their UK-based Bentley subsidiary won Le Mans at its third attempt—resulting in huge global publicity and an enormous growth in sales, which has not diminished since.

Current Industry Position

The German motorsport and performance engineering marketplace was estimated at £3 billion in 2003 (MRA, 2004c). Germany has a very strong base of road-car manufacturing, including VAG, BMW, Mercedes, Opel and Porsche, and has a significant pool of automotive-engineering expertise situated around Stuttgart and Munich. Massive investment by Toyota F1 in Cologne has focused attention on the growing strength of the German motorsport industry.

Toyota, like Ferrari, is unique in producing both chassis and engine for F1 under the same roof. German OEMs involved in F1 include BMW, who produce engines for the wholly BMW-owned former Sauber team in Switzerland from their German-based facilities, and Mercedes, who currently part-own McLaren F1 and use their wholly owned UK specialist Ilmor (now renamed Mercedes High Performance Engines) as engine supplier to the team. There are also a significant number of world-class F1 suppliers in Germany, including Sachs (clutches), BBS (wheels), Bosch (electronics), Mahle (pistons) and Eibach (suspension).

The German Motorsport Industry

Outside F1, Audi and Bentley, part of VAG, have enjoyed significant sports-car success, including winning six consecutive Le Mans 24 Hours, and success in the USA. Audi and Bentley engines and chassis, however, have been partly built and developed outside Germany, relying on British and Italian specialists. This reliance on outside chassis and design specialists, particularly in the area of aerodynamics and composites, points to two areas of weakness for the German motorsport industry.

Rumours persist of a VAG team to be entered in F1, based in Germany, and building its own engines and chassis. Similarly, Porsche has opened a new factory at Leipzig with a test track built to F1 standards.

Mercedes activities, outside F1, are based around the successful DTM saloon car series; an essentially German-based national championship that also had German OEMs Opel and Audi as competitors until 2005, when Opel pulled out. Mercedes DTM cars are built by AMG, a formerly independent motorsport specialist, which is now wholly owned by Mercedes. Opel had a similarly wholly owned motorsport specialist in Germany, OPC, to construct its DTM cars, while Audi uses the independent German motorsport specialist, Abt, and the in-house Audi Sport to build its DTM cars. A significant proportion of all three OEMs' DTM cars are sourced from outside the country, particularly from motorsport specialists in Italy and Britain.

German Motorsport Value Chain Analysis

Table 2.11 summarizes the motorsport value chain applied to the current German motorsport industry. Following the table, each cell of the table is discussed to complete a comprehensive empirical description of the German industry.

Regulation of Sport

Motorsport in Germany is regulated by the Deutsche Motor Sport Bund (DMSB), the nationally designated organizing body recognized by the FIA. All German motor clubs involved in motorsport are members of the DMSB and follow DMSB and FIA rules and procedures for organizing and administrating motorsport in Germany, including safety matters.

Supporting Service Industry

The German-based support-service industry is stronger than that in Italy but does not match that available in the UK. Due to the importance of F1 in Germany and the number of German corporate F1 sponsors, marketing and marketing-support services in Germany are strong. Driver management at the highest levels is world class, in part due to the highly successful Schumacher brothers and their German-based management.

Table 2.11 **The German Motorsport Value Chain**

Value chain position	Companies/organizations involved in supply chain
1. Regulation of sport	
Regulatory bodies	DMSB
Safety panels	DMSB, FIA
2. Supporting service industry	
Logistics	—
Markets and merchandizing	WH Sport International, Sport + Markt, P&W, MSM, WWP
Personnel and human resources (driver management)	Weber Management
Other (racing school, insurance and risk management, finance, accountancy, legal)	—
3. Constructors	
F1	Toyota
Rally	VW
Sportscar	Porsche, Audi Sport
Kit car	—
Other	Saloon—AMG, Audi Sport, Abt, OPC; Off road—VW, X-Raid
4. Constructor suppliers	
Engines	Toyota, BMW, Spiess, AMG
Electronics	Bosch, 2D Debus and Diebold
Materials	HF Carbon
Design Services	Porsche
Transmission	Getrag
Brakes/suspension	Sachs, Eibach
Safety systems	Recaro, Matter
Tyres	Continental
Fuel/lubrication	Veedol, Liqui Moly
Other	—
5. Entrants (licensed)	
Race team	DTM, GP2, F3
Individual participants	10,000
Clubs	Local and regional
Drivers	Michael Schumacher, Ralf Schumacher, Nick Heidfeld, Nico Rosberg, Sebastien Vettel
6. Events	
F1	Nurburgring, Hockenheim
WRC	Deutschland

(*Continued*)

Table 2.11 **(Continued)**

Value chain position	Companies/organizations involved in supply chain
Historic	Norisring, Nordschleife, HRA, Oldtimer, Youngtimer
Saloon	DTM
Club	Weak
Other	–
7. Event suppliers	
Circuits (construction, safety)	Tilke
Event management/ infrastructure	ADAC
8. Distribution	
Media	F1 TV—RTL; Magazine—*Sport Auto*
9. Consumption	
Viewers	F1 viewing figures per race event 2005: 6.9 m (*Source*: Sports Marketing Surveys)
Spectators	Medium
Participants	Low

Constructors

Toyota remains the only F1 constructor based in Germany with a massive organization similar in size to Ferrari. Below the level of F1, German constructors are not involved to any depth in WRC.

There is a strong sportscar presence headed by the worldwide sportscar racing presence of the Porsche factory, which has a long history of motorsport involvement. Much of Porsche's worldwide racing-car construction is done in Germany. In contrast, the other sportscar constructor in Germany is Audi Sport, who have a strong Le Mans and American sportscar racing pedigree over recent years, but rely on UK- and Italian-based suppliers for some of their cars, but not their engines.

German-based constructors like X-Raid (BMW) and VW Racing have an involvement in the Paris-Dakar Off Road Rally and the FIA Off Road Championship.

Constructor Suppliers

Within the engine supply chain in Germany, the Toyota F1 facility also includes an engine build and development facility. Also in F1, BMW Motorsport in Germany supply engines for the Swiss-based BMW team, formerly known as Sauber. Mercedes F1 engines for the McLaren team are built in the UK by the Mercedes-owned Mercedes Benz High Performance Engines, formerly Ilmor.

The major championship outside F1 that German-based constructor suppliers are involved in is the German-based DTM championship. Here German firms like AMG and Spiess supply engines to, respectively, the Mercedes and the former Opel DTM teams.

The German component supply chain to the engine builders is strong in parts. Mahle produce pistons, Schrick camshafts and Bosch electronics for F1 involvement. These firms are global motorsport suppliers with world-class reputations, who also supply components for motorsport involvement below the level of F1.

A further area of supply-chain strength is in safety. Recaro produce seats for road cars and motorsport use and Matter prepare and strengthen production car shells for competition use. In addition, both Sachs and Eibach produce competition suspension for a global market, while Sachs also produce clutches for competition use from F1 involvement, down through the motorsport hierarchy.

Entrants (Licenced)

Toyota has the only F1 team to be based in Germany at Cologne. The largest numbers of entrants within Germany by value are the DTM teams. Although the DTM championship races across Europe, all the OEMs involved, the series' administration and virtually all the teams are German-based. The most well known of these DTM teams are AMG and Joest.

Outside of F1 and DTM, German entrants are not well represented in WRC due to the low involvement of German-based competition-car suppliers. Within single-seat racing below F1, in championships like GP2 and the World Series by Renault, German teams are very rare compared to those from the UK, Italy or France. In the Euro F3 Series, created in 2003 from a merger of the national series in France and Germany, German teams like Mucke Motorsport are to be found.

In sportscar racing German entrants are strong due to the history of involvement of Porsche in global sportscar racing, for example the various one-make factory-supported national Supercup series. Porsche racing has a very strong national presence in Germany, leading entrants to venture out from this onto the European and global stage.

The number of individual license holders, quoted by the DMSB at around 10,000 across all four-wheeled motorsport disciplines, is among the lowest in Western Europe. It is around half that of Italy, the next lowest, and some way behind France and the UK. This low figure is exacerbated by the relatively few permanent road-racing circuits available in Germany, compared to those available in the UK, France and Italy, particularly when compared to the population size of those countries relative to Germany.

Events

Events are relatively strong within Germany, which is due partly to the recent success of Michael Schumacher. F1 is now very popular in the country and this allowed it to host two Grand Prix a year until 2007. One, entitled the European Grand Prix, was held at the Nurburgring, while the German Grand Prix was held at Hockenheim. From 2007, the Grand Prix will alternate between the two facilities, which are Germany's oldest and most significant, particularly the Nurburgring.

The recent expansion of the WRC has also spawned, for the first time, a German-based round of the WRC, which has proved successful.

German historic motorsport events are strong, as they are in much of Europe. Events in Germany include high-profile meetings based at venues of historic significance for German and world motorsport. The once-a-year Norisring street race is one example, while the original 14-mile Nordschliefe circuit at the Nurburgring is also the site of much history within world and German motorsport, and organizes events like the Oldtimer GP to reflect that heritage. German national historic racing also occurs across the range of motorsport disciplines.

The DTM is by far the strongest German-based motorsport series of events. With strong German-based OEM support, the series draws large crowds to the majority of the championship rounds that are held in Germany. Expert estimates suggest that the series could be worth up to five times the value of the British based BTCC. Consequently, the DTM is the strongest domestic four-wheeled motorsport series in Europe by value.

Drag racing is popular in Germany with a well-supported round of the FIA European Drag Racing Championship at Hockenheim and one of the strongest European national series.

Due to the low levels of competitors and shortage of permanent circuits, club motorsport involvement is not particularly strong in Germany.

Event Suppliers

The main global event supplier of repute in Germany, in an otherwise weak part of the supply chain, is the international circuit designer Tilke, which has been responsible for many F1-standard tracks built in recent years. Promotion of F1 events is by the ADAC automobile club, while DTM events are promoted by an organization comprised mainly of the OEM manufacturers involved in the series.

Distribution

Distribution of the F1 television rights is by the RTL organization. *Sport Auto* is one of the main motorsport specialist magazines in the German market.

Consumption

TV viewing figures for F1 are among the highest due to the Schumacher effect (although he retires in 2007). Similarly, large TV audiences occur for the

> **German Motorsport Industry Case Study: Mercedes AMG GmbH**
>
> AMG was set up to engineer, design and develop racing engines in 1967. The company's early sporting success was with modified Mercedes saloon cars. This relationship presaged a successful partnership with Mercedes. Initially, AMG built on this sporting success by offering modified Mercedes road cars and aftermarket work on similar road-going cars for the general public. By the late 1980s, AMG returned to top-line motorsport by acting as a factory team in saloon car racing and sportscar racing for the Mercedes company. AMG continued to offer a lucrative series of modified Mercedes road cars, as well as operating a highly successful racing team running Mercedes saloons. By the mid-1990s AMG had evolved from modifying Mercedes road cars to being a virtual manufacturer of specialist road-going Mercedes in its own right. This relationship between AMG and Mercedes was formally solidified in 1999, when Mercedes bought AMG outright, the company now being known as Mercedes AMG GmbH. The main fields of activity of Mercedes AMG are:
>
> - the design and development of high-performance road-going vehicles;
> - the manufacture of AMG series vehicles in conjunction with DaimlerChrysler manufacturing facilities;
> - the manufacture of competition cars for the DTM series; and
> - the operation of two of the teams that run Mercedes DTM cars.
>
> The company now produces 18,500 road cars a year and has 500 employees based in Affalterbach.

domestic DTM series. Spectator figures are high, both for F1 events and the DTM, and for one-off events like Hockenheim's round of the FIA European Drag Racing Championship.

SWOT Analysis: German Motorsport Industry

Following description of the German motorsport value chain, a SWOT analysis summarizes some of the key aspects of the position on the global grid (Table 2.12).

Table 2.12 **SWOT of the German Motorsport Industry**

Strengths
1 Strong manufacturer involvement and competition between OEMs
2 Rising domestic motorsport recognition due to Schumacher effect
3 Very strong precision engineering capability in Germany more widely
4 Very professional OEM-supported national series, strongest in Europe
5 "Autobahn" culture of fast cars
6 Tradition of enhanced motorsport branding (AMG-Mercedes; BMW M-Series)

Weaknesses
1 Few independent motorsport specialists. e.g. Mercedes now owns AMG, a formerly independent Mercedes motorsport specialist
2 Few permanent circuits and low participant involvement
3 Few independent wind tunnels
4 Strong green lobby
5 Club motorsport not strong/well organized
6 Conservative engineering tradition
7 High labor costs and restrictive labor regulation

Opportunities
1 OEM involvement builds German network of motorsport subcontractors
2 Knowledge transfer from UK partners to Germany
3 Some state support for motorsport infrastructure e.g. Lausitzring circuit in former East Germany

Threats
1 Low cost East European engineering
2 EU labor laws
3 Loss of "Schumacher effect"

Conclusion: The German Motorsport Industry

Recent years have seen the expansion of a strong OEM-driven national industry based upon a combination of domestic and overseas OEM investment and a high-quality automotive supply chain and technical workforce increasingly geared to the requirements of motorsport. The industry lacks an independent, flexible and entrepreneurial network of firms and this is highlighted by the substantial use of specialists from the UK and Italy. The sport, as measured by grass roots participation, remains relatively weak. A new era of OEM-dominated motorsport would see the German industry particularly well placed to further compete on a global scale.

The Italian Motorsport Industry

Table 2.13 provides the global metrics for the Italian motorsport industry. The fifth largest national motorsport industry, comprising 4 percent of world industry turnover, the industry has significant global representation in terms of

Table 2.13 **The Italian Motorsport Industry in 2005**

Indicators	Italy 2005	% of world total
Total value of annual motorsport turnover for engineering and services	£2.0b	4.0
Motorsport turnover as % GDP	0.21 percent	—
Permanent paved circuits (including ovals over ¼ mile but not kart)	10	1.7
Competition license holders	19,000	—
Global chassis constructors (F1, WRC, WTCC and A1GP)	3	13.5
Number of racing series		
— Global	F1; WRC; WTCC	—
— Regional	GP2; FIA GT; LMS; Rally	—
Global motorsport events (F1, WRC, WTCC and A1GP)	5	9.0
Average F1 viewing figures per race event (*Source*: Sports Marketing Surveys)	6.8 m	13.0
Average WRC viewing figures per event (*Source*: wrc.com)	1.33 m	2.5

constructors, racing series and events. Viewing figures and participation remain relatively high.

A History of the Italian Motorsport Industry

The large Italian road-car production companies, like FIAT, Alfa Romeo and Lancia in the north of the country, have a long heritage of involvement in post- and pre-war motorsport. From the late 1940s to the early 1960s, Italy became the center of world motorsport. This center was based around the city of Modena in the region of Emilia Romagna, and can be historically compared in importance to the UK's Motorsport Valley® of today (see Angus, 2001a; 2001b).

The famous automotive names of Maserati, Lamborghini and Ferrari were based around Modena, together with less well-known names like DeTomaso and Stanguellini. Just down the road in Bologna were OSCA and the short-lived ATS, while into the 1990s Bugatti also chose Modena as a base. The importance of Modena became such that from the mid- to late 1950s the town's racetrack graduated to holding a non-championship Grand Prix. The track provided a focal point for the Italian motorsport industry in the same way that Silverstone has done in Britain, until planning restrictions curtailed activities at the Italian track. The history of the motorsport industry in Italy can be usefully subdivided into three parts according to the type of car constructor involved:

- *Type One: Large Italian road-car manufacturers in motorsport.* This would include, for example, the names of Alfa Romeo, Fiat and Lancia. This sector is also expressed geographically in that the motorsport arms of these companies were, or are, mainly based around Milan and Turin, near to the parent road car-producing companies. These companies arose in the 1920s.

- *Type Two: The low-production, high-performance, road-car industry.* This would include names such as Ferrari and Maserati, for example, which produce very low numbers of highly specialist and expensive road cars. This sector also has a geographic expression in that many of these companies were, or are, based in and around Modena. These companies arose in the 1930s.

- *Type Three: The specialist motorsport constructor.* This category includes names like Dallara, Tatuus, Minardi and Coloni, which originated in the 1970s.

Companies from the first two eras existed alongside one another before being joined by the specialist motorsport constructors during the 1970s.

Current Industry Position

The annual turnover of the Italian motorsport industry was estimated at £2 billion in 2003 (MRA, 2004b). Ferrari, based near Modena, is the longest-running team in Formula One, while, in the lower categories of single-seat competition and sportscar racing, firms like Dallara and Tatuus have overcome a formerly dominant UK position.

One of the most important single-seat categories outside F1 is now the Indy Racing League (IRL) in the USA. Products from Dallara, based near Parma, numerically dominated this series in 2005, while the firm also provides the one-make chassis to the IRL's feeder category, the Infiniti Pro Series. In the junior single-seat category of Formula 3, important as an F1 feeder series in Europe and South America, Dallara has dominated the category worldwide for the last decade. Outside IRL and F3, Dallara exclusively supplies chassis to the F1 supporting GP2 and the World Series by Renault.

Below F3, the single-seat categories have a significant presence from the Milan-based Tatuus organization. The company's relationship with Renault means that Tatuus is responsible for that company's one-make chassis in many countries throughout the world. Tatuus will also provide the one-make chassis for a new single-seat series supporting the WTCC from 2007.

The country also has an increasing presence in European and USA sportscar racing represented, for example, by firms like Picchio and Osella.

Important Italian component suppliers include Magneti Marelli, an electronics specialist, Brembo, a brake supplier, and Fondmetal Technologies, an aerodynamic consultancy, all three of which have a very high international presence both inside and outside F1. Aerodynamic research within motorsport is particularly strong within Italy, with private motorsport wind tunnels available at Dallara and Fondmetal Technologies, and a joint venture between Dallara and Fondmetal Technologies called Aerolab producing another commercial tunnel in Italy. Finally, the Italian karting industry is the acknowledged world leader in its field.

Italian Motorsport Value Chain Analysis

Table 2.14 summarizes the motorsport value chain applied to the current Italian motorsport industry. Following the table, each cell of the table is discussed to complete a comprehensive empirical description of the Italian industry.

Table 2.14 **The Italian Motorsport Value Chain**

Value chain position	Companies/organizations involved in supply chain
1. Regulation of sport	
Regulatory bodies	CSAI
Safety panels	FIA, CSAI
2. Supporting service industry	
Logistics	—
Markets and merchandizing	—
Personnel and human resources (driver management)	—
Other (racing school, insurance and risk management, finance, accountancy, legal)	Henry Morogh Racing School
3. Constructors	
F1	Ferrari, Minardi/Toro Rosso
Rally	Fiat (NTechnology)
Sportscar	NTechnology, Osella, Picchio, Michelotto
Kit car	—
Other	*Single seat*—Dallara, Tatuus; *Saloon/ GT*—NTechnology, JAS
4. Constructor suppliers	
Engines	NTechnology, JAS, ORAL Engineering, Novamotor, Ellegi Motor

(Continued)

Table 2.14 **(Continued)**

Value chain position	Companies/organizations involved in supply chain
Electronics	Magneti Marelli, Efi Technology, MAHTechs, Tecno Elettra, FIAMM
Materials	ATR, Belco Avia
Design services	Dallara, Pininfarina, Bertone, ITALDesign, Zagato, Ghia
Transmission	CIMA
Brakes/suspension	Brembo
Safety systems	Sparco, OMP, Sabelt
Tyres	Pirelli, Marangoni
Fuel/lubrication	Agip, Selenia
Other	*Wheels*—Tecnomagnesio, MIM, OZ, Fondmetal, Speedline, Bellotto; *Aerodynamic*—Dallara, Fondmetal, Aerolab; *Karting*—Vega, Comer, IAME, Italsystem, PCR, Pavesi, Vortex, Biesse, Birel, CRG, Jollykart, Maranello Kart, Tony Kart, Trulli
5. Entrants (licensed)	
Race team	GP2, F3, LMS
Individual participants	19,000
Clubs	—
Drivers	Jarno Trulli, Giancarlo Fisichella
6. Events	
F1	Imola, Monza
WRC	Sardinia
Historic	Mille Miglia, Targa Florio, Coppa Milano-Sanremo, CIA
Saloon	Superproduction, CIVT
Club	—
Other	Karting Strong
7. Event suppliers	
Circuits (construction, safety)	—
Event management/ infrastructure	ACM, SAGIS, Peroni Promotions
8. Distribution	
Media	F1—RAI, Magazine—*Autosprint*
9. Consumption	
Viewers	F1 viewing figures per race event 2005: 6.8 m (*Source*: Sports Marketing Surveys)
Spectators	Medium
Participants	Medium

Regulation of Sport

Motorsport in Italy is regulated by the Commissione Sportiva Automobilistica Italiane (CSAI), the nationally designated organizing body recognized by the FIA. All Italian motor clubs involved in motorsport are members of the CSAI and follow CSAI and FIA rules and procedures for organizing and administrating motorsport in Italy, including safety matters.

Supporting Service Industry

The Italian-based support service industry is not particularly strong. Within the area of logistics, for example, more components are carried from the UK to Italy than the other way around and UK-based logistics firms have the dominant presence in this international shipping process. Local-based firms play a part in the logistics of the domestic motorsport industry, but the specialist logistics firms found in the UK are not as prevalent in Italy.

Marketing and driver management are carried out within Italy, but not generally by Italian-based firms. For example, the marketing and driver arrangements of Ferrari are carried out outside Italy, although the marketing of Ferrari itself is now back in-house in Maranello. Many Italian circuits have driver training schools but none are of particular international significance.

Constructors

Italian motorsport can be split into two networks. Encapsulating one network is the international scale and scope of the Ferrari F1 team, employing almost 1,000 personnel and with a 2005 total budget of over $300 million. Relatively little within the Ferrari F1 supply chain is linked into the rest of the Italian motorsport industry, although there are small signs this may be changing.

Outside the Ferrari F1 network is the internationally linked network of smaller firms, headed by the single-seat specialists Dallara and Tatuus. Outside of the world of single-seat racing are the saloon, sportscar and rally builders NTechnology, and the sportscar builders Osella and Picchio. This non-F1 network also supplies much of the domestic motorsport needs within Italy, supported by a network of very small constructors like Reggiani and Ombra, who supply the national market only.

Constructor Suppliers

The far-reaching strength of the UK motorsport industry within Europe can be seen by the presence of many UK-based constructor suppliers within Italy. The UK firms supply the market through three major Italian distributors or direct to the end user when required. The overall reliance on a UK supply chain does hide some Italian supplier strengths, for example, the composite supplier ATR. The firm supplies composite parts for Ferrari (F1 and road), Dallara and Tatuus in Italy and Porsche in Germany. In addition, Brembo is a global competitor in the braking field, supplying Ferrari, among others, and also now owning UK-based AP Racing, manufacturing clutches and brakes.

Aerodynamic research in motorsport within Italy is relatively strong with three key international suppliers outside the Ferrari F1 networks. Dallara have long been involved in international motorsport aerodynamic consultancy, as have Fondmetal Technologies, a subsidiary of the Fondmetal wheel-making organization. In 2004, both Dallara and Fondmetal Technologies increased their role in the supply of international motorsport aerodynamic consultancy by opening a jointly owned wind tunnel called Aerolab.

Italy is also Europe's key supplier of safety equipment, with firms like Sparco, who employ 300 personnel in Italy, being joined by OMP and Sabelt. These firms make all kinds of safety equipment for motorsport, from personal safety items like helmets and overalls, to larger items like full-vehicle roll cages.

Perhaps the most significant subsector of the motorsport supply chain within Italy is that for karting. Italy is the acknowledged center of the world kart industry, which is viewed as the lower rung of the single-seat racing segment. The Italian kart industry dominates short-circuit karting throughout the world, with Italian chassis firms such as Biesse, Birel, CRG, Jolly Kart, Maranello Kart, Tony Kart and Trulli backed up by Italian engine suppliers like Comer, IAME, Italsystem, PCR, Pavesi and Vortex. The Italian kart-tire supplier Vega also has a significant international market share. The Italian kart industry is the third largest sector within the Italian motorsport industry by value, behind only the single-seat segment and performance engineering, and is a key motorsport sector exporter.

Entrants (Licenced)

Italian team entrants play a large part on the stage of international motorsport. At the top of world motorsport are the two Italian-based F1 teams, Torro Rosso, formerly Minardi, owned by the Austrian soft-drinks brand, Red Bull, and Ferrari, which together comprised 20 percent of the F1 grid in 2005. In WRC, Italy is poorly represented, with only Fiat's low-key involvement in the JWRC. From 2007, Fiat will enter the Eurosport-owned and sponsored International Rally Championship (IRC).

In other international European-based single-seat formulae, like GP2, Nissan World Series and Euro F3, Italian teams such as Coloni, Durango, Prema Powerteam and Team Ghinzani are key competitors. International GT championships also have a strong presence from Italian teams, with Scuderia Italia and GPC Squadra Corse contesting the LMS and FIA GT Series. Autodelta, the works Alfa Romeo touring-car team, is also a prolific winner in the WTCC.

Outside circuit racing, the main international presence of Italian motorsport teams is in the competitive karting segment. Here, reflecting the Italian industry dominance in this sector, Italian teams are highly competitive on the European and World Kart championship stage.

The CSAI claim there were approximately 19,000 license holders across all four-wheeled motorsport disciplines in 2003. This puts Italy some way behind France and the UK in Europe, but ahead of Germany. All European countries lag some way behind the huge numbers of motorsport participants claimed for the USA. The strength of karting as a sport in Italy goes some way to make up for the relative weakness of the grass roots of Italian motorsport when compared to that in, for example, the UK. In addition, Italy's strong motorsport heritage and the strength of grass roots karting means that it can always lay claim to many drivers competing on the international stage at any one time.

Events

Motorsport events are strong within Italy. Of the 19 F1 events taking place in 2005, two took place within Italy. The first is the Grand Prix at Monza, now one of the most famous and oldest Grand Prix on the calendar, dating back to the 1920s. The second is the San Marino Grand Prix held at Imola, an event with a quarter of a century's heritage. In WRC, Italy's event was historically the San Remo round of the World Championship. In recent years this event has been transferred to the island of Sardinia.

Historic motorsport events in Italy are popular. This is partly due to Ferrari being a national symbol within Italy, and this strength extends back into Italian motorsport heritage. The brand, Ferrari, within motorsport is strong not just because of the success it has had in the past, but also due to its continuing to win at the highest level within motorsport today. Other marques within Italian motorsport history are also respected on a global scale, with names such as Alfa Romeo, Lancia, Lamborghini, Maserati and De Tomaso reflecting both a heritage of Italian motorsport and of road-going Italian supercars.

Italian historic motorsport events can be split into two segments. The first segment is "revival" historic motorsport events such as Targa Florio and Mille Miglia. The history of these events, and the strength surrounding the history of the Italian marques, combines to make them among the most successful on the international historic motorsport calendar. They are high profile, attracting high net worth individuals, and historic cars and sponsorship from the heritage departments of global OEMs.

The second Italian historic segment is at club level. The Italian domestic historic motorsport scene encapsulates events in rallying, speed events and racing. The last of these captures the highest profile within Italian domestic motorsport. The main race series is called the Campionato Italiano Autostoriche (CIA), and is for historic racing saloons.

Saloon racing within Italy is weak compared to the strength of the German-based DTM series. The main championships are called CIVT and the less technically sophisticated Superproduction. Sportscar racing occurs in GT and the unique sportscar category.

Club motorsport events are relatively weakly supported within Italian motorsport but this is partly offset by the grass roots support of domestic Italian karting events. In addition, national-level Italian kart championships are recognized as some of the best and most well attended in the world.

Event Suppliers

Event suppliers in Italy are mainly local and domestic in origin. The two Grand Prix are promoted respectively by the Automobile Club of Monza, for the Italian Grand Prix held at Monza, and by SAGIS for the San Marino Grand Prix held at Imola. Many national-level motorsport events are promoted by the Rome-based Peroni Promotions organization. The WTCC, a new global series, is managed from Italy, but owned by Eurosport TV.

Distribution

RAI televises the highly partisan Grand Prix coverage in Italy. Similarly, although there are a number of specialist motorsport magazines, like *Autosprint*, these magazines' coverage tends to be most extensive for the home-based team of Ferrari. Independent, non-Ferrari-based coverage within Italy is difficult to find in the print media.

Consumption

Motorsport consumption in Italy leans very strongly toward the coverage of Grand Prix, and Ferrari's involvement in those events. Viewing figures have historically been high, but more recently, and paradoxically in spite of Ferrari's success, these figures are dropping. Two-wheeled motorsport viewing consumption remains high, but club-level spectator involvement in four-wheeled motorsport is not strong, a situation similar to that in many European countries.

Italian Motorsport Industry Case Study: Dallara

Dallara is a small racing-car chassis manufacturer and consultant based to the south of Parma that employs around 100 people. Founded in 1972, the company has become a major competitor to UK companies like Lola and formerly Reynard and Ralt. Dallara describes itself as a British motorsport company that just happens to be based in Italy. Like many UK companies, it is a small, highly flexible organization that relies on outside subcontractors for many major components sourced from the UK and, increasingly, from within Italy. Products from Dallara dominate the Indy Racing League (IRL), for example, while the firm also provides the one-make chassis to the IRL's feeder category, the Infiniti Pro Series. In the junior single-seat category of Formula 3, the company has led the category worldwide for the last decade. Outside IRL and F3, Dallara exclusively supply chassis to the F1-supporting GP2 series and the World Series by Renault. The company is also a leading supplier of aerodynamic and chassis consultancy services to the motorsport arms of large OEMs like Audi and Toyota.

SWOT Analysis: Italian Motorsport Industry

Following description of the Italian motorsport value chain, a SWOT analysis summarizes some of the key aspects of the position on the global grid (see Table 2.15).

Table 2.15 **SWOT of the Italian Motorsport Industry**

Strengths	Weaknesses
1 Strong independent industry subgroupings hidden under the glamor of Ferrari (e.g. Tatuus, Brembo)	1 Current predominance of the Fiat empire, and strength of Ferrari, inhibits a more balanced network of motorsport firms
2 Success of Dallara expanding expertise and reputation in "one-make" single-seater market	2 Motorsport technological paradigm lost to UK 40 years ago
3 Karting industry and sport	3 Small manufacturing base and sometimes poor-quality products means restricted supply of specialist subcontractors in key areas
4 Strong domestic interest in motorsport	4 August shutdown
5 Performance engineering cluster around Modena	5 Can have quality and delivery problems
6 Passion surrounding Ferrari	
7 World-class stylists	
8 Motorsport heritage	

Opportunities	Threats
1 Expansion of Italian motorsport into new markets e.g. China	1 EU labor laws
2 Continuing success of single-seat exporters	2 Externally, Italian motorsport is overwhelmingly seen as Ferrari
3 World market for aerodynamic expertise	3 Low-cost East European engineering base
4 Lower labor costs	
5 Italian motorsport "brand"	

Conclusion: The Italian Motorsport Industry

Renowned for the brand of Ferrari, and its karting industry, the Italian motorsport industry has experienced a slow but steady expansion of other world-class constructors and suppliers such as Minardi, Dallara, Tatuus, NTechnology, Pirelli, Brembo, Fondmetal Technologies, Sparco and Sabelt. It remains a center for the production of low-volume, high-performance road cars and has a motorsport heritage and passion that is the envy of the world. Nevertheless, it remains fragmented and looks to the UK, in particular, for much of its expertise and supplies.

The French Motorsport Industry

Table 2.16 provides the global metrics for the French motorsport industry. The last of our frontrunner nations, with an annual motorsport turnover of some £1.5 billion, the industry hosts a number of racing events, and has a national passion for rallying based upon its historic success.

Table 2.16 **The French Motorsport Industry in 2005**

Indicators	France 2005	% of world total
Total value of annual motorsport turnover for engineering and services	£1.5b	3.0
Motorsport turnover as % GDP	0.13 percent	—
Permanent paved circuits (including ovals over ¼ mile but not kart)	9	1.5
Competition license holders	54,000	—
Global chassis constructors (F1, WRC, WTCC and A1GP)	2	9.0
Number of racing series		
— Global	F1; WRC; WTCC	—
— Regional	GP2; FIA GT; FIA Rally	—
Global motorsport events (F1, WRC, WTCC and A1GP)	3	5.4
Average F1 viewing figures per race event (*Source*: Sports Marketing Surveys)	3.8 m	7.2
Average WRC viewing figures per event (*Source*: wrc.com)	15.7 m	31.0

A History of the French Motorsport Industry

In the pre-World War I era of motorsport, France was very strongly represented in both sporting and industry terms. In sporting terms the ACF, the Automobile Club of France, was heavily involved in the organization of the first Grand Prix, while, within the motorsport industry, some of the most successful pre-World War I teams were those fielded by the OEMs like Peugeot, Renault, Panhard and Darraq.

In the post-World War I period, French OEMs were again heavily involved in motorsport, with the likes of Talbot, Delage and Delahaye moderately successful in international sportscar racing until the 1950s. In contrast, Bugatti, in the 1920s and 1930s, was one of the first companies in the world to become involved purely in the manufacture of purpose-designed cars for motorsport. Bugatti helped change the paradigm of international motorsport, from one that was OEM-dominated to one where a well-funded privateer could be competitive.

World War II and the rise of the German manufacturers ended the success of Bugatti and, post-World War II, the company failed to gain the financial viability to successfully re-enter motorsport. Instead, Gordini carried on the tradition of the small motorsport specialist in the post-war era in France. Gordini were successful in sportscars and moderately successful in F1 until the company ran into financial difficulties and was taken over by Renault, with a view to its acting as an in-house motorsport specialist.

With the demise of Delage, Delahaye, Talbot and Gordini, French presence in the international motorsport arena remained relatively subdued until the arrival of Matra in the late 1960s. Matra was a government-owned defence and aerospace conglomerate that built F1 engines with success in the late 1960s, winning several F1 Grand Prix events with Tyrell. They also initially built chassis, and later successful international sportscars, throughout the 1970s. While the sportscars were highly successful, their F1 chassis was only moderately so, and they subsequently became an F1 engine supplier to one of the few specialist French F1 teams, Ligier, who were only moderately successful. Matra withdrew from frontline motorsport in the early 1980s.

Renault was also a government-owned OEM, and followed Matra by re-entering international motorsport in the mid-1970s. Renault revolutionized F1 by introducing turbocharged engines, developed successfully for international sportscar racing. The company initially made both engine and chassis in F1, with limited success, before concentrating fully on engine supply to a number of UK specialist F1 chassis manufacturers in the 1980s, such as Lotus, Williams and Benetton. Renault is now involved again as an F1 engine and chassis manufacturer—having bought out the UK-based Benetton team for that purpose—and has won the F1 Constructors' Championship two years running, 2005 and 2006.

Peugeot, part of the PSA Group, re-entered international motorsport in the mid-1980s with a very successful rallying program. The firm has also been involved in the 1990s as a successful international sportscar entrant and as an F1 engine supplier. The F1 engine was supplied unsuccessfully to various UK specialist F1 teams before being sold off to a private engine company, Asiatech, a few years ago. The Asiatech engine, built at the former Peugeot premises in France, was unsuccessful and the Asiatech venture closed in late 2002. Peugeot continued as a very successful WRC constructor, winning three consecutive titles in 2000, 2001 and 2002, before pulling out of the sport at the end of 2005 to concentrate on a diesel-engined Le Mans program for 2007.

Citroën is also part of the PSA Group. They had an intermittently successful in-house rally program for many years, but in the last few years have become a world-class competitor in the WRC, winning the constructors' title three times in a row—2003, 2004 and 2005.

The number of truly independent French motorsport specialists has always been relatively low in comparison to French OEM motorsport involvement. Some of the few specialists have grown up around the world-famous Le Mans sportscar race, such as the former Rondeau, with Courage continuing this trend.

In F1, the independent specialists are again relatively few. The former Ligier team enjoyed much state patronage when it competed in the 1970s through to the 1990s. In the late 1990s Ligier was taken over by the former French F1 World Champion Alain Prost. The team did not enjoy any greater success than previously, and slid into bankruptcy in early 2002, after rumours that Prost had considered moving the entire organization to Motorsport Valley® in the UK.

Current Industry Position

The turnover value of the French motorsport and performance engineering market in 2003 was estimated at £1.5 billion (MRA, 2004a). Historically, French motorsport has gained significant funding from French OEMs, tobacco companies and oil companies. Over the last ten years finance from oil and tobacco companies has significantly reduced, leading to the loss of a generation of F1 drivers and a significant part of the domestic industry.

While Renault now has a significant presence in F1 after the OEM bought Benetton in the UK outright in 2001, the team and chassis production are still based in the UK, with engines produced in France. France's last surviving F1 team, Prost Grand Prix (formerly Ligier), closed early in 2002. Renault engines are produced in Viry Chatillon, France, at Renault Sport and, while these are now the only high-profile F1 involvement in France, this hides a strong French presence as engineering suppliers to the F1 industry.

Within the F1 engine supply chain, Mecachrome is a long-standing partner of Renault. Mecachrome is an aerospace engineering company that also supplies the high-technology end of the motorsport market. In the past it has acted as a manufacturer of F1 engines in its own right, utilizing Renault F1 technology when Renault decided to cut its F1 involvement. Nowadays, it acts as a highly regarded subcontractor to the F1 engine program of Renault and, it is rumoured, other OEM F1 engine programs.

Another highly regarded F1 engine supplier based in France is Chambon, who produce crankshafts, and are part of the Performance Motorsports Inc group (part of the Dover Industries Group of the USA) that also includes Perfect Bore, J.E. Pistons and Carrillo Rods. Also within the French-based F1 engine supply chain is JPX, a firm that supplies F1 pistons, valves and specialist coatings, but is now itself part owned by Mecachrome. Mecachrome recently bought the Swiss-based Mader Racing engine specialists, who exclusively build engines for the F1-supporting GP2 series and, from 2007, will supply the one-make engine for a new single-seater series supporting the WTCC.

Carbon Industrie is another French aerospace engineering firm (alongside Mecachrome) involved in motorsport. Other French aerospace-related aerodynamic research establishments include ONERA and Institut Aerotechnique. Carbon Industrie is one of three manufacturers of carbon brakes to F1. Additionally, there are also smaller motorsport-related aerodynamic consultancies like the Sardou Group.

In 2005, French tire company Michelin supplied 60 percent of the F1 grid alongside Japanese rival Bridgestone. From 2007, the whole F1 grid will revert to a one-tire formulae, supplied exclusively by Bridgestone.

Outside F1, France also has a very strong presence in the World Rally Championship, providing both the Peugeot WRC team, based at Velizy, and the increasingly competitive Citroën WRC team, based in Versailles. However, Peugeot pulled out of WRC at the end of 2005 in order to concentrate on a 2007 Le Mans program. It is rumoured that the new Suzuki WRC team may be located in France to take advantage of the rally skills and experience of employees currently not required by Peugeot. Elsewhere in the French motorsport industry, Mygale has a significant presence in Formula Ford and builds the chassis for the various Formula BMW series.

In sporting terms the Le Mans 24 Hours remains the world's premier sportscar race, and attracts domestic sportscar constructors like Courage. In addition, the former F1 circuit Paul Ricard in the south of France is being developed as a permanent F1 test facility under Bernie Ecclestone's ownership. Toyota's F1 team has a permanent base there.

French Motorsport Value Chain Analysis

Table 2.17 summarizes the motorsport value chain applied to the current French motorsport industry. Following the table, each cell of the table is discussed to complete a comprehensive empirical description of the French industry.

Table 2.17 **The French Motorsport Value Chain**

Value chain position	Companies/organizations involved in supply chain
1. Regulation of sport	
Regulatory bodies	FFSA
Safety panels	FFSA, FIA
2. Supporting service industry	
Logistics	—
Markets and merchandizing	Trajecting, Grand Prix Group
Personnel and human resources (driver management)	TNTZ
Other (racing school, insurance and risk management, finance, accountancy, legal)	Winfield
3. Constructors	
F1	None
Rally	Citroën
Sportscar	Courage, ORECA, Pecarolo
Kit car	—
Other	*Saloon*—Solution F, ORECA, SNBE, Danielson Engineering; *Off road*—Ralliart France, Schlesser; *Single seat*—Mygale, Martini/Ligier
4. Constructor suppliers	
Engines	Renault Sport, Pipo Moteur, SODEMO, Mecachrome, Solution F, Moteur Huger
Electronics	Atex, XAP
Materials	—
Design services	Solution F, Danielson Engineering, Nogaro Technologies, Sardou Group
Transmission	SADEV, Mecachrome
Brakes/suspension	Carbone Industrie
Safety systems	Stand 21
Tyres	Michelin
Fuel/lubrication	Elf, Total, Motul
Other	*F1 Engine Supply Chain*—Chambon, JPX, SOREVI, ICC
5. Entrants (licensed)	
Race team	Renault Sport, Citroen Sport
Individual participants	54,000
Clubs	ACO
Drivers	Sebastian Bourdais, Franck Montagny, Sebastian Loeb

(*Continued*)

Table 2.17 **(Continued)**

Value chain position	Companies/organizations involved in supply chain
6. Events	
F1	Magny Cours
WRC	Corsica
Historic	Le Mans, Tour Auto, Pau, Angouleme, Serie VH, VdeV, Grand Prix de L'Age d'Or
Saloon	Supertourisme
Club	—
Other	Karting sport strong but Italian equipment used
7. Event suppliers	
Circuits (construction, safety)	—
Event management/ infrastructure	FFSA, Excelsis SA, SRO, TPO, Rayon d'Action
8. Distribution	
Media	F1 TV—TF1; Magazine—*Auto Hebdo*
9. Consumption	
Viewers	F1 viewing figures per race event 2005: 3.8 m (*Source*: Sports Marketing Surveys)
Spectators	Medium
Participants	High

Regulation of Sport

Motorsport in France is regulated by the Federation Francaise du Sport Automobile (FFSA), the nationally designated organizing body recognized by the FIA. All French motor clubs involved in motorsport are members of the FFSA and follow FFSA and FIA rules and procedures for organizing and administrating motorsport in France, including in safety matters.

Supporting Service Industry

The supporting service industry in France appears weaker than the UK and possibly Germany. There are a number of marketing and sponsor agencies surrounding F1 and one key F1 driver-management organization.

Constructors

There are currently no F1 chassis constructors based in France. Renault's F1 constructor is based in the UK and the last French-based constructor, Prost, closed in 2002. France's main motorsport constructors in 2005 are the factory-based

WRC involvement from Peugeot Sport and Citroën Sport, although Peugeot pulled out of the WRC after 2005 to concentrate on a Le Mans program. The Citroën Sport entry is a relatively recent effort, while Peugeot re-entered the sport in the late 1990s after a gap of a decade or so. These two teams comprised half the competitive WRC teams in 2005.

French constructors are also well placed in other areas of off-road motorsport. Mitsubishi's Paris–Dakar vehicles are built in France, as are the Paris–Dakar Schlesser buggies. In addition the successful French winter ice-racing series, the Trophee Andros, has spawned a number of constructors for the series, ORECA and SNBE among them.

The history of the Le Mans 24-hour sportscar event means that there are French constructors involved in preparing sportscars for this event. ORECA supplies the road-based Chrysler Viper and specialist prototypes are produced in smaller numbers by organizations like Courage.

France has a unique saloon car championship, utilizing purpose-built space-frame chassis and modified road car-derived engines. Several French-based constructors supply this series, namely, Solution F, ORECA, SNBE and Danielson Engineering.

Finally, in the single-seat categories outside F1, France has two constructors of note. One is Mygale, which is notable for supplying all the chassis for the BMW-supported Formula BMW on a worldwide basis. Mygale also supply chassis for the French-based Formula Campus junior single-seat series and chassis for the Formula Ford category. Mygale are interested in producing F3 chassis in the future. Also of interest is the revived Ligier/Martini organization, which builds small numbers of F3 and sportscar chassis and low-cost chassis for racing schools.

Constructor Suppliers

In the engine supply area of the supply chain France is well represented. Renault's F1 engines are built in France and France plays host to a number of world-class F1 engine-component suppliers like Mecachrome, JPX and Chambon. Other French companies notable for supplying F1 are the carbon brake manufacturer Carbon Industrie and Michelin (until 2006).

Outside the F1 engine supply chain, firms like Pipo Moteur build engines for the Peugeot Sport WRC car, and Huger build engines for the one-make single-seat Renault Sport category. France's domestic motorsport scene is well supported by engine builders like SODEMO and Solution F in, for example, the Supertourisme category. Mecachrome are also involved in engine supply to the F3000 replacement single-seat category GP2, although Mecachrome's Swiss-based subsidiary, Mader, will actually build the engines.

SADEV is a key supplier of motorsport transmissions in France. SADEV supply gearboxes to all Renault's one-make motorsport categories and to other one-make racing formulae in Europe like the Alfa 147 Cup. Mecachrome, the large aerospace technology company currently extending its motorsport involvement, are also to move into the realm of transmission supply, by building gearboxes for the new GP2 series mentioned above.

Solution F, Danielson Engineering, Nogaro Technologies and the Sardou Group provide small-scale performance engineering consultancy to a mainly domestic audience. These companies are not, however, of the scale of the UK's Ricardo MCT or Prodrive AT.

The remaining key members of France's constructor supply chain are the fuel and lubricant companies Elf, Total and Motul. Elf has a particularly high international profile due to its association with Renault Sport.

Entrants (Licenced)

The main entrants in 2005 in France were the three WRC and JWRC teams from Peugeot Sport, Renault Sport and Citroën Sport. Renault is an F1 entrant but their team is based in the UK. In the European-based single-seat series below F1, namely GP2, the World Series by Renault and the F3 Euroseries, French teams are well represented by names like ASM, Saulnier and Paul Belmondo.

The history of the Le Mans 24-hour race and the more recent Le Mans Series means that French teams like Courage and Pescarolo are well represented. Peugeot have also decided to enter Le Mans and the LMS from 2007. France has a strong national GT series that leads entrants into Le Mans and the FIA GT championship.

In the domestic Supertourisme series, French entrants like Solution F and Pescarolo Sport predominate. Many teams involved in Supertourisme are also involved as entrants in the successful winter-based Trophee Andros Ice Racing Series.

At the level of the individual entrant, the FFSA claim that there are 54,000 license holders across all four-wheeled motorsport disciplines in France, a significantly larger number than in any other European country, the UK included.

Events

F1 is weaker in France than in many other European countries and it almost lost the Grand Prix entirely from its Magny Cours venue in 2004. However, the economic benefits of the Monaco Grand Prix also accrue to the regions of southern France surrounding the principality. Rallying may be stronger, with the French round of the championship on the isle of Corsica, and the famous Monte Carlo rally being based in the principality of Monaco, but utilizing mainly French roads.

The most important motorsport event in France is the famous Le Mans 24-hour sportscar race, which attracts a quarter of a million spectators a year. Probably second in popularity is the Paris–Dakar off-road event. While much of the Paris–Dakar takes place outside French borders, those stages that do take place in France attract a high level of attention. Similarly impressive, but on a lesser scale, is the Trophee Andros, a winter ice-racing championship unique to France.

Historic motorsport, as in many other European countries, is growing in France. The key events are the Tour Auto and events held at the Le Mans circuit. The Tour Auto is a five-day road-based event, like the Italian Mille Miglia. The event attracts a large contingent of international participants. The various racing events held at the Le Mans circuit attract a great deal of attention due to the current status and historic importance of the Le Mans 24 Hours. France also has a strong heritage of motorsport, with some of the most famous circuits in Europe alongside Le Mans, such as the Pau street circuit in the South of France.

Below the international historic circuit-based events, the FFSA organizes a five-round Serie VH (Historic Vehicle) championship at the main French circuits. There is also a French Endurance Championship for Historic sportscars entitled the French HSR Endurance Championship.

The key saloon car championship in France is the technically unique Supertourisme series. This championship runs as part of the French governing body's Super FFSA series of events.

Renault's proposal, first put forward in 2005, to initiate a series of ten free European-based circuit events utilizing only Renault-based championships is another sign of the French OEM's innovative use of motorsport to promote its road cars, alongside its initial championing of Renault-based one-make series. Spectator attendances at these events have been very high.

Event Suppliers

The FFSA has had to take over the promotion of the French Grand Prix as, if it had not, the event looked likely to be lost by its former promoter. The Stephan Ratel Organization (SRO), based in the UK, promotes the highly successful French GT series, alongside the FIA GT series and the British GT series. The Peter Organization promotes historic motorsport events in France, including the successful Tour Auto.

Distribution

TF1 supplies the F1 feed to the French domestic TV audience. While popular in France, TV viewing for F1 does not rival Germany, for example. *Auto Hebdo* is one of a number of highly regarded motorsport print media specialists in the country.

Consumption

While TV consumption for F1 may be average, demand for unique French motorsport events like the Le Mans race, Paris–Dakar and Trophee Andros

> **French Motorsport Industry Case Study: Citroën Sport**
>
> Citroën is part of the large French OEM PSA Group, which also incorporates Peugeot. As such, PSA and Citroën have always had a greater or lesser degree of governmental involvement. Citroën has a long tradition of involvement in long-distance rallying, dating back to the 1950s, usually utilizing in-house preparation facilities, rather than specialist subcontractors. Citroën Sport was set up as a wholly owned subsidiary in 1989 and initially utilized equipment from fellow PSA Group company Peugeot to compete in long-distance rallying events like the Paris–Dakar rally. In the late 1990s the World Rally Championship (WRC) became more and more high profile and OEMs began to take an increasing interest. Slowly Citroën Sport's involvement increased in the WRC until, in 2003, it submitted a high-profile three-car entry incorporating the drivers Colin McRae and Carlos Sainz. Citroën Sport's main competitor until the end of 2005 was the similarly PSA-owned reigning World Rally Champions, Peugeot Sport. Citroën Sport is based in Versailles and employs approximately 250 personnel. Like Peugeot Sport, the Citroën Sport WRC car has a small but significant part of its supply chain based in Britain.

goes some way to make up for this. Participation is high according to FFSA figures, and the number of circuits and club motorsport events are higher than Germany and Italy, albeit behind the UK.

SWOT Analysis: French Motorsport Industry

Following description of the French motorsport value chain, a SWOT analysis summarizes some of the key aspects of the position on the global grid (see Table 2.18).

Conclusion: The French Motorsport Industry

The French industry incorporates world-class motorsport involvement (F1 engines and WRC) closely related to the fortunes of (government-supported) domestic OEMs. Outside this domain, the limited network of motorsport specialists has shrunk in recent years due to the poor home market, the vagaries of French multinational involvement and Italian and UK competition. Le Mans is a world-class brand and Paul Ricard circuit is a strong competitor for testing purposes.

Conclusion: The Frontrunners

Table 2.18 **SWOT of the French Motorsport Industry**

Strengths
1 Strong manufacturer and "government" (via Renault) involvement means F1 engines and WRC is strong
2 Le Mans a world-class brand name
3 Strong karting infrastructure
4 Renault's innovative motorsport programs
5 Bernie Ecclestone's Paul Ricard testing facility (south of France—good weather, few planning restrictions)
6 High number of motorsport participants
7 High reputation events (Le Mans, Paris–Dakar)

Weaknesses
1 Reliant, relatively, on state involvement through manufacturers and very open to change of competition policy from large corporations. Recently many state-backed corporations have reduced their motorsport involvement to the detriment of the French motorsport industry
2 The single seat specialists like Martini and Mygale have been under pressure from the Italian firms Dallara and Tatuus
3 Poor home market and recent closures (Prost, AMT, ROC) mean very few motorsport specialists
4 Tight labor laws and consequent production costs
5 Not much high-tech development in motorsport
6 Few entrepreneurs

Opportunities
1 Renault very proactive in emerging markets, e.g. S. America, China; Renault also building a sporting empire through national and European championships, to the detriment of suppliers outside the loop. Seeking to integrate F1 success in to repositioned OEM brand
2 Le Mans expansion through Panoz, a USA sportscar organizer, licensing the name for a USA-based series (the ALMS)
3 WRC viewing figures the highest in the world

Threats
1 National capability may be adversely affected if OEMs lose interest
2 Withdrawal of Peugeot and Citroen WRC teams in 2006
3 EU labor laws
4 French 35-hour working week

Conclusion: The Frontrunners

As we write, the frontrunner nations remain overwhelmingly dominant in the supply of the world's motorsport products. Between them they account for 75 percent of the world market, 91 percent of the global chassis constructors and

41 percent of the global racing series events. Globalization has seen the expansion of the global racing series—there are now four—and the expansion of the number of countries that they now visit (to 29 countries). Yet even here, while the six frontrunner countries represent only a fifth of the nations now on the global motorsport circuit, they host two-fifths of events.

Within the indicators, different frontrunner nations stand out for different reasons (see Table 2.19). The USA market is more than double that of any of its competitor frontrunners, it has large numbers of participants and viewers but remains, fundamentally, domestic in its outlook. The UK still remains the center of global production, with fully 50 percent of global chassis constructors and the highest number of circuits supporting international motorsport activity. It does so with no domestic OEM of any note but as the recipient of

Table 2.19 **The Frontrunner Countries in 2005**

Indicators	USA	UK	Japan	Germany	Italy	France
Total value of annual turnover motorsport engineering and services	£13.0b	£6.0b	£4.0b	£3.0b	£2.0b	£1.5b
Motorsport turnover as % GDP	0.17%	0.5%	0.15%	0.20%	0.21%	0.13%
Global chassis constructors	0	11	0	3	3	2
Permanent paved circuits (including ovals over ¼ mile but not kart)	243 (182 ovals and 61 road)	19	19	6	10	9
Competition license holders	443,000	30,000 *participants* (not license holders)	30,000	60,000	10,000	19,000	54,000
Global series events	2	4	2	5	5	3
Average F1 viewing figures per race event 2005 (*Source*: Sports Marketing Surveys)	0.32 m	2.6 m	3.2 m	6.9 m	6.8 m	3.8 m
Average WRC viewing figures per event 2005 (*Source*: wrc.com)	Not known	1.60 m	2.13 m	0.48 m	1.33 m	15.70 m

substantial OEM investment from the other frontrunner nations. Indeed, for the frontrunners France, Germany and Japan it is the action of their domestic OEMs that has supported the fortunes of their national industries.

In France, the motorsport industry is heavily reliant on the actions and profitability of its domestic OEMs and their investment in international success. Production networks as far as they exist are reliant on the OEM market needs and viewing figures for global series map closely to those areas of OEM-driven national success. In Japan, high rates of participation in domestic motorsport create a significant market but on a global scale the policy of outsourcing vehicle production to those areas of highest expertise (the other frontrunner countries) means no global chassis constructors and no global suppliers of any note beyond engine production.

In some senses, the German industry is a mixture of the two, combining an international constructor and performance engineering core based on the domestic OEMs (plus Toyota) with OEM overseas investment and partnership (principally in the USA and UK). Within this core sits a growing, and increasingly independent, set of world-class motorsport suppliers. The paradox in Germany remains high viewing figures and joint largest share of global events coupled with low participation rates.

Which leaves Italy—home of the strongest motorsport brand in the world, Ferrari, and a national industry best characterized as a fragmented version of the other frontrunner industries. Still retaining domestic OEMs—with a history of motorsport involvement—current financial weaknesses provide a highly uncertain investment environment for OEM support for the motorsport industry. In contrast, if one other trend is noticeable within the motorsport industries of the frontrunner countries, it is the inroads made into the global market share of motorsport by a new breed of Italian constructors and suppliers.

And it is this global market—and the share held by the frontrunner countries—that is the target of attack from the next group of nations on the Global Starting Grid … the Midfield.

PART THREE

The Midfield

Introduction: The Midfield

The second tier within our Global Starting Grid is that of the midfield—a set of national motorsport industries or regional markets of moderate size, which, it will be shown, have limited purchase on the global motorsport industry. Headed by Australia, this group of five can boast significant racing heritage but penetration of these nations' industries into global motorsport markets is very limited at present.

Significant, also, is the limited international material and data that currently exists on these national industries. Within the following Part Three, the global metrics are applied to benchmark each of the midfield nations using that data that could be accessed. Each nation's industry is reviewed before the completion of a SWOT (strengths, weaknesses, opportunities and threats) analysis and final summary.

The Australian Motorsport Industry

Table 3.1 provides the global metrics for the Australian motorsport industry. The industry has a significant annual turnover value of £1.5 billion (the equivalent of France) and hosts global events, but delivers a small viewing audience and is home to no global chassis constructors.

History and Current Industry Position

Motorsport has a long history in Australia stretching back to before World War I. The early competition was of an informal nature, involving racing activity such

Table 3.1 **The Australian Motorsport Industry in 2005**

Indicators	Australia 2005	% of world total
Total value of annual motorsport turnover for engineering and services	£1.5b	3.0
Motorsport turnover as % GDP	0.44 percent	–
Permanent paved circuits (including ovals over ¼ mile but not kart)	15	2.5
Competition license holders	22,000	–
Global chassis constructors (F1, WRC, WTCC and A1GP)	0	0
Number of racing series — Global — Regional	 F1; WRC; A1GP Champcar; FIA Rally	 – –
Global motorsport events (F1, WRC, WTCC and A1GP)	3	5
Average F1 viewing figures per race event (*Source*: Sports Marketing Surveys)	0.5 m	0.9
Average WRC viewing figures per event (*Source*: wrc.com)	0.33 m	0.7

as hillclimbs and occasional events on horse-racing tracks. After World War I, Australian motorsport concentrated on intercity record breaking utilizing public roads.

At this early stage in Australia's motorsport history, track racing began at circuits like Maroubra and Phillip Island. In the 1930s, the first event was held at the Bathurst circuit, home of the now famous Bathurst 1000, the "Great Race" for modified saloon cars, called V8 Supercars. Early versions of the Great Race were held at Phillip Island until the event moved permanently to Bathurst in 1963 and solidified the race in the calendar of Australia's leading sporting events and among the world's most famous motorsport events. Historically, Bathurst galvanized a rivalry between Australia's two OEMs, Ford and Holden (GM). This long-standing brand rivalry, which continues to this day, has tilted the direction of Australian motorsport strongly toward saloon-based road racing.

Historically, Australian motorsport has been strongly linked to the UK motorsport industry, partly by a common language and partly through the political ties of a former British colony. The Australian three-time Formula One World

Champion Jack Brabham was perhaps the first to epitomize this linkage on an international stage. An accomplished driver on the Australian national motorsport scene, he traveled to the UK in the mid-1950s, initially to join Cooper, where he won two GP World Championships in 1959 and 1960 and, ultimately, to establish his own team. In 1966 he became the first driver to win a Formula One World Championship driving a car of his own manufacture. His team went on to win again the following year, and both championships were won using the Australian Repco 3-litre engine. Integral to this story was the involvement of outstanding Australian designer Ron Tauranac. Tauranac joined Brabham in the UK in 1960 before he created the Ralt single-seater manufacturer (also in the UK), which became one of the most successful global racing-car producers.

This transfer of personnel, both drivers and engineers, between the UK and Australia continues to this day, with the latest examples being the involvement of the UK's Prodrive and Triple 8 teams in Australia's V8 Supercar series, and the continued utilization of many Australian engineering personnel in UK-based teams, epitomized by Williams F1's current technical director Sam Michael. Tom Walkinshaw, a well-known figure in the UK motorsport scene, owns Holden Special Vehicles (HSV) so the rivalry between the Ford and Holden brands, which is the mainstay of Australian motorsport, is effectively a further example of the global reach of the UK's Motorsport Valley® community.

International motorsport events in Australia are headlined by the Australian Grand Prix, formerly held in Adelaide, but now in Melbourne. The Australian Grand Prix has consistently been one of the most well-run and -attended races on the F1 calendar. Australia also holds a WRC event, although at time of writing this event appears to be taking a sabbatical in 2007, due to pressure on the calendar from other countries to run WRC events. In addition, since 1991 the USA-based Champcar series annually organizes a highly popular event at Surfers Paradise, attracting crowds in excess of 300,000 each year.

The Confederation of Australian Motorsport (CAMS) runs national motorsport in Australia. CAMS' main motorsport series is the V8 Supercar series, and its supporting series, the V8 Development series. In 2005, 1.7 million people attended V8 Supercar events as spectators with single race attendance at the most popular events hitting 300,000 (cams.com.au). The series is mainly Australia-based, with one round in New Zealand and a recent international expansion in to China in 2005 in what was a one-off event. From 2006 the series has signed a multi-year deal to run an event in Bahrain at the newly established circuit used for the F1 race.

The historic OEM rivalry between Holden and Ford continues at lower levels of national motorsport series in championships like the Performance Cars Series, and the recently established V8 Utes championship (a "Ute" being the same as a pick-up truck). The Australian Touring Car Challenge also features a fair number of GM and Holden products, but also showcases cars from European OEMs.

Within GT racing, Australia also has a strong national GT series, utilizing mainly imported cars like Vipers, Ferraris and Porsches. In addition, a strong one-make national Porsche Carrera Cup exists with committed OEM support.

Single-seater racing is not as popular as saloon car racing, but nevertheless is represented by a number of categories. At the top of single-seat racing in Australia is Formula 4000, which uses the same modified Holden road-car engine in UK-built chassis, raced formerly in Formula 3000 and Formula Nippon. In 2006 these were mainly Reynards but the series was very poorly supported.

Below Formula 4000 in terms of speed, but probably above it in terms of prestige, is the Australian F3 Championship, from which Australian drivers attempt to reach the international arena and F1. As elsewhere in the world, most chassis are from the Italian-based Dallara firm, although entries for the championship were barely in double figures in 2005.

Below F3, Australia national motorsport has state-based Formula Ford Championships and a successful National Formula Ford Championship, from which drivers such as Mark Webber have emerged. Formula Ford chassis utilized in Australia are split roughly equally between UK-built Van Diemen chassis, and Australian-built Spectrum chassis. It is interesting to note a global development as, in 2006, Spectrum chassis started to make an impression in the prestigious UK Formula Ford Championship. The entry-level single-seat series in Australia is Formula Vee, a thriving championship at the state level, dominated by the domestically built Jacer chassis.

Outside circuit racing, Australia has a thriving national rallying championship and hosts a round of the FIA Asia-Pacific Regional Rally championship. These events are supported by state and local championships. Most cars utilized in these series are imported cars from Japanese manufacturers—Mitsubishi, Toyota, Suzuki and Subaru. Australian national motorsport also supports karting, drag racing and off-roading, with a similar series of national, state and local championships.

Australia has a strong short dirt oval series of championships, headlined by purpose-built sprint cars of a type similar to that prevalent in USA short oval racing. Short oval racing is organized by the National Association of Speedway Racing, who claim 1 million paying spectators a year and some 10,000 licensed participants (nasr.com.au). This would make short oval racing in Australia the strongest of its type, outside the USA.

Most of the Australian motorsport industry is domestically biased, with one or two notable exceptions. V8 Supercars utilize an international supply chain due to USA-like engine technology and large team budgets. Other domestic saloon car series will utilize a more domestic-oriented supply chain due to cost and logistical constraints, but still utilize some overseas components. Within V8 Supercar, chassis and gearboxes will be Australian-sourced, with the gearbox suppliers, Hollinger, being one of the few Australian firms operating in the global supply chain. The electronics supplier Motec is another Australian motorsport firm with international linkages.

Within Australian GT racing, European suppliers like Porsche and Ferrari dominate the category in Australia.

Most of the single-seat categories are supplied from a European base, with the honorable exception of Spectrum chassis in Formula Ford and Jacer in Formula Vee. Most equipment used in Australian rallying will be from a Japanese- or a UK-based supplier. Finally, within oval racing, suppliers will be part domestic, and part USA-based, reflecting the origin of some of the short oval-based series power units.

At the national level, there is a growing industry being stimulated by certain state governments, who have come to recognize the value of the technology and international income that can be generated by motorsport.

SWOT Analysis: The Australian Motorsport Industry

Following description of the industry, a SWOT analysis summarizes some of the key aspects of the position on the global grid (see Table 3.2).

Table 3.2 **SWOT of the Australian Motorsport Industry in 2005**

Strengths	Weaknesses
1 Strong domestic championships with emphasis on saloons (V8 Supercars)	1 Limited single-seat expertise at regional and international level
2 Reasonable level of participants	2 Aerodynamics and composites technology
3 Reasonable domestic saloon-based supply chain	3 Reliance on USA and UK suppliers
4 Short dirt oval series strong (second only to USA)	4 Hollinger and Motec notable exceptions to the lack of membership of the international motorsport supply chain
5 Strong links to UK motorsport industry	
6 Interest in off-road and rally events	
Opportunities	**Threats**
1 Domestic series going regional into Asia	1 Withdrawal of GM or Ford from national level motorsport
2 Exporting saloon-based supply chain	2 "Green" technology
3 Off-road events utilizing geography of country	
4 Specialist firms develop global supply chains	

Conclusion: The Australian Motorsport Industry

Australia has a strong domestic headline series with V8 Supercars and is tentatively expanding this series overseas. Most Australian motorsport suppliers operate in a domestic market only, with European and USA-based suppliers dominant in international forms of racing. A few notable exceptions exist, such as Hollinger, Motec and Spectrum.

Australian motorsport is strongly biased toward saloon cars, to the detriment of single-seat categories like F3 and F4000. Only the national Formula Ford series and regional Formula Vee series really thrive in this sector of the marketplace. Off-road events and rallying are relatively strong in Australia, reflecting the opportunities to utilize Australia's great natural resources.

The significant reliance on the Holden and Ford brand battle, for much domestic motorsport, could prove problematic if one or other loses interest in motorsport as a promotional tool. On the positive side, historically strong industry linkages with UK motorsport provides access to a leading global center of motorsport knowledge.

The Spanish Motorsport Industry

Table 3.3 provides the global metrics for the Spanish motorsport industry. A medium-sized industry of some £1 billion annual turnover, it hosts three global series events and the global constructor SEAT Sport.

History and Current Industry Position

Motorcycling has historically been far stronger in Spain than four-wheeled motorsport. Fernando Alonso's recent success in F1 has changed this to a degree, but motorcycling still holds the primary attention of the Spanish motorsport enthusiast. The world-leading Moto GP series is owned and has been successfully developed by Spanish-based Dorna.

Global events in Spain revolve around the highly successful F1 Grand Prix at Barcelona, which has one of the highest spectator attendances of all, partly due to the Alonso effect and also due to astute marketing. Spain also has a prominent WRC event. Rallying has long been popular in Spain, partly due to Carlos Sainz's success in WRC.

Four-wheeled national motorsport events in Spain split into three main areas of interest: circuit racing; rallying and off-road events. Circuit racing has a strong national Spanish GT championship, one of the better-supported GT championships in Europe. Single-seater racing has a reasonably strong national F3 championship, supported by a series called Master Junior Formula, similar to

Formula BMW in conception. Master Junior drivers arrive in motorsport from the Spanish karting scene.

Saloon racing is popular is Spain, particularly one-make championships, due mainly to the involvement of the Spanish OEM SEAT. SEAT Sport is the biggest, and one of the very few, international motorsport firms in Spain. SEAT Sport builds cars for, and supports, many one-make SEAT championships throughout Europe, as well as a national GT team, a WTCC and BTCC team, and various rallying and off-road event entrants.

Within one-make saloon racing in Spain, SEAT supports the SEAT Leon Super Cup, a series mirrored in many other European countries. Other one-make saloon racing in Spain includes that supported by Renault (Clio) and two strongly supported series from Hyundai (Coupe and Getz). Below the national-level championships, Spanish circuit racing appears relatively weak, with only the odd regional-level saloon car championship.

Rallying is arguably stronger in Spain than circuit racing, with two strong national championships—an Asphalt championship, solely utilizing tarmac surfaces, and a Gravel championship (non-tarmac surfaces). Similarly, off—road events are particularly strong in Spain, with relatively large numbers of entrants.

Most of the motorsport equipment utilized in Spain is imported, and the international motorsport industry in Spain is limited to little more than SEAT

Table 3.3 **The Spanish Motorsport Industry in 2005**

Indicators	Spain 2005	% of world total
Total value of annual motorsport turnover for engineering and services	£1.0b	2.0
Motorsport turnover as % GDP	0.17 percent	–
Permanent paved circuits (including ovals over ¼ mile but not kart)	9	1.5
Competition license holders	Not known	–
Global chassis constructors (F1, WRC, WTCC and A1GP)	1	4.5
Number of racing series — Global — Regional	 F1; WRC; WTCC GP2	 – –
Global motorsport events (F1, WRC, WTCC and A1GP)	3	5.4
Average F1 viewing figures per race event (*Source*: Sports Marketing Surveys)	4.2 m	8.0
Average WRC viewing figures per event (*Source*: wrc.com)	0.83 m	1.7

Sport. SEAT Sport is a prolific producer of saloon cars for the WTCC and BTCC and various one-make saloon car championships, including the Spanish. It also produces specialized GT cars for the Spanish GT championship, as well as various rally vehicles for national series. SEAT Sport builds most of their chassis at their Spanish base, but accesses a European-based supply chain, particularly the UK and Germany, for components such as engines, gearboxes and electronics.

Most cars in the GT championship, SEAT's small involvement aside, are from Ferrari and Porsche, and the supply chain reflects the origin of these OEMs. The single-seat racing supply chain is entirely international, with the F3 chassis being from the Italian Dallara firm, with Japanese Toyota engines and the Master Junior Formula utilizing German-built chassis from Schubel and German BMW engines.

Rallying again utilizes an international supply chain, with cars mainly coming from Subaru and Mitsubishi. Many UK specialists (for example, MMSP and Prodrive) are involved in supplying this market, given their position as the appointed global rallying specialists for these particular OEMs. SEAT has a strong role in Spanish national rallying, but accesses an international supply chain for many of their components.

Mostly vehicles from Japanese OEMs Nissan, Mitsubishi, Toyota and Isuzu contest the strongly supported Spanish Off-Road championship but many of the specialist suppliers for these vehicles are based in other parts of Europe, particularly in France, Germany and the UK.

SWOT Analysis: The Spanish Motorsport Industry

Following description of the industry, a SWOT analysis summarizes some of the key aspects of the position on the global grid (see Table 3.4).

Table 3.4 **SWOT of the Spanish Motorsport Industry in 2005**

Strengths	Weaknesses
1 Motorcycling	1 Reliance on OEM (SEAT)
2 National GT, F3 and saloon racing all strong	2 Little domestic motorsport industry
3 Support of OEM (SEAT)	3 Motorsport second to motorcycle sport
4 Reasonable number of circuits	4 Little activity below national level
Opportunities	**Threats**
1 "Alonso" effect	1 Loss of motorsport investment from SEAT
2 Off-road and rallying nascent domestic supply chain?	2 Loss of Spanish drivers in global series

Conclusion: The Spanish Motorsport Industry

Motorsport is still under the thumb of motorcycling in Spain, but the Alonso effect has increased F1 viewing and spectator figures. The question remains as to whether or not this will translate in to increased four-wheeled motorsport participation. Rallying is possibly stronger than circuit racing in Spain, with circuit racing itself equalled by interest in off-road events.

SEAT is the main global motorsport firm in Spain so if ever they (or their parent company, VAG) change the direction of its motorsport policy, motorsport in Spain could suffer substantially. National-level racing is reasonably strong, with several strong championships, but, below this, club-level circuit motorsport remains relatively weak.

The South American (Brazil and Argentina) Motorsport Industry

Table 3.5 provides the global metrics for the South American motorsport industry, comprising the two nations of Brazil and Argentina and a substantial history of motorsport.

Table 3.5 **Motorsport in South America in 2005**

Indicators	South America 2005	% of world total
Total value of annual motorsport turnover for engineering and services	£1.0b	2.0
Motorsport turnover as % GDP	0.24%	—
Permanent paved circuits (including ovals over ¼ mile but not kart)	Argentina—33; Brazil—13	8
Competition license holders	Not known	—
Global chassis constructors (F1, WRC, WTCC and A1GP)	0	0
Number of racing series		
— Global	F1 (Brazil); WRC (Argentina)	—
— Regional	FIA Rally	—
Global motorsport events (F1, WRC, WTCC and A1GP)	2	3.6
Average F1 viewing figures per race event (*Source*: Sports Marketing Surveys)	Argentina—Not known; Brazil—9.6 m	Brazil—18.3
Average WRC viewing figures per event (*Source*: wrc.com)	Argentina—0.94 m; Brazil—Not known	Argentina—1.9

History and Current Industry Position

Motorsport, in both Brazil and Argentina, began by racing modified road cars on public roads over the great distances afforded by the scale of the continent. It was in the 1950s that the sport began to move toward circuit racing as permanent circuits began to be built.

International motorsport events in South America revolve around the F1 Grand Prix in Brazil and the WRC event in Argentina, both long-standing events with high spectator attendances. Below these international events, the Sudam F3 Championship races in both Brazil and Argentina, and has a record of success in launching young South American drivers on international careers. Within rallying and off-road motorsport, there are growing South American championships, which contain rounds in Brazil and Argentina.

Turning to the national position of Brazilian motorsport, a starting point should be to note that Brazil has a long and successful track record of sending young drivers from Brazil to the UK to learn their craft. This started with Emerson Fittipaldi in the early 1970s and continued with Nelson Piquet and Ayrton Senna, to name the most successful.

The most popular circuit-based series in Brazil is a saloon-racing series for V8 stock cars. This is a series supported by the GM and Mitsubishi OEMs, which attracts large numbers of spectators. Many Brazilian drivers who made the trip to Europe to establish their careers end up in this series on their return to Brazil. The cars are highly modified silhouettes of production cars.

Renault, which has substantial manufacturing interests in Brazil, supports a strong presence in Brazilian motorsport, including a one-make Renault Clio saloon car championship and a Formula Renault single-seat championship. The latter is the main single-seat championship, which acts as a feeder to the Sudam F3 Championship previously mentioned.

Below circuit racing, Brazil has one of the strongest karting championships outside Europe. The aforementioned Fittipaldi, Piquet and Senna and many other professional drivers have all graduated from here. There is a well-supported national karting championship, into which state championships feed. The Brazilian governing body, the Brazilian Motorsport Confederation (CBA), estimate that Brazil has 2,000 licenced karters, and five times as many who "fun" kart.

Outside circuit racing in Brazil, rallying is expanding from a relatively low base. Importers from OEMs like Subaru, Peugeot, Fiat, Mitsubishi and VW have become involved in recent years. Similarly, off-road competitions are increasing in popularity, with involvement from OEMs like GM and Mitsubishi in both national and regional series.

It is worth noting that the most popular form of motorsport is truck racing, which attracts huge crowds and all the major OEMs. Road transport affects the whole of South America to a great degree, due to the difficulties of moving product throughout the region, hence the use of motorsport to increase brand share among truck drivers and owners.

The Brazilian motorsport industry has a number of domestic suppliers, but is not international in nature. Domestic manufacturers mainly supply karting, while single-seat categories like F3 and Formula Renault use imported Italian chassis, although all engines in F3 come from the Argentinean firm Berta. This company travels the world to secure new technology for its products.

In saloon car racing, the one-make Renault Clios are prepared for racing by local specialists. The main national racing series is V8 Stock Car, and here chassis and gearbox come from Argentina, while engines come from the USA.

Rallying suppliers are mainly European in origin, reflecting the locations of the competition departments of OEMs like Subaru, VW, Mitsubishi and Peugeot. Off-road suppliers reflect a similar supply chain, while teams will usually construct vehicles locally.

Motorsport in Argentina is far stronger than in Brazil, although perhaps not as internationally known due to the lesser numbers of Argentinean drivers who have launched successful international careers. Motorsport in Argentina developed from the public road races of the 1930s and 1940s, where drivers such as Fangio made their name, toward circuit racing in the 1950s.

In the 1950s, the sport was government funded by President Peron, who utilized motorsport to raise the international profile of the country. This patronage had two main outlets—it gave support to drivers such as Fangio to come to Europe and helped develop a grass roots Argentinean motorsport infrastructure.

The results of this grass roots infrastructure can still be seen to this day, with a large number of circuits, and what is believed to be a large number of competitors. Although official numbers are hard to come by, it is estimated that there are as many as 11,000 race cars in the country (Performance Racing Industry magazine, various).

Circuit racing is the most popular form of motorsport in Argentina, with a very large number (33) of permanent road-racing tracks—a very high proportion for the population—and as many as 100 regional dirt tracks. The two most important categories in national circuit racing in Argentina are both saloon-racing categories. The first, entitled TC3000, is for highly modified cars similar to NASCAR-style vehicles. The second category is entitled TC2000 and is for less-modified saloons similar to the European Super Touring-style regulations. It is claimed that spectator numbers at these events can reach 50–60,000 in total (Performance Racing Industry magazine, various).

There are many other saloon-racing categories in Argentina that feed these two categories. TC Pista 1, TC Pista 2 and Turismo Nacional are multi-manufacturer series, while Top Race is a one-spec series utilizing different manufacturers' body shapes. Below these series are approximately 20 regional feeder series, with car counts ranging between 20 and 100 cars per series (Performance Racing Industry magazine, various). Some of these series are one-make (like the Renault Megane championship), while others are multi-manufacturer.

Single-seat racing in Argentina has Sudam F3 at the apex of the sport. The Argentinean national feeder series to F3 is the popular Formula Renault series. Overall, however, single-seat racing in Argentina is not as popular as saloon racing. Like Brazil, beyond circuit racing, rallying and off-road events are becoming more popular, with national- and regional-level championships becoming stronger.

The Argentinean motorsport industry is large and has a number of international suppliers—IASA, Ferrea and Sainz Performance being the main names—all supplying engine components of various types. Berta is probably the best-known Argentinean motorsport firm due to its involvement in F1 in the 1970s. Berta now builds all the engines for the Sudam F3 series, all the cars and Jaguar-based engines for the Top Race saloon-racing series and supplies many other national and South American motorsport series (for example, engines and chassis for the Ford-based TC2000 entry). It also has the only motorsport wind tunnel in South America.

In the major saloon racing series TC3000, many components are supplied from either a USA or a national supply chain, while suppliers to TC2000 are domestic and European-oriented, due to the similarity in regulations to European saloon-racing formulae. The comprehensive domestic supply chain mainly supplies the lower-level championships.

In single-seat racing, Berta supplies all Sudam F3 engines, while chassis come from the Italian company Dallara. Interestingly, Formula Renault is not a one-spec chassis formula as in many countries, and is instead supplied mainly by South America's only volume single-seat producer, the Argentinean firm Crespi.

The rallying and off-road supply chain reflects that to be found in many countries, where locally based teams utilize Subaru, Nissan and Mitsubishi cars, prepared from a European-sourced supply chain.

SWOT Analysis: The South American Motorsport Industry

Following description of the industry, a SWOT analysis summarizes some of the key aspects of the position on the global grid (see Table 3.6 overleaf).

Conclusion: The South American Motorsport Industry

A strong motorsport presence in both Brazil and Argentina belies particular country differences. Grass roots karting is stronger in Brazil than Argentina, and Brazil has an impressive record of producing drivers for international motorsport. Rallying and off-road competitions are roughly equal in each country, with both

Table 3.6 **SWOT of the South American Motorsport Industry in 2005**

Strengths	Weaknesses
1 Argentina has a strong domestic industry	1 Relatively few really international motorsport firms
2 Very strong circuit racing scene in Argentina	2 Industry tends to be low-tech and fabrication based
3 Argentina very strong on track infrastructure	3 Berta has the only motorsport wind tunnel in the region
4 Brazil has strong international heritage in drivers	4 Crespi the only South American single-seat manufacturer
5 Brazilian karting one of strongest in world, utilizing domestic equipment at national level	

Opportunities	Threats
1 Argentina is an exporter of proprietary engine products to USA	1 Export of USA racing culture down through Central America?
2 Argentinean saloon-based supply chain (Berta?)	2 Sport first to suffer under weak economic conditions
3 Brazilian karting industry	3 Economic instability of region reduces inward investment opportunities, which could enhance knowledge transfer

segments growing. Single-seat racing in each country is, again, similar but secondary to saloon-based series. As is the case with much of the motorsport industry above karting, Argentina has a stronger presence in the single-seat industry segment (Berta, Crespi) than Brazil.

Both countries have strong saloon-car series but Argentina has strength in depth. This reflects the greater grass roots infrastructure of cars, circuits and drivers in Argentinean motorsport. Furthermore, the Argentinean motorsport industry does play a (relatively unknown) role in the global motorsport industry. It has a handful of global suppliers and, bar karting and driver development, outstrips its Brazilian neighbor.

The Mexican Motorsport Industry

Table 3.7 provides the global metrics for the Mexican motorsport industry. The industry remains relatively undeveloped, with a motorsport turnover as a percentage of GDP that places it in second to last place on the Global Starting Grid.

Table 3.7 **Motorsport in Mexico in 2005**

Indicators	Mexico 2005	% of world total
Total value of annual motorsport turnover for engineering and services	£0.5b	1.0
Motorsport turnover as % GDP	0.13 percent	—
Permanent paved circuits (including ovals over ¼ mile but not kart)	20	3.3
Competition license holders	Not known	—
Global chassis constructors (F1, WRC, WTCC and A1GP)	0	0
Number of racing series		
— Global	WRC; WTCC; A1GP	—
— Regional	Champcar	—
Global motorsport events (F1, WRC, WTCC and A1GP)	3	5.4
Average F1 viewing figures per race event (*Source*: Sports Marketing Surveys)	Not known	—
Average WRC viewing figures per event (*Source*: wrc.com)	0.76 m	1.5

History and Current Industry Position

Motorsport in Mexico entered the international arena with the short-lived Carrera Pan Americana event in the 1950s that attracted international entries and attention. This event utilized race cars running on open roads and has now been revived as a historical motorsport event. Mexico also became known for the Baja California off-road event, which is still being run as part of the six-round SCORE off-road championship. SCORE is a USA-based championship, half of whose events take place in the USA and half in Baja California in Mexico. Mexico's off-road terrain is also utilized as a result of the successful addition of a WRC round to the series in 2004.

Within world motorsport but away from off-road and rally events, Mexico also held a round of the WTCC and A1GP in 2005. The USA-based Champcar series also holds events in Mexico, though from 2007 this will be reduced to one event per year.

Joint series with the USA highlight how Mexico's geographic proximity, and its role as a partner in the NAFTA trade group, has seen its motorsport influenced by trends from the USA. From 2006, NASCAR will hold one event a year in

Mexico, initially a Craftsman Truck event, which will, from 2007, become a Busch series event. These will be supported by a Grand-Am sportscar round, a series similarly under the wing of the NASCAR-controlling France family.

The leading national series in Mexican motorsport—the Corona Series—is similarly influenced by USA-style racing. The series takes after NASCAR and races half on ovals and half on road circuits. Drag racing has a strong presence in Mexico and another NASCAR-like pick-up series headlines the National CARreras circuit-racing series package. This series of championships holds events for pick-ups, Formula Vee single-seaters and a one-make Ford Ka championship.

Alongside NASCAR-like series, saloon car racing in Mexico includes a production saloon car series, called Mexico Touring, which races on road circuits. In addition to the one-make Ka series, mentioned above, is a one-make series for VW Beetles based at the Monterrey circuit. Finally, within the saloon-racing segment, there is a well-supported national series for historic cars.

Single-seat racing is less well supported in Mexico. The most prestigious series that visits Mexico below A1GP and Champcar is the Pan-Am Formula Renault 2000 Series. This is a Central and South American series, four rounds of which are held in Mexico as well as visits to Brazil or Argentina. From 2007, a Formula Renault 1600 category is due to support the headline 2000 series. The main national Mexican single-seat series is the aforementioned Formula Vee championship, part of the National CARreras racing package.

Outside circuit racing, off-road events are well supported, particularly in Baja California, as a result of the USA-based SCORE championship. Mexico has a national rally championship, but it appears to be poorly supported, although Peugeot does support a one-make 206 championship in the country.

The motorsport industry in Mexico appears to comprise mainly local teams and importers of overseas equipment. Much of the supply chain is imported from either the USA or Europe and there are no Mexican international motorsport firms. Within saloon car racing, those series utilizing NASCAR-style equipment like pick-ups and the Corona Series access a USA-based supply chain. Local championships for Kas and Beetles utilize a less expensive locally based supply chain, where costs dictate that international suppliers are not necessary.

European rally suppliers are sourced through local distributors, reflecting the home base of the motorsport equipment used by OEMs such as Mitsubishi, Renault and Peugeot. Similarly, off-road suppliers are Europe- or USA-based.

SWOT Analysis: The Mexican Motorsport Industry

Following description of the industry, a SWOT analysis summarizes some of the key aspects of the position on the global grid (see Table 3.8).

Table 3.8 **SWOT of the Mexican Motorsport Industry in 2005**

Strengths
1 NASCAR linkages via series and events
2 Off-road potential of terrain—Baja California
3 WRC event and good viewing figures

Weaknesses
1 Little domestic industry
2 No international industry
3 Single-seat racing weak compared to position ten years ago

Opportunities
1 Oval/NASCAR expansion through to Central America?
2 Supply of low/medium-spec generic technology due to producer cost advantage
3 Expansion of off-road/rallying
4 Mexican drivers in USA

Threats
1 Proximity of USA industry puts domestic industry in shadow
2 Infrastructure poor—tracks closing and some poorly run

Conclusion: The Mexican Motorsport Industry

As part of NAFTA, which has created "duty free trade" between Mexico, the USA and Canada, Mexico is rapidly growing as a major automotive manufacturing and assembly base. It seems likely this will lead to global motorsport companies, seeking to supply the vast USA motorsport market, increasingly locating some activity in Mexico to take advantage of the low labor rates and high skills available. In turn, this may lead to a growth in the Mexican motorsport industry itself as engineering knowledge expands.

Internationally, Mexico is increasing its presence on the world stage through events like WRC, WTCC and A1GP. Additionally, there are an expanding number of "regional" events sourced out of the USA, with tentative expansion of NASCAR into Mexico, a headline NASCAR-like national series and the half Mexican-, half USA-based SCORE Off-Road championship, incorporating the famous Baja California event.

Below these series, Mexican motorsport appears relatively undeveloped, with no international motorsport supply chain, few national level suppliers of any note and, overall, a "shadow" effect from the geographically proximate USA industry.

The South African Motorsport Industry

Table 3.9 provides the global metrics for the South African motorsport industry. While South Africa barely achieves global presence on these headline figures, its racing history and position as an economic power within Africa has seen the

Table 3.9 **Motorsport in South Africa in 2005**

Indicators	South Africa 2005	% of world total
Total value of annual motorsport turnover for engineering and services	£0.5b	1.0
Motorsport turnover as % GDP	0.42 percent	—
Permanent paved circuits (including ovals over ¼ mile but not kart)	9	1.5
Competition license holders	6,000	—
Global chassis constructors (F1, WRC, WTCC and A1GP)	0	0
Number of racing series — Global — Regional	 A1GP FIA Rally	 — —
Global motorsport events (F1, WRC, WTCC and A1GP)	1	1.8
Average F1 viewing figures per race event (*Source*: Sports Marketing Surveys)	0.12 m	0.2
Average WRC viewing figures per event (*Source*: wrc.com)	Not known	—

development of a substantial industry, which contains a number of firms of international stature.

History and Current Industry Position

Motorsport in South Africa has always had a relatively high profile in the continent. An F1 Grand Prix was held until the early 1990s, and there are continuous moves to bring an F1 event back to the country. Several high-profile South African entrepreneurs are the investors behind the new A1GP series, and South Africa's one A1GP event per year is currently its only slot on the global motorsport calendar.

Below global events, South Africa is well represented regionally, with rounds of both the FIA regional rally championship and the Off-Road World Cup. This representation in off-road events is reflected in strong national series for off-road events and rallying, with support from OEMs VW, Toyota, Ford and Nissan. In 2006, the nascent Eurosport-backed International Rally Championship (IRC) held its first round in South Africa.

Within circuit racing, the leading series in South Africa is the Super Series (formerly known as the Power Tour), which gathers together the leading circuit-racing series under one umbrella. The leading championship is the V8 Supercar

Series, which is a highly modified saloon-based series with regulations similar to the USA's Trans Am series, not dissimilar to NASCAR, with tube-frame chassis and V8 engines. Supporting this are championships for production cars, supported by a variety of OEMs, a one-make VW Polo championship, a national Formula Ford championship and a one-spec sportscar series called Shelby Can-Am.

National circuit-racing championships exist for both single-seat and saloon cars. Notable in the former category is the long-standing and successful Formula Vee Championship, and a championship for historic single-seaters organized by the HRCR, which also organizes two national historic saloon series.

At a local level, circuit racing is split into provinces, with varying numbers of circuit-racing championships in each one. This ranges from the sole Eastern Province regional circuit-racing championship for saloon cars, to the more numerous Northern Region series for single-seat categories like Formula Vee, Formula Ford, Formula GT (like VW Super Vee) in single-seaters, and saloon car series for historic cars and Lotus.

National rally and off-road championships in South Africa also comprise a number of strong regional series for both categories. There are short oval tar and dirt championships at national and regional levels, which are popular events.

The motorsport industry in South Africa has a number of global players, particularly in off-road, rallying and in composites more generally. Nissan bases its global off-road competition development in South Africa, and VW and Toyota have strong rally development bases, particularly for the new and promising S2000 category. At a regional and national level these South African-based suppliers will supply the local market, as do distributors for European-based motorsport specialists for vehicles like Subarus and Mitsubishis.

South African composite firms, developed by their large domestic defence industry, are also being used in the global motorsport supply chain. One of the beneficiaries of such expertise is the niche vehicle industry in South Africa. The Superperformance/High-tech Automotive Group is the third largest independent car manufacturer in the world, building 700 cars a year, including Cobra replicas and the new Le Mans Coupe, as well as bodies for the UK-based Noble sportscar.

Within circuit racing, the top-line Super Car series is linked to a USA-based supply chain, reflecting the USA-style technical regulations of the formula. Staying within the headline Super Series, Formula Ford chassis are supplied from UK-based Van Diemen and French-based Mygale. The one-spec Shelby Can-Am series was originally designed, and its chassis built, in the USA, but today the class is virtually completely supplied from a locally based supply chain, which supplies everything from the production Nissan 350Z-based engine to the bodywork.

Outside the national Super Series, various domestic suppliers are involved in national- and regional-level circuit-racing series. For example, a number of Formula Vee chassis (Rhema, Lantis) are made domestically, as are some Formula Gti chassis (DAW). Within regional saloon car racing domestic and international supply chains are used by the competitors, reflecting the origin of the car's manufacture. Finally, it is worth noting that the Speads range of single-seat and sportscar chassis are manufactured in South Africa and are sold successfully in the UK and USA.

SWOT Analysis: The South African Motorsport Industry

Following description of the industry, a SWOT analysis summarizes some of the key aspects of the position on the global grid (see Table 3.10).

Table 3.10 **SWOT of the South African Motorsport Industry in 2005**

Strengths	**Weaknesses**
1 Strong niche vehicle industry 2 Composites already used by UK companies 3 Impressive grass roots motorsport 4 Large brands willing to invest in racing (Sasol, Wesbank, Vodafone) 5 Off-road and rally car production 6 Motorsport center of African continent	Isolated position for regional motorsport linkages unless rest of Africa comes on stream
Opportunities	**Threats**
1 South African firms moving toward international motorsport supply chain 2 S2000 going global via Eurosport IRC? 3 Key position if rest of Africa develops motorsport culture	Political and economic problems of African continent

Conclusion: The South African Motorsport Industry

To some extent, the strong domestic South African motorsport industry falls below the radar of the global metrics—but this is by sheer volume alone. The industry has a small but successful presence in the global motorsport supply chain, especially within global rallying and off-road car production supply chain, and in the composites industry more widely.

South Africa also has a strong involvement in the global performance engineering industry through its composites expertise and both the production of, and supply to, niche vehicles.

Within the sport, South Africa has a good level of competitor support at a regional level across the circuit-racing, short oval, rallying and off-road segments. This is reflected in strong national series within these racing disciplines.

Conclusion: The Midfield

The Midfield provides a number of countries with significant racing heritage and domestic industries. Nevertheless, what is striking is their combined limited share of the global market. Their combined *total* motorsport turnover, at £4.5 billion, represents less than 10 percent of the global market and between them they contain only one global chassis constructor (Table 3.11).

If one theme runs through the majority of this tier it is their valuable position as "major regional gateways" to racing markets and cultures—into the regions of Australia, South America, Africa and, in Mexico's unique case, to North America. The question that remains is how great their potential for growth is in the global regions within which they sit.

Here, their greater purchase of global racing events (a 21 percent global share) and the growth of cross-border championships provide tentative signs of the process of globalization in motorsport consumption markets where consumption leads as a driver.

Table 3.11 **The Midfield Countries in 2005**

Indicators	Australia	Spain	South America	Mexico	South Africa
Total value of annual turnover motorsport engineering and services	£1.5b	£1.0b	£1.0b	£0.5b	£0.5b
Motorsport turnover as % GDP	0.44%	0.17%	0.24%	0.13%	0.42%
Global chassis constructors	0	1	0	0	0
Permanent paved circuits (including ovals over ¼ mile but not kart)	15	9	Argentina, 33; Brazil, 13	20	9
Competition license holders	22,000	Not known	Not known	Not known	6,000
Global series events	3	3	2	3	1
Average F1 viewing figures per race event 2005 (*Source*: Sports Marketing Surveys)	0.5 m	4.2 m	Argentina—Not known; Brazil—9.6 m	Not known	0.12 m
Average WRC viewing figures per event 2005 (*Source*: wrc.com)	0.33 m	0.83 m	Argentina, 0.94 m; Brazil, Not known	0.76 m	Not known

Within vehicle production, too, examples exist of growing national industries (Australia, Brazil, South Africa) finding a niche in the international division of labor and providing specialist expertise. Overall, however, such elements are the exception to the rule of international imports or domestic supply.

Finally, one other challenge unites this tier—holding their position in the face of new kids on the global grid who are coming through the field—and it is to this final tier of the Global Starting Grid that we turn in Part Four.

PART FOUR

Coming Through The Field

Introduction: Coming Through the Field

The final tier within our Global Starting Grid of 16 is the five countries or global regions Coming Through the Field—Malaysia, the Gulf Region, China, Turkey and the Czech Republic. In the main, this is a set of newcomers to the world of motorsport, and the critical issue is whether these truly represent new regions of growth for the global industry.

Again, there remains very limited international material and data on these nascent national industries. One interesting example, however, is Malaysia, which has identified the potential value of creating a motorsport industry and put in place a strategy and sustained program of activity to achieve its position on the Global Starting Grid.

Within the following Part Four, the global metrics are applied to benchmark each of the Coming Through the Field nations, using the limited data available. Each nation's industry is reviewed before the completion of a SWOT (strengths, weaknesses, opportunities and threats) analysis and final summary.

The Malaysian Motorsport Industry

Table 4.1 provides the global metrics for the Malaysian motorsport industry. Worth only 1 percent of the global market, Malaysia hosts two global racing events.

History and Current Industry Position

Motorsport has a longer history in Malaysia than many recall. It hosted popular motorsport at the Shah Alam circuit and also Johor Bahru, in the South, for

Table 4.1 **Motorsport in Malaysia in 2005**

Indicators	Malaysia 2005	% of world total
Total value of annual motorsport turnover for engineering and services	£0.3b	1.0
Motorsport turnover as % GDP	0.45 percent	—
Permanent paved circuits (including ovals over ¼ mile but not kart)	2	0.3
Competition license holders	Not known	—
Global chassis constructors (F1, WRC, WTCC and A1GP)	0	0
Number of racing series		
— Global	F1; A1GP	—
— Regional	FIA Rally	—
Global motorsport events (F1, WRC, WTCC and A1GP)	2	3.6
Average F1 viewing figures per race event (*Source*: Sports Marketing Surveys)	0.26 m	0.5
Average WRC viewing figures per event (*Source*: wrc.com)	Not known	—

many years. Domestic motorsport has been very low key, concentrated mainly on motorcycle racing, while international participation has also remained limited. Motorsport has been used in the last ten years, by the national government, to exemplify and expand industrial activity in high-tech development and innovation and to improve the country's international image.

The Malaysian government (through the Malaysian Airport Authority) funded the building of the state-of-the-art Sepang F1 circuit as part of a successful drive to gain a World Championship Grand Prix. This has provided location incentives targeted specifically at overseas motorsport companies.

Most recently Petronas, Malaysia's state-owned petroleum and gas corporation, announced a Motorsport Technical Center in Bangi, near Sepang, which will train Malaysian engineers and include an R&D section. Overall, Malaysia has sought to develop both its low-key domestic motorsport scene and its involvement in international motorsport.

At the domestic level it has sought to build club-level karting, motorcycle racing and club-level motor racing. This is based mostly around the preparation of domestic cars, principally Proton, and a number of domestic rally championships utilizing some imported cars and domestic manufacturers. These events are held principally on the two permanent racing circuits in Malaysia.

At the level above these domestic racing championships, Malaysia holds rounds of regional series like the Asian Festival of Speed (AFOS). AFOS includes series for touring cars (ATCC), Porsche one-make (Carrera Cup) and two one-spec single-seat championships (Formula Renault V6 and Formula BMW).

Linking major Malaysian manufacturers with existing motorsport specialists in other countries has helped to develop Malaysia's involvement in international motorsport. Proton, the state-owned car manufacturer, for example, has taken this approach in the field of performance engineering by purchasing the Lotus Group, based in the UK. It has grown the company but also successfully transferred to Malaysia high-performance knowledge to benefit its local culture. Proton entered a car in the BTCC from 2002—4 and, although the car was designed and built in the UK by a specialist team, the team had a policy of employing Malaysian personnel where possible. In motorcycling, Proton has in the past employed Proton Team KR, based in the UK, to build both chassis and engine for the MotoGP series.

Other international motorsport linkages included the links of Petronas, the Malaysian state-owned oil company, with the former Sauber F1 team through sponsorship of the team's purchase of its Ferrari F1 engine. The company also developed joint Sauber-Petronas engineering projects linked to road-car production. In a similar way, in the field of motorcycling Petronas has employed UK-based specialist Team Foggy to build the chassis for its World Superbike campaign, while Swiss engine specialists developed the engine. A third element of international motorsport involvement has been the sponsorship of F1 teams by a variety of Malaysian public bodies.

Nevertheless, there are currently no Malaysian motorsport industry specialists operating independently on the world stage.

SWOT Analysis: The Malaysian Motorsport Industry

Following description of the industry, a SWOT analysis summarizes some of the key aspects of the position on the global grid (see Table 4.2 overleaf).

Conclusion: The Malaysian Motorsport Industry

The country has seen a recent and sustained drive by the government to build an international motorsport presence from a very limited base—but so far with limited success. This support has achieved a Grand Prix calendar date and several high-profile ventures, alliances and sponsorships in high-technology international motorsport.

The program has gained international profile and exposure for this modernizing nation but very limited success in attracting motorsport inward investment

Table 4.2 **SWOT of the Malaysian Motorsport Industry in 2005**

Strengths	Weaknesses
1 Strong and recovering economy	1 Sparse domestic motorsport industry
2 Large state corporations willing to invest	2 State controls most of the road car production
3 Government support for motorsport as R&D for domestic industry and national profile raiser. Owns Sepang F1 track	3 Only two tracks
4 Tax incentives for motorsport investment (e.g. no import duty on karting equipment)	4 Unclear as to whether private sector entrepreneurs exist to take motorsport industry forward

Opportunities	Threats
1 Possible location for low cost quality components?	1 Withdrawal of government support
2 Malaysia becomes the motorsport focus for Asia	2 Government initiatives fail to develop domestic interest in motorsport

and there has been no development of Malaysian motorsport specialists to date. There are encouraging signs of a growth in participation through the active formation and growth of club/leisure-level motorsport and the development of racing schools and karting tracks.

The Gulf Region (Bahrain, Qatar, Dubai) Motorsport Industry

Table 4.3 provides the global metrics for the Gulf Region motorsport industry. The region has a combined turnover worth less than 1 percent of the global market but hosts two global racing events.

History and Current Industry Position

The Gulf Region has long been on the radar of international motorsport for its well-supported role in the FIA Regional Rally Series and its round of the FIA Off-Road World Championship, the UAE Desert Challenge.

In contrast, motor racing has been restricted due to the lack of suitable circuits. In 2004, however, three new circuits debuted, one each in Bahrain, Dubai and Qatar. Of these, the most global profile is enjoyed by the Bahrain International Circuit, which has hosted an annual round of the F1 World Championship since 2004. This new circuit has also attracted other international events like GP2, FIA GT and, from 2006, Australian V8 Supercar and drag racing.

The Dubai circuit also gained a round of the A1GP in the 2005. However, no rounds are to be held in the Gulf Region for the 2006/07 A1GP series. In 2006, Dubai held a round of the FIA GT series, but this will not be repeated in 2007.

Table 4.3 Motorsport in the Gulf Region in 2005

Indicators	Gulf Region 2005	% of world total
Total value of annual motorsport turnover for engineering and services	£0.3b	0.6
Motorsport turnover as % GDP	0.38 percent (for all three countries combined where Dubai GDP is included as total GDP of UAE)	—
Permanent paved circuits (including ovals over ¼ mile but not kart)	Bahrain (1); Qatar (1); Dubai (1)	0.5
Competition license holders	Bahrain (230); Others not known	—
Global chassis constructors (F1, WRC, WTCC and A1GP)	0	0
Number of racing series — Global — Regional	 F1; A1GP GP2; FIA GT; FIA Rally	 — —
Global motorsport events (F1, WRC, WTCC and A1GP)	2	3.6
Average F1 viewing figures per race event (*Source*: Sports Marketing Surveys)	Not known	—
Average WRC viewing figures per event (*Source*: wrc.com)	Not known	—

The Losail circuit in Qatar concentrated initially on attracting MotoGP rather than four-wheeled motorsport. The main international exception to this was the hosting of a round of the Grand Prix Masters series in 2006. Other motorsport in Qatar includes a national rally championship supported by a one-make Mitsubishi championship, although entries are not high. Motorsport in Qatar, aside from rallying, comprises a saloon-based sprint series.

Motorsport at a national level in Bahrain is focused on the new Bahrain circuit and its National Racing Championship. This championship comprises four events; two are for single-seat series, Formula Arabia (formerly Zip Ford equipment) and Formula BMW, and two are for one-make saloon/sportscar series (Mini Cooper and Caterham).

Outside circuit racing, Bahrain also holds a sprint championship and a drag-racing championship. More specialized international drag-racing cars are showcased at the once-yearly Bahrain International Drag Racing event, attracting international participants. The circuit also allows members of the public to use its drag strip on "Test and Tune" events.

Motorsport in Dubai revolves around the Dubai circuit. The circuit holds a national multi-event championship for both VW Polos and Radical Sportscars. Outside circuit racing, Dubai holds a national karting championship and a number of endurance karting events.

All motorsport events utilize imported equipment and there is no international motorsport industry in the region, aside from the track infrastructure.

SWOT Analysis: The Gulf Region Motorsport Industry

Following description of the industry, a SWOT analysis summarizes some of the key aspects of the position on the global grid (see Table 4.4).

Table 4.4 **SWOT of the Gulf Region Motorsport Industry**

Strengths	Weaknesses
1 Track infrastructure	1 Little domestic industry
2 Financing	2 Weak grass roots
3 Government support	3 No evidence of entrepreneurial drive to develop the industry
4 Regional rally series	
Opportunities	**Threats**
1 Historic business linkages in high-tech defense industry to Europe	1 All competing for the same international series
2 Build linkages to other high-tech initiatives in the region	2 Withdrawal of government support

Conclusion: The Gulf Region Motorsport Industry

The region boasts a set of world-class circuits, which have attracted several high-profile events, particularly F1 in Bahrain. Bahrain apart (F1, V8 Supercar), the region is struggling to maintain these international events due to the global competition. Grass roots motorsport is weak though growing, and the domestic industry remains nascent. Some efforts are being made to stimulate grass roots involvement, particularly with circuit racing and drag racing in Bahrain, rallying in Qatar and karting and circuit racing in Dubai. Bahrain has recently announced plans to grow its engineering and educational base around the race circuit.

The Turkish Motorsport Industry

Table 4.5 provides the global metrics for the Turkish motorsport industry. The region has a combined turnover worth less than 1 percent of the global market but hosts two global racing events.

History and Current Industry Position

Global motorsport events started relatively recently in Turkey, with their first world championship event being a WRC event in 2003. This was held until 2006 when it was withdrawn from the calendar due to competition for places on the WRC calendar from other events. Turkey had long held international rallies, the first being in 1972, and the country still holds a round of the FIA Regional Rally Championship. It also has a strong national rally championship, mainly using imported equipment.

Circuit racing in Turkey attracted global events by the opening in 2005 of the new circuit at Istanbul Park. There are two other circuits in Turkey, which host national events only. The new Istanbul circuit attracted an F1 Grand Prix from 2005, as well as a round of the WTCC and other international series like FIA GT, LMS and the F1-supporting GP2 in 2005. This impressive start was faltering slightly by 2007, with only an F1 event (with GP2) and a WTCC event confirmed.

National circuit racing comprises three main series that compete at all three circuits. The first is the TR Track championship, comprising an F3 championship, the premier single-seat series in Turkey, a production saloon championship, and a one-make series for Fiat Sienas. The second series incorporates two one-make saloon car series, the SEAT Cup and the women-only VW Polo

Table 4.5 **Motorsport in Turkey in 2005**

Indicators	Turkey 2005	% of world total
Total value of annual motorsport turnover for engineering and services	£0.3b	0.6
Motorsport turnover as % GDP	0.18 percent	—
Permanent paved circuits (including ovals over ¼ mile but not kart)	3	0.5
Competition license holders	Not known	—
Global chassis constructors (F1, WRC, WTCC and A1GP)	0	0
Number of racing series — Global — Regional	 F1; WRC; WTCC GP2; FIA GT; FIA Rally; LMS	 — —
Global motorsport events (F1, WRC, WTCC and A1GP)	3	5.4
Average F1 viewing figures per race event (*Source*: Sports Marketing Surveys)	Not known	—
Average WRC viewing figures per event (*Source*: wrc. com)	1.07 m	2.14

Cup. The last series incorporates two one-make saloon car championships for locally built Fiat 124s, one open championship and one for women only, and a one-make Caterham series.

Outside circuit racing and rallying there are low-key championships for drag racing, utilizing modified production cars, and a growing karting scene with a national series.

Other than events utilizing locally built cars (Siena, 124) most equipment is imported into Turkey and there are currently no international motorsport firms in Turkey.

SWOT Analysis: The Turkish Motorsport Industry

Following description of the industry, a SWOT analysis summarizes some of the key aspects of the position on the global grid (see Table 4.6).

Table 4.6 **SWOT of the Turkish Motorsport Industry in 2005**

Strengths	Weaknesses
Istanbul circuit regarded as one of world's best "new" circuits	1 Few tracks
	2 Weak domestic motorsport industry
Opportunities	**Threats**
1 Joining EU?	1 Turkish national politics (2006 F1)
2 VW and SEAT involved already	
3 Link between East and West motorsport	2 Withdrawal of indirect government support

Conclusion: The Turkish Motorsport Industry

Turkey's recent motorsport history is based on drawing international events to the country. The short-lived WRC event raised the profile of motorsport in Turkey, and the opening of the part-government-funded Istanbul Park Circuit and the gaining of the F1 event, raised this further still.

Grass roots motorsport is relatively weak but growing, with the involvement of one-make championships like VW and SEAT drawn to the facilities of the new Istanbul Circuit. Apart from local distributors and preparation, the motorsport industry in Turkey is at a very early stage of development.

The Chinese Motorsport Industry

Table 4.7 provides the global metrics for the Chinese motorsport industry. The region has a combined turnover worth less than 1 percent of the global market but hosts two global racing events. The critical figure for the current Chinese motorsport industry is a motorsport turnover figure of a mere 0.03 percent GDP in a rapidly expanding economy, predicted to be the largest in the world by 2020.

History and Current Industry Position

Motorsport in China is at a low level, and there is little domestic industry. It seems China's motorsport strategy has two approaches. First, it will attract high-profile international events to the country in order to raise their global profile. China gained the rights to host a F1 Grand Prix in 2004 on a brand-new circuit in Shanghai. In addition, the circuit attracted a round of the Australian V8 Supercars championship (Australia's premier motorsport series) in 2005. In 2003, a non-championship round of the Japanese GT Championship was held on a temporary street circuit in Shanghai. In 2007, a round of the Champcar World Series will be held at Zhuhai, together with a round of the FIA GT Championship at the same circuit. In the 2005/6 championship, A1GP held a round at Shanghai, joined the following season by a street race in Beijing, making two A1GP races in China in one season.

Table 4.7 **Motorsport in China in 2005**

Indicators	China 2005	% of world total
Total value of annual motorsport turnover for engineering and services	£0.25b	0.5
Motorsport turnover as % GDP	0.03 percent	—
Permanent paved circuits (including ovals over ¼ mile but not kart)	4	0.7
Competition license holders	Not known	—
Global chassis constructors (F1, WRC, WTCC and A1GP)	0	0

Number of racing series
  — Global
  — Regional
	
	F1; A1GP
	FIA GT; FIA Rally
		
		—
		—

Global motorsport events (F1, WRC, WTCC and A1GP)	2	3.6
Average F1 viewing figures per race event (*Source*: Sports Marketing Surveys)	3.3 m	6.3
Average WRC viewing figures per event (*Source*: wrc.com)	3.74 m	7.5

Outside circuit racing, China holds a round of the FIA Regional Rally Championship called the China Rally. China formerly held a round of the WRC, but the event was removed from the calendar due to organizational difficulties.

The second aspect of China's motorsport strategy is to build domestic-level participation. Motorsport in China starts with karting, organized in conjunction with Hong Kong motorsport authorities. The pinnacle of circuit-based motorsport in China is the China Circuit Championships (CCC). The CCC incorporates a Touring Car Championship, a one-make VW Polo championship, Formula Campus and Formula Renault.

Below this national championship, Formula Racing Developments runs a lower-level one circuit-based series for Formula Renault, Formula Renault Campus and Renault Spyder.

One rung above these domestic circuit-racing championships are rounds of the Asian-based Asian Festival of Speed championship (AFOS), which are held at the Goldenport, Shanghai and Zhuhai circuits, among a championship held at ten Asian circuits. AFOS includes series for touring cars (ATCC), Porsche one-make (Carrera Cup) and two one-spec single-seat championships (Formula Renault V6 and Formula BMW). Another regionally based series that has rounds in China is the Pan Delta Super Racing Festival, incorporating rounds of the Asian F3 championship, the Hong Kong Touring Car Championship and a one-make Lotus Challenge. Finally, an Asian Formula Renault championship, with most rounds run in China, has also been established.

For 2007, a newly announced national motorsport concept called CF2000 is to commence. This seeks to develop young Chinese driver talent to take forward onto the international stage. Interestingly, the company uses a new single-seater car entirely manufactured in China—the first of its kind.

Other Chinese domestic motorsport, outside circuit-based racing, includes rally events, particularly a Chinese national championship organized by the Chinese governing body, the Federation of Automobile Sports China (FASC). One of these rounds is held in Shanghai and is sponsored by the Shanghai Volkswagen Automotive Sales Company. This championship attracts entries from across Asia, utilizing mainly imported cars.

There are currently no Chinese motorsport industry specialists competing on the world stage.

SWOT Analysis: The Chinese Motorsport Industry

Following description of the industry, a SWOT analysis summarizes some of the key aspects of the position on the global grid (see Table 4.8).

Conclusion: The Chinese Motorsport Industry

China is a very recent entrant into the world of international motorsport. The size of the potential domestic car market, and the growth of OEM interest, has

Table 4.8 SWOT of the Chinese Motorsport Industry in 2005

Strengths
1 Huge long-term potential, due to size of population, when road car market expands
2 Shanghai auto engineering complex with OEM joint ventures

Opportunities
1 OEM migration includes motorsport activity
2 Low-tech motorsport components
3 Expand domestic participation and consumption of motorsport due to large audience potential
4 Build skills base for labor-intensive activities such as composites

Weaknesses
1 Low level of road car ownership
2 No domestic motorsport industry
3 Relatively poor population for motorsport in medium term
4 No specialist motorsport press as yet

Threats
1 Other new global entrants in low-cost production
2 Central government clampdown on regional government capital projects

driven rapid movement to hosting of international events at newly built facilities. The recent growth of the Shanghai automotive engineering complex, including the Shanghai circuit, is expected to continue. There is the long-term potential for specialist motorsport production driven by the orientation of OEMs to this potentially vast market. Grass roots motorsport, although growing, is currently at a low level.

It would seem likely that some motorsport companies will source supplies from China in the future alongside automotive and high-technology developments. It is probable that, as local engineering knowledge grows, this will lead to local companies producing and selling motorsport products on a world stage.

The Czech Motorsport Industry

Table 4.9 provides the global metrics for the Czech motorsport industry. Uniquely among this tier of countries, the industry has a global chassis constructor. In addition, although the country hosted no global series events in 2005, this situation was to change in 2006 and 2007.

Historic and Current Industry Position

Motorsport in the Czech Republic has a long history, having developed, like many mainland European countries, from city-to-city races in the early 20th century, which utilized public roads. International motorsport has also had a long presence, though the country has rarely attracted a global motorsport series.

Within circuit racing, the country only has two circuits, Most and Brno, with Brno holding events of an international standard. In 2005, no world motorsport events were held in the country but, in 2006, rounds of the WTCC and A1GP were held at Brno, and this looks likely to be repeated in 2007. Brno will also host a long-standing round of the FIA GT series. A round of the German DTM series was held in 2005.

National-level circuit racing revolves around a number of saloon and GT championships and a less well-represented single-seater scene. The most prestigious circuit-racing championship in the country is a combined saloon/GT championship, with a capacity split at 1600cc. Below this multi-marque series are two one-make saloon car championships, the long-standing Skoda Octavia Cup, and a new series for BMW 1-series. Single-seat circuit racing has one multi-make class for up to 1400 cc engines.

Outside circuit racing, the Czech Republic has held a round of the FIA Regional Rally Championship for some time. Rallying is traditionally strong at a national level, with two national championships, Rally and Sprint Rally, and well-supported regional and local events. The strength of rallying in the country is reflected in very strong TV viewing figures for the WRC.

Motorsport equipment used in the Czech Republic is split between imported equipment and domestically produced products, mainly from Skoda. The headline GT/saloon series utilizes imported cars like Ferrari, Porsche, BMW and Mercedes, but also includes a strong element of Skoda Octavias. The two-one make saloon

Table 4.9 **Motorsport in the Czech Republic in 2005**

Indicators	Czech Republic 2005	% of world total
Total value of annual motorsport turnover for engineering and services	£0.20b	0.4
Motorsport turnover as % GDP	0.34 percent	—
Permanent paved circuits (including ovals over ¼ mile but not kart)	2	0.3
Competition license holders	Not known	—
Global chassis constructors (F1, WRC, WTCC and A1GP)	1	4.5
Number of racing series		
— Global	None	—
— Regional	FIA GT; FIA Rally	—
Global motorsport events (F1, WRC, WTCC and A1GP)	0	0
Average F1 viewing figures per race event (*Source*: Sports Marketing Surveys)	0.7 m	1.3
Average WRC viewing figures per event (*Source*: wrc.com)	3.35 m	6.7

car series are split equally between the domestic OEM Skoda and BMW. In the one single-seat category, chassis manufacture is split between overseas firms like Van Diemen and small Czech domestic producers like Fiks. In rallying, many cars are imported from the usual rally producers like Subaru, Mitsubishi, VW and Peugeot, but there is also a strong contingent from the domestic OEM Skoda.

The sole international global motorsport firm in the Czech Republic is Skoda Motorsport (part of VAG, but with input from German-based VW Motorsport). Until 2005, Skoda maintained a works presence in WRC, but this has since been downgraded to a works-supported private team presence. Skoda has a strong presence in national motorsport, evidenced by the one-make Skoda Octavia Cup in circuit racing, and the many Octavias in national and regional rallying and in the leading saloon/GT circuit racing series.

It should be noted that the Czech Republic's strong history of engineering, good universities and a growing automotive industry has led firms like Ricardo to set up satellite automotive/performance engineering specialists in the country.

SWOT Analysis: The Czech Motorsport Industry

Following description of the industry, a SWOT analysis summarizes some of the key aspects of the position on the global grid (see Table 4.10).

Table 4.10   **SWOT of the Czech Motorsport Industry in 2005**

Strengths	Weaknesses
1 Active OEM—Skoda	1 One of the two OEMs, Skoda, involved in many areas of motorsport (other is PSA)
2 Strong engineering base	
3 Motorsport history (Skoda, Tatra)	
4 Relatively strong grass roots	2 Only two circuits for 10 million population
5 Strong WRC viewing figures	
Opportunities	**Threats**
1 Performance engineering consultancies	1 Skoda pull out of motorsport
2 Low-cost generic motorsport components utilizing skilled workforce at lower labor rates	2 Loss of one of the two circuits
	3 Potential low-cost advantage in comparison to the frontrunner countries is surpassed by new global competitors

Conclusion: The Czech Motorsport Industry

Of the two OEMs involved in the Czech Republic (PSA and Skoda), Skoda has a very strong motorsport presence, including in international rallying. Circuit racing only has two venues but one, Brno, is of global standard and is attracting global series events. The domestic industry has a potentially strong offering in performance engineering in which automotive engineering crosses with motorsport activity. As their domestic automotive manufacturing base grows it is likely that motorsport production will as well.

Conclusion: Coming Through the Field

A distinctive theme among the majority of these countries is that they are all at a relatively early stage in building an interest in the business of motorsport; in effect, they are growing their industries from a very low base (Table 4.11). With the exception of the Czech Republic, they are all following government-funded, explicit strategies to achieve growth in the motorsport sector.

Table 4.11 **The Coming Through the Field Countries in 2005**

Indicators	*Malaysia*	*Gulf Region*	*Turkey*	*China*	*Czech Republic*
Total value of annual turnover motorsport engineering and services	£0.3b	£0.3b	£0.3b	£0.25b	£0.2b
Motorsport turnover as % GDP	0.45%	0.38 percent (for all three countries)	0.18%	0.03%	0.34%
Global chassis constructors	0	0	0	0	1
Permanent paved circuits (including ovals over ¼ mile but not kart)	2	Bahrain (1) Qatar (1) Dubai (1)	3	4	2
Competition license holders	Not known	Not known	Not known	Not known	Not known
Global series events	2	2	3	2	0
Average F1 viewing figures per race event 2005 (*Source*: Sports Marketing Surveys)	0.26 m	Not known	Not known	3.3 m	0.7 m
Average WRC viewing figures per event 2005 (*Source*: wrc.com)	Not known	Not known	1.07 m	3.74 m	3.35 m

Conclusion: Coming Through the Field

In many cases, strategy has been led by the development of racing infrastructure capable of grabbing a part of the global market—perhaps an event in one of the global series and, in particular, a Formula One Grand Prix. Initial success has been achieved through bringing on-stream a new group of national consumers. In the relentless march of globalization, however, the challenge is of these global series continuing to move to other destinations, as they are always in search of new markets and locations.

In contrast, developing domestic participation, and the basis upon which to develop a motorsport industry to compete globally, is proving to be a longer-term, and more difficult, goal. It is, therefore, this next stage in their development that will determine whether or not they will be able to create and sustain a viable motorsport value chain in the long term.

Nevertheless, there remains one country within this tier that has the potential to rapidly shift the immediate future of the global motorsport industry and that is, of course, China. While it, too, has been led by the desire to capture the global exposure of a Grand Prix, the potential global driver is the development of a Chinese domestic market which, in volume terms, is likely to transform a global marketplace, currently characterized by "batch" production of very small numbers of niche vehicles.

And, in turn, the rise of China in the new global economy reminds us of those other potential entrants of similar scale still waiting to get on to the Global Starting Grid; namely, India and Russia. A daunting and interesting prospect for all involved.

PART FIVE

Motorsport Going Global

"Globalization in motor sports is, probably, the most exciting frontier for people passionate about cars and racing that I can ever remember."
Herb Fishel (*Source*: interview with authors)

"No customer will stay if you fail to supply the winning car, regardless of price or where your business is based."
Gian Paolo Dallara (*Source*: interview with authors)

"I see everything that comes along as an opportunity. Globalization clearly offers a larger and exciting new marketplace for us all."
David Richards (*Source*: interview with authors)

"There can be no place for complacency, when there are very clever people out there with the will and determination to fight for their place in the global world of tomorrow."
Pat Symonds (*Source*: interview with authors)

"To compete in this new global race, you must be aware that there is a fire burning in the belly of good people in all these emerging nations. We must be awake to this."
Sir Jackie Stewart (*Source*: interview with authors)

"We must accept global trade is two-way and a positive force for business. We have to raise our game when we find new global competitors performing better than we are. In this way, globalization forces continuing improvement in our businesses."
Peter Digby (*Source*: interview with authors)

PART FIVE: MOTORSPORT GOING GLOBAL

All the quotes in the following section are drawn directly from interviews with the above individuals.

In Part Five, Motorsport Going Global, we pull together our conclusions to consider what directions the global motorsport industry might be heading toward in to the future. Part Five draws on both the framework and empirical data outlined in the previous parts to the book. But we have also applied the insights offered by six leading motorsport figures, all of whom draw on their considerable experience at the international level, to reflect on where the industry is heading and the challenges it faces going forward.

The world of Formula One is represented through Sir Jackie Stewart who, as a world champion in 1969, 1971 and 1973, pioneered the dominance of the Ford Cosworth DFV in the series. But Sir Jackie's achievements following his driving career are certainly equally as impressive. He worked globally as a motorsport expert and commentator for many years following his retirement before he undertook what he describes as the greatest challenge of his life. Establishing the Stewart Grand Prix team from scratch in the late 1990s and subsequently selling the team for a significant, undisclosed, sum to the Ford Motor Company in 1999. Unlike many short-lived teams, Stewart GP were highly competitive from the start, finishing third at the Monaco Grand Prix in their first year, and winning at the Nurburgring in 1999. Since he sold the team, Stewart has continued to work in the sport, most recently as President of the British Racing Drivers Club at Silverstone and now representing the Royal Bank of Scotland in their sponsorship of the Williams F1 team.

Pat Symonds is probably known to many F1 fans as the strategy guru who helped guide Fernando Alonso to his second world title and Renault's second consecutive championship win in 2006. In 1994, with Benetton, he helped Michael Schumacher to his first win! Pat is well placed to comment on the future of motorsport as, like many of his peers, such as Ron Dennis at McLaren, he has worked his way up from being a Race Engineer for Schumacher during his time at Benetton to Director of Engineering at Renault F1. Pat is a qualified engineer with an MSc from Cranfield University.

Of course, the motorsport industry is a lot more than Formula One, so we have representation from those who have reached senior and influential positions in other parts of the industry. David Richards, founder and Chairman of Prodrive, presides over one of the largest specialist motorsport companies in the world. Prodrive works with a range of global clients, including Subaru, Ferrari, Ford, BMW, Porsche and Aston Martin. David's initial personal experience centered on World Rallying, in which he became a world champion co-driver to Ari Vatanen; later he became Team Principal of both the Benetton and British American Racing F1 teams.

Herb Fishel, formerly Head of Racing at General Motors, provides an important North American input to our analysis of the changing motorsport industry. We cannot highlight all Fishel's accomplishments during his 40-year career at General Motors but, as an example, he led GM to the triple crown of racing by winning the Daytona 500, the Indianapolis 500 and the 24 Hours at Le Mans, all in the same year. Herb was Director of Motorsports for General Motors during the time they were actively competing in the Indy Racing League, NASCAR, drag racing and Le Mans. Herb, therefore, provides a further important perspective in terms of the manufacturer's view of the process and the fundamental creed of "Race on Sunday, sell on Monday", which has driven much of the global investment in motorsport.

Gian Paolo Dallara is founder and Chairman of one of the most successful global race car manufacturers: Dallara. While being based in Italy, less than 15 percent of the company's sales occur there. Dallara has made inroads into every major motorsport region in the world, and in 2006 supplied all the chassis used in the GP2 single-seat series. Currently developing their presence in China, Dallara are likely to be at the forefront of any new trends and technologies in race car manufacture.

A similar global perspective is provided by Peter Digby, the Managing Director of Xtrac, the highly successful transmission specialist manufacturer that acts as a key supplier to many teams competing in Formula One, World Rally Championship and Le Mans, among many other series. Xtrac's technological breakthrough in high-performance transmission design has made them a dominant force in world motorsport and underlines the need to continually innovate in order to stay on top of their game. Xtrac encapsulates the typical Motorsport Valley® firm in the UK, in that they operate within the local cluster, yet supply and support global markets.

We use interviews with these six experienced motorsport practitioners to explore some of the key trends and alternative business models that may emerge, or combine, to create the future of the motorsport industry. They define some of the challenges and opportunities that these present. We interviewed each individually, asking them a series of questions relating to the globalization of the motorsport industry. Here we summarize some of the key themes that emerged from these discussions.

Globalization in Motorsport: A Driving Force for Change

Our experts strongly agreed on the trend toward globalization and the opportunities it presents. However, there were marked differences as to where the motorsport industry currently sits on the road to globalization. For David Richards the position is clear, the motorsport industry is already global:

> The whole world has become a single market. In the past, you could sell a product into Europe knowing your American competitor would not be interested, but no

longer. Modern communication, price structures and the knowledge that the Internet provides, mean we must see the world on a global basis. You are fooling yourself if you don't have a global pricing policy and still believe there are discreet markets that can pay premiums. At Prodrive, we have such a single-pricing policy. Say, for example, we produce 100 Group N cars per year—with one going to Russia, one to the Middle East and another to China—it would be ridiculous to set different pricing policies or specifications on each of these. We lay out our stall on a global basis accepting we will be compared on that basis.

Gian Paolo Dallara shares this perspective, emphatically:

Most certainly our business is global. We are involved in racing on every continent and have a web of agents and personnel handling our interests. With modern communications and transport infrastructure, it is no longer a problem to operate globally. For instance, it is now possible to freight products anywhere in the world in a very short time. My products can be delivered throughout Italy within 12 hours, in Europe within 20 hours, in the United States the next day and just a little more for Japan. Our customers are global and our suppliers are becoming even more global. To remain successful in this business you must be able to communicate worldwide and understand globally developing situations early.

Dallara totally thinks and operates globally, in fact, we probably make less than 15 percent of our sales in Italy. Our strongest market, at present, is the USA with Europe a close second, particularly the UK and Germany. Of course, Japan is always important. Recently we have been particularly successful with German manufacturers such as Porsche, Audi and Bugatti.

Yet, in contrast, Herb Fishel's background with a major global OEM allows him to see the motorsport industry at a relatively early stage in the globalization process:

Pieces are in place today but, as yet, the industry is not globally mature. The opportunity is there for automotive manufacturers and suppliers, together with promoters, sanctioning organizations and even racers themselves, to develop and influence the new global model. Right now, I see this as an evolving and very important activity.

Moreover, Herb identifies a strong global desire for participation in motorsport activities at many levels:

I don't see from area to area, region to region, any lack of passion, enthusiasm or excitement about cars. If that is a given, then they are going to pursue, with that very interest and enthusiasm, whatever vehicles and race products they can find or make. These regions are growing fast and this speed will create new automobiles and racing products, at a similarly fast rate. Japan has had a well-developed, mature market for many years. I am not sure I see that growing, or where they go from here, but they have great circuits and motorsport is well established. They are very innovative in new forms of racing—just see what they have recently created with drifting.

In India, Thailand, Russia, China and Latin America, where there has been a lower automotive manufacturing base, I see slower growth in motorsport. However, as their manufacturing and supply bases grow, and this is happening very quickly, so the pace for motorsport will accelerate as people purchase locally built cars.

Pat Symonds shares Herb Fishel's perspective on the emergence of a global industry, but he recognizes larger companies (such as David Richard's Prodrive) are already there. It is, he argues, the small and medium-sized enterprises that still need to grasp what globalization really means for their business:

> Globalization in motorsport is no different to globalization in any other industry— it is a reality and our future. Globalization may have started with the larger companies but it is rapidly spreading down through medium-sized companies and will inevitably, soon, affect smaller companies.

By contrast, from the specialist supplier perspective, Peter Digby sees the industry operating as a series of regional zones coupled with a number of global characteristics:

> There certainly is [globalization], but it doesn't embrace the entire world. I witness Europe, America and Japan and some emerging countries actively intertrading with each other. But Australia, South America and South Africa, for example, tend to be more isolated and appear to be looking after themselves. While, mostly, our industry operates globally, some elements remain regional, looking after their own championships and television rights, but using European cars and powertrains, for example.

For Pat Symonds of the World Champion Renault F1 Team, the fact that his team owners are a global manufacturer means they too have a global perspective on the impact of their activities:

> As automotive manufacturers globalize it makes sense for them to be involved with a sport that is global. At Renault, our targets for the future are clearly set. We now produce around 2.5 million cars a year, and have targets for over 3 million cars a year in 2009. We are not going to achieve those just selling into France, UK, Italy and Spain—so we have to move outside to new markets. The global publicity generated by our becoming 2005 and 2006 Formula One World Champions is very important to Renault, which has set its sights on further globalization.

He underlines an important distinction, made by many observers in the industry and supported by the benchmarking analysis in this book, that in the

USA, the industry tends to operate on a regional, or perhaps a national basis:

> Talking of motorsport in general, not just F1, North America is the exact opposite of global—it is strictly national. This applies not only to motorsport, but also to all US sports, where they create a World Series that is, in reality, a domestic championship.

So, with some exceptions, we can see the influence of globalization—Motorsport Going Global—in many of the views expressed by these expert practitioners. Using some concepts from our earlier framework, for example, the Motorsport Value Chain, we can explore some of the issues they raise in more depth. This leads us to consider the following aspects. With *consumption*, we start with the marketplace and our experts' views on the nature and development of consumption of events through spectator live audiences, TV or other media and also their consumption of motorsport merchandize. *Supply* concerns the production of all the inputs that create a motorsport event, such as the cars and their respective technologies, the circuits and other supplies and services that allow the event to take place. Within both supply and communication with consumers *technology* remains a key driver in motorsport and we elaborate on the debate regarding the role and importance of technology in motorsport. Thereafter, we consider issues surrounding the *management* of globalizing motorsport businesses. This was not a predefined issue but one that emerged from the comments and observations of our experts. Finally, we condense all their views into a number of *visions of the future*, and elaborate on some of the potential scenarios that may describe the future of the global motorsport industry.

Consumption

Although it is widely accepted that changes in technologies relating to the supply side of motorsport are an inherent part of the industry, it is also important to recognize substantial changes in the way motorsport events are disseminated to the public at large. David Richards sees some important changes occurring with regard to the nature of media networks, which have important implications for the consumption of motorsport events:

> The most significant thing, right now, is the growth of television networks. Gone are the days when there was a limited choice of channels, with motorsport restricted to just one. As motorsport is a minority sporting activity it will, inevitably, mostly appear on dedicated sport satellite channels. We have to accept this segmentation when producing motorsport programs and look at things in a different way.

He underlines the importance of recognizing the significant differences between global motorsport events and those local or regional activities, which underpin the development of the industry and are equally important to sponsors:

> There will always be the premium sport events—Olympics, World Cup football, Wimbledon and Formula One—and premium sports will always be allocated TV time. These are global sports events that take place on an annual basis. They understandably demand premium slots on terrestrial TV, secure substantial income, and, by appearing on the main channels, take a high market share.
>
> The remainder of motorsport will need to change the way it sells itself to TV, as it will appear on specialized channels, possibly even those totally dedicated to motorsport. Here, the financial side is fixed, as there will be no license income. I expect partners will take advertising or directly sponsor these TV programs, a concept that is becoming very much the norm in America.
>
> Programming must be created in a different way, as TV advertising is becoming less and less effective, as viewers can now automatically skip the adverts. Promotional material will be built into program content either through signage, on-screen mentions or program sponsorship.
>
> The World Rally Championship, www.wrc.com, currently has 800,000 individual subscribers each month—a significant audience and a global one. This is a well-targeted and segmented community, suffering none of the wastage from a scattered approach of advertising, so allowing sponsors to approach, directly, a very interesting audience, as a result.

David underlines that just because a particular country or region has no event or driver represented in a series, this does not mean there are no opportunities for growth in consumption:

> A car manufacturer will look at one of my motorsport programs, saying "… but you don't go to my key markets". I reply, "Our communication strategy is extremely effective in reaching your target markets, even though the actual events may not take place in them."

He goes on to articulate a process of global development in consumption:

> You can prioritize three critical elements to secure national interest—a driver, a team and an event. The number-one priority is to get a driver of local significance and importance participating in a championship, then to secure a locally based team to participate and succeed. Finally, an event should be created to take place in that territory.

From a Formula One perspective, Pat Symonds is unequivocal as to the role of the driver in creating consumption. This is exemplified by the level of viewing figures in Germany during Michael Schumacher's recent reign and now the growth in Spain following the ascension of Fernando Alonso:

> Certainly there will soon be change. We need to visit a few more countries, but remember, essentially, F1 is a global television sport. We attract great interest in each country when we appear, and even more so when we use drivers from that area. F1 has grown enormously in Spain as a direct result of Alonso's success. India, a country that really has no previous interest in F1, suddenly gets an F1 driver and everyone knows about him. We clearly need to attract drivers from a wider group of nations.

Many experts agreed that it is important motorsport is enjoyable for those who actually attend as spectators, as well as those who view the events through other media. In the same way as a crowd at a football event enhances the atmosphere of a match, so the same is true in motorsport. For many, including Gian Paolo Dallara, this is a badly neglected part of the equation:

> Organizers must do more for spectators, both those who watch on television and those who attend a race. Events like Le Mans or F1 are still able to attract many thousands of spectators, but these people cannot enjoy the competition as much as they should.
> At Monza, in Italy, spectators see very little, they just hear the noise (or the sound if you prefer); in fact, they see more by watching on television. It is surprising that even in the very expensive F1 Paddock Club, guests only have a 30-minute visit into the paddock area, where they see very little and rarely meet a driver.
> In the USA, the racing fan gets just the opposite. They get close to the drivers, who are contracted to attend open autograph sessions, and fans are encouraged to get close to the cars. European organizers will have to change and think differently to satisfy spectators, and allow them to get closer to, and more involved in, the action.

The growth in spectator numbers in the USA in recent years, in drag racing and NASCAR, emphasizes this point very effectively. Accessibility is everywhere at these US events, but this approach is not currently mirrored in other areas of the world.

A further problem with the nature of consumption is the complexity sometimes created by the regulations, as Gian Paolo comments on the nature of Formula One:

> In Italy, there are several weekly racing magazines so their 400,000 readers should understand F1, but I am not sure many do. In F1 it is very hard for anyone to really understand the actual competition. All we see are the results, which fail to explain why Alonso and Schumacher are so much faster than everyone else. All the teams want to do is win races; they just don't care about entertaining the crowds.
> We simply must change our "race product," or we will lose audience and our income. These new global markets will not replace this business, as they have no

historical interest, so we have to take our motorsport product to the people, just as they do in the USA.

In NASCAR, the race cars look similar to production cars. In Europe, we have a history of racing being a technological challenge and this is the spirit behind F1. It is likely that, in emerging countries, racing with cars similar to the ones used by the spectators will be, initially at least, more attractive. What, for sure, we have to learn from motorcycle motorsport, is to have races that are often won on the last corner.

So there seems to be a developing consensus that motorsport is losing its connection with the marketplace. This has to be of serious concern for any industry, but in motorsport, it raises the question as to who the real consumer is? For David Richards, it is the consumer of automotive products that is top of the agenda in his motorsport business:

Today, and in the future, the motorsport public need to see that the car in the showroom represents, in some way, the sporting image they see on the track. If this connection is not very clear, then the money invested in motorsport has been wasted. There must be an integrated program. It is wrong to go racing without a communication program for the consumer so they can understand the relationship. Conversely, if the performance car in the showroom has no continuing and obvious motorsport link or heritage then it will not fit the customers' perception.

Supply

Our central focus throughout this book has been the motorsport industry, which includes all the elements needed to create a motorsport event but, in particular, the specialist vehicles that race on circuits, roads and other terrains. So how will the balance of the supply side change in the future? What are the key drivers for creating these changes?

From our experts, we see some distinctive and contrasting positions. David Richards is very clear that the UK-based Motorsport Valley® business community will remain at the forefront of motorsport supply, but with some changes in terms of the overall supply chain:

In future, Britain will remain the powerhouse as far as intellect and design for motorsport. However, elements of manufacturing, for example composites, will be outsourced to more efficient supply bases in other countries, then assembled here to add the value and provenance of the UK.

The Italians have a great motorsport heritage and the French try but have not proved to be very effective. It's very expensive to operate in Germany and they just don't have the right motorsport culture. I accept the Americans are good but they don't operate to the same level of sophistication as we do. Similarly, if we look at the Far East, it's no coincidence that no Japanese car manufacturer has a globally significant motorsport program based in Japan—they outsource and base them around the world.

God forbid, if Toyota had chosen to locate their Formula One team in Motorsport Valley UK—we'd all be looking for jobs by now! They would have taken Formula One by storm and dominated it for a long time to come—as it is they are paying a heavy price for their choice of location.

Peter Digby also sees the UK and the US remaining as the key sources of supply for motorsport, but he underlines some important caveats relating to labor costs:

UK and US motorsport companies may source some product from lower-cost areas, but the general servicing, assembly and customer relationships will remain where they are now.

Wherever a supplier faces a high labor content, say in carbon fibre, or a chassis for Formula Ford or Formula 3, then it should be worth setting up a manufacturing facility where costs are cheaper. Motorsport, for example, may favor Eastern Europe, but their costs and labor rates are escalating from around 20 percent to at least 40 percent of UK rates, so some of the cost advantage has already disappeared. Right now, for the lowest costs, India and China are the best. I feel China is the biggest threat or opportunity, as it has such an enormous labor resource, and is unlikely to raise its labor cost significantly for some time.

David Richards underlines this by pointing out the longer-term dangers of salary inflation in the UK motorsport industry:

Recent extraordinarily high salary awards in the UK motorsport sector cannot be sustainable. These will create a shift of certain activities, probably in commodities required, such as composites or basic machining, to less expensive areas. My original argument remains that while the intellect remains here, our dominance will still be strong, and this UK region will still be the center of excellence in global motorsport.

Gian Paolo Dallara also underlines the important difference between the labor costs of relatively simple components, which can be supplied from stock, and the need for highly agile supply chains to respond to quickly changing customer demands:

Not in the near future [will countries like China become dominant] because they currently don't have the flexibility of delivery and engineering needed for motorsport. In ten years time, this will change and we will be buying from these countries, for sure. At the moment we buy only simple components, like bearings, where we find the quality is perfectly OK.

But we need very flexible suppliers. For example, we received an order for four IRL cars on February 20 and had to deliver them four weeks later! China just could not react quickly enough for that demand, or for such a small volume.

However, others see a different picture emerging—one where the source of supply becomes irrelevant, and where technologies and knowledge are commonly accessible, available anywhere in the world. For example, Herb Fishel sees a very different story emerging to that of David Richards:

> As soon as racing products become a commodity, they can be built anywhere. At the SEMA or PRI shows, many of the products seen are manufactured globally, and not in the USA. As the global racing scene evolves, there is nothing to stop this supply base expanding quickly to embrace a wide range of countries that will be able to create their own racing series, based on these products.

Pat Symonds also recognizes the potential threat of commoditization and the emergence of new technologies and areas of production:

> Traditionally, the supplier base for global motorsport has been in the UK but there is an enormous risk of complacency here, and a danger the supplier base will move elsewhere. The UK motorsport industry relies on experienced specialists with a particular mindset, but today these skills are more globally available.
>
> In the past, you needed designers with flair and craftsmen with real ability. Today, you still need good designers, but advanced equipment now available tends to equalize the good and the less good. Manufacturing is more computerized, as are fabrication techniques. These used to be such basic skills at the very heart of building race cars, but now there are more rigid composite technologies and machining.
>
> We see US-based companies that have serviced their national amateur racing scene for so many years, becoming serious international players. They have drive that contrasts starkly with the complacency of the UK. UK motorsport companies should be worried and very aware of this and must work a damn site harder to retain their successful position.
>
> We have a fantastic supply chain here in the UK, really second to none, which should give strength and security for a long while, but you can see the impetus growing in the USA. The UK industry shouldn't just stand and watch.

Sir Jackie Stewart shares similar concerns for the motorsport industries of France and Germany and underlines that competition is operating at a national, governmental level, as well as that of individual firms:

> I worry about the future of motorsport in France and Germany. With all their resources and strength, Renault still choose to base their F1 team here in Oxfordshire and BMW of Germany chooses Switzerland with Sauber. In my racing days, Matra of France would never have done that, as the whole project was jointly owned by the government and private enterprises, but they've let such things go.
>
> For the UK to develop to its full capacity, our government has to take a stronger interest, because that's certainly what China and India will do. We will no longer be

measured against our European competitors in Italy, France or Germany. There is a now a new game with powerful new players, and we, together with our government, have to rise to that challenge.

Linked to these ideas, David Richards also sees the dissemination of local knowledge through satellite operations and moving skilled staff around the world:

> We could well create satellite operations around the world. If our client is based in China, then we may have an operation annexed to their facility for certain specific projects. So, over a long period of time, this could quietly become a significant base of operations. We will certainly be outsourcing some components to Eastern Europe, Turkey and possibly the Far East, but I still believe the hub of all our motorsport activities will remain in the UK.

In summary, we can see the experts defining a global division of labor within the supply of motorsport—based on the need to be close to market for servicing clients, the continued location of the highest value-added activity in the global centers of excellence and a growing outsourcing of those activities and supplies that can be commoditized to take advantage of cheaper cost locations.

Technology

Here again we have some contrasting views, perhaps polarized between the positions of David Richards and Herb Fishel. David is pretty unequivocal that motorsport does not provide a basis for technology development in road cars:

> No. This area [motorsport as a contribution to technology development] has now gone, it is just a perception created by the sport. The technology on road cars today is way ahead of motorsport. Formula One teams are not using any revolutionary technologies at all. They simply manage known technologies in an extraordinarily detailed way, using minutiae to fully exploit the structure of the regulations. This approach is the difference between success and failure.
>
> In fact, technology has become the bane of motorsport and has to be curtailed, as it is totally irrelevant. Technology in motorsport should either be relevant, or used to communicate to our audience so they can understand and enjoy the sport better.

In contrast, Herb Fishel sees the advancement of technology and process engineering as the one critical area where motorsport can contribute:

> There is, as yet, no measurable return from a technology, a process or a component standpoint. The really great things about building and racing a race car—the unique design approach, the rapid development, the innovative engineering, the accelerated processes—all these are the intangibles behind creating a winning solution.

Say a manufacturer invests $250 millon to $500 millon in motorsport and measures their return on the marketing value alone—just consider what could happen when that same manufacturer measures the same investment but based on new areas of return. In addition to all the marketing benefits, they also gain feedback on the development of a new hybrid powertrain, a new electronic integration control unit, a rapid manufacturing process that improves production efficiency.

Honda has always placed a high priority on the educational and competitive value that benefits its engineers through their involvement in motorsports. Many of their top executives, like Nobuhiko Kawamoto, managed motorsports programs during their early career.

Audi will be a long-term major global player. They do a great job in connecting current production and future products to their race programs. As an example, take their form of direct injection pioneered and developed for Le Mans and then put into their production cars. In the same way, they are working hard and successfully on diesels now—winning Le Mans at their first attempt with a diesel-engined car. Audi has a good blueprint showing how to connect production to race cars, which I respect.

Porsche's recent investment in the Volkswagen Audi Group (VAG) has great promise for both organizations. Such a partnership, which can take advantage of Porsche's methodology to create a different line of vehicles from a price and performance point, will be at the leading edge. I believe Porsche is on top of their game and are a long-term motorsport player.

We need to converge the thinking of those in race car design together with those in production vehicle design, where the race car embodies leading-edge automotive technology. It could be in a powertrain, body configuration, some unique handling or suspension design. If, in fact, the race car became their advanced research laboratory then the manufacturer would have invested in something that is invaluable to them in accelerating the critical product cycle.

Possibly one example where this can be seen today is in safety. Safety research is very expensive and OEM activity in this area is extremely valuable to the racing community. The extreme conditions of racing, however, provide valuable lessons for the OEMs. Drivers are now able to survive horrific incidents by virtue of this two-way safety research relationship. The FIA Foundation has used income from F1 to fund a specialized Safety Institute, led by Professor Sid Watkins, to lead in this area. Results and knowledge go back to the production world to give automotive engineers further momentum in their work.

For Pat Symonds, the real contribution is more about the ethos of motorsport rather than direct technology transfer, but he uncovers an unusual challenge in terms of getting people to move on from motorsport:

> I know, from personal experience, it's possible to put engineers through motorsport who go on to become industry leaders. The ethos of motorsport is of real value within any industry, not just automotive. Such skills may play an even more important role

as companies consolidate and grow larger with a corresponding need for more dynamic management. I'd like to think such transfers will happen, but you've got to get the engineers to agree to leave motorsport and move into industry first—and that's not easy!

He goes on to raise an important cautionary note concerning the way in which OEMs relate to motorsport:

I'm not certain motorsport will interact well as OEMs continue to globalize. There may be some movement from the engineering side, and certainly in the work ethic, but probably none in overall management. You have to imagine someone, probably not trained as a professional manager, managing a relatively small team of high-performance engineers, all incredibly motivated and working with excellent financial backing. Then try and translate that situation into a global company with, speaking bluntly, a large number of averagely motivated workers, watching every euro! This environment is so very different, hence my doubt such expertise will transfer easily.

Pat Symonds feels motorsport, potentially, misses some important opportunities relating to new technologies:

In motorsport, we have been slow in terms of tearing up the drawings and starting again. No matter what your views are on energy shortages in the future, energy will become more and more expensive. When we recently changed F1 engine rules, I was disappointed diesels were not considered more closely as diesel engines power most European OEMs' cars now.

I am keen on hybrid technology, and believe this could play an important part in our future. We are already seeing interesting regenerative braking concepts on the market but, as yet, not operating too well. This technology, while still in its infancy, is an area where motorsport could contribute to development and add an exciting new aspect to racing.

It would be fascinating to have, effectively, a small energy store on the race car to use tactically, at certain times in the race. An improved lap time, a better overtaking opportunity or a better start—whatever the choice, each would add an interesting tactical dimension. At the same time, once motorsport is involved, we will demand the solution is smaller, lighter and more powerful and so this will, usefully, help drive the OEMs in that direction.

When we speak of energy, the headline is always that a Formula One engine uses huge amounts of energy or fuel. Yet drill down below that headline, and we find that the specific energy consumption of an F1 engine is really outstanding, far better than many road cars. In F1, we seem willing to allow negative and incorrect publicity of our high fuel usage without reminding the world of our excellent energy efficiency. This has to change.

In motorsport, fuel (and energy) efficiency is something we really care about and about which we have a great deal of knowledge. For example, at Renault, we study each engine control system in all our nightly reports and de-briefs. We report, exactly, the percentage of fuel going into each control system and then assess carefully its "energy" value. We are very, very energy efficient and conscious. We simply don't publicize this aspect of our work—that's probably a mistake in today's world, as we ought to tell someone about it.

The Motorsport Valley® cluster in the UK is an important part of motorsport. It has worked so well for many years and I see no reason to alter the model. Technologies will change—for example, fabrication is less important now than composites—but they can all develop within a cluster, keeping machining and design close by, with a specialist in each area of expertise. The goal has to be to make sure this UK cluster is better than any newly emerging ones in other countries.

Pat Symonds makes some further comments, which connect with David Richards's earlier observations on the importance of "visible" technology:

On this basis, some of our current, somewhat obscure, material research is not really worth pursuing. The average spectator is not excited knowing an upright is made from a metal matrix composite, rather than titanium or steel. They can enjoy, see, hear and understand interesting aerodynamics or even advanced engine technology with engines running at over 19,000 rpm. This technology is attractive, noisy, visible and this is where we should concentrate.

Shifting technologies present threats as well as opportunities. One particular issue is where particular specialist component areas become subsumed into integrated, modular technologies in an overall drive to bring down costs. Sir Jackie Stewart raises an interesting concern here relating to the future of specialist component suppliers, such as Xtrac:

Xtrac has become an excellent company purely based on its motorsport business and a demand for that high standard of quality gearbox. I think they will need help from government to enable them to take the next big step. They need to find new ways of creating transmissions, because I think the gearbox, as we know it today, is going to be finished. In time, there will be no specialist gearbox companies, as technology moves toward becoming a powertrain, where gearbox development will be an important part of the engine program and manufacture. I have no idea why no one has yet moved in that direction but it has to happen.

Motorsport Management

A further area of comment by our experts, and one we had not anticipated, covers the role of senior management in the globalizing motorsport industry.

Pat Symonds sets out the paradox of conservative management in an innovative and high risk-taking sport:

You're making the assumption that motorsport has good management capabilities—sometimes you have to question that! History has not shown management within F1 in a particularly good light, to be honest.

There have been some F1 teams that have endured but many more that failed, as they haven't seen the future and moved strategically forward to meet it. It's very important to keep a clear lookout to see what's coming. Surprisingly, for such a dynamic sport, there's a remarkable amount of conservatism in management. Globalization presents a huge challenge to those who are conservative.

David Richards seems to agree and sees the answer in the transfer of managerial knowledge from other sectors:

The one weakness in this industry is at senior management level. More and more leading companies are employing managers from outside motorsport, so we are addressing this weakness.

As leading motorsport businesses move from their entrepreneurial stage to a more corporate level, they reach a dangerous and precarious period. If overall funding, and the industry at large, cannot sustain the next level then it will collapse. I believe we will see such a change in Formula One over the next couple of years, as the current operating scale of Formula One teams is simply unsustainable. Smaller teams, run efficiently and with the right calibre of people, will succeed—but that change will create an enormous imbalance.

However, Sir Jackie Stewart sees a potential danger in "managerialism" diluting the essence of the motorsport drive and passion for risk-taking and innovation:

We see Ron Dennis taking a lawyer from Baker McKenzie and other management skills from British Aerospace, because he feels he needs this. He can still be the figurehead but knows he needs other top-line ingredients to be successful beyond a certain level.

However, the problem is that the more you bring in such so called expertise, the further you are from employing and using the passion that is absolutely vital to this business. In my experience, such development has a generally negative effect. In this business and sport you have to demand passion, just as in the arts, where there is passion, enthusiasm and energy. This ingredient is simply not synonymous with corporate management structures.

Peter Digby is more positive about the quality of management in motorsport. He underlines the fact that change, a huge area of challenge for managers in conventional industries, is an area in which many in motorsport thrive:

Motorsport definitely attracts entrepreneurial management. Some are charismatic intuitive managers, some are "wheeler dealers" like Eddie Jordan, and even Sir

Frank Williams in his early days. We now have some excellent managers in this business that, I am confident, will rise to the globalization opportunity.

Most motorsport people enjoy change—in fact, they almost seem motivated by it! However, change per se can cause real problems as it forces through new ideas. We will have to identify individuals who have the ability, then invest in training, and push them forward to progress. As an example, Xtrac sends employees to work in our USA branch, and they come back far more experienced. We only have a small USA team so they learn to do everything—dealing with customers and suppliers, packing the truck and so on.

Peter Digby raises some interesting issues on the challenges of doing business with organizations from very different cultural backgrounds, a key aspect in the globalization of the motorsport industry:

Xtrac is currently restricted as our staff are generally inexperienced in international sourcing. We prefer to engage a UK importer or agent to source our overseas requirements rather than do it ourselves. We must change, certainly for China and India, and will have to open our minds and make more effort. We don't need a wholesale change of culture, but we do need to bring in new specialities and skills.

A further important point made by Gian Paolo Dallara is that, to develop their business, managers must not lose sight of the fact that success in competition is fundamental to motorsport. Manage costs, yes, but never forget that the fundamental need is producing product to win races:

In this business, as with any other, if you are not competitive you will be beaten anyway. At Dallara, we expect to work very hard to stay ahead. We know we must constantly build winning cars if we are to survive—if we fail to do that, then we will collapse. Every day is a new competition.

While there is currently a great deal of focus on the need to reduce costs, at the end of the day, as it has always been in motorsport, whoever makes the better car will succeed—even if it is a little more expensive.

Visions of the Future: *Motorsport Going Global*

So what do these experts see as the future of motorsport? Is it, in any way, close to our "Motorsport 2035" scenario? As we stated at the start of the book, any forecast in such a complex multi-faceted industry is likely to be wrong—but where could things be going, and who are likely to be the winners and losers in these differing scenarios?

As a first step when considering the business model of motorsport, we should reflect back to the original development of the motorsport industry in the UK. This is summarized in Figure 5.1.

Figure 5.1 **Historical Model of Motorsport Industry Development**

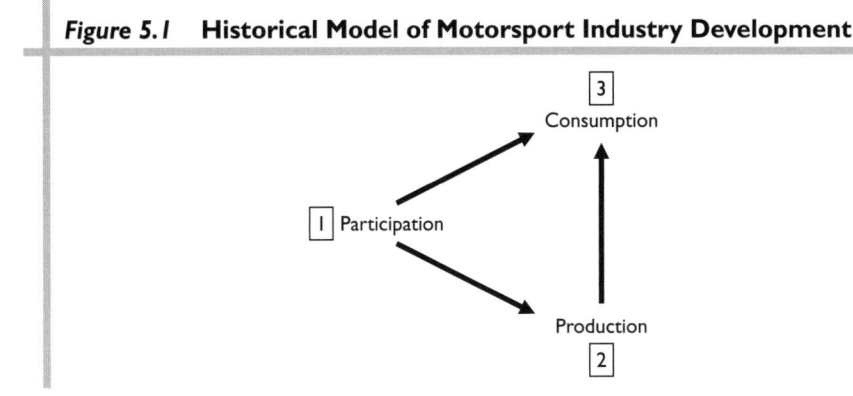

```
                            3
                        Consumption
                          ↗      ↑
                         ↗       ↑
            1 Participation      ↑
                         ↘       ↑
                          ↘      ↑
                         Production
                            2
```

In this "historical" framework, we see three core elements of motorsport—*participation* (taking part in motorsport events), *production* (producing motorsport equipment, technology and services) and *consumption* (viewing the motorsport event, or consuming motorsport-related products).

The UK motorsport industry, from the outset, was driven by the active participation of enthusiasts from whose demand developed the cottage industry of "garagistes." These very small businesses began assembling cars using modified basic and standard components, combined with bespoke engineering. This, in due course, developed consumption and an audience from publicity of racing events, which attracted growth in brand sponsorship, which in turn fed the production activities of the motorsport industry. It is interesting to note that, in their conversations, our experts develop some alternative models to the way the industry will operate in the future, reflecting the changing world of the industry. We describe these as the "consumer-led" business model and the "production-led" business model.

Motorsport Going Global: Consumer-Led Business Model

Figure 5.2 outlines our understanding of a consumer led business model.

Essentially this model attempts to illustrate the ideas put forward below by David Richards. This suggests that motorsport should be seen as a mechanism by which a wide array of products is presented to particular consumer segments. In this model, motorsport is a brand-development mechanism that allows products and services to develop their brand awareness and associations by utilizing the particular connotations associated with, and provided by, motorsport:

> Motorsport must attract the next generation and needs a younger consumer audience. If the teenagers of today become more influenced by environmental, efficiency,

Figure 5.2 **Motorsport Going Global: Consumer-Led Business Model**

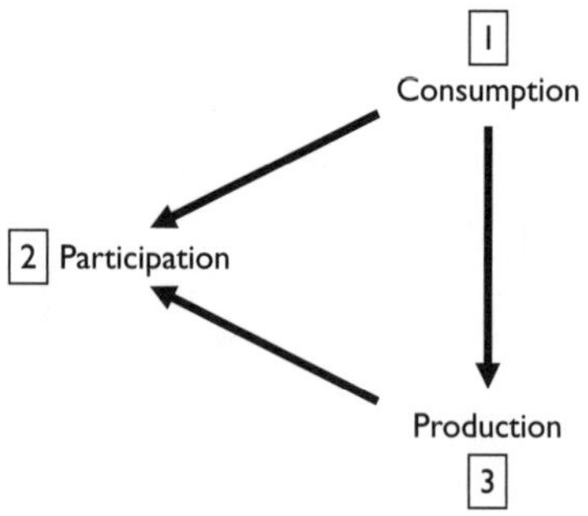

```
         [1]
     Consumption
      ↙        ↓
[2] Participation
      ↖        ↓
              Production
                [3]
```

practicality and cost issues rather than the image that motorsport delivers, then we could be on a hiding to nothing. Consequently, motorsport must be sure to retain its relevance for the future.

It is relevant to the delivery of technical feedback from cars that the public recognize. It also has relevance as entertainment, with powerful imagery, to enhance a brand image. Motorsport has to address both these issues over the next decade, or it will operate in a declining market.

Young people change their buying habits fast. As soon as car manufacturers see motorsport having no significant impact on their brand by appealing to a young age group then they will, quite rightly, move away. I am sure we will soon witness at least one major car manufacturer making a bold statement that motorsport is no longer relevant to their future plans, as they focus on leading the field on green issues. Now who that will be, we will know within the next three years.

In European motorsport, the key players are motor manufacturers, as we currently know them, whereas in American motorsport, car manufacturers have less brand significance, as it is consumer brands that are prevalent in NASCAR. This will change, in the future, because car manufacturers will look to invest less in motorsport as it becomes less relevant to them. We will have to replace their investment with non-tobacco consumer brands.

As an advertising medium, motorsport is, in reality, very expensive when compared with conventional advertising. I expect to see more brands coming into motorsport that have difficulty communicating their message, by conventional means, to the specific 18—35-year-old male consumer segment. For example, we may see more pharmaceutical brands, as this is a clearly targeted audience of theirs.

The biggest threat, in a world that communicates on a second-by-second basis, is that ideas are stimulated and spread very quickly. See how fast young people change their habits, whether buying on the Internet, in music or even on cultural issues. A Japanese 18-year-old now looks like an American or British 18-year-old. If that group becomes disillusioned by the relevance of motorsport, and changes their buying habits as a result, then motorsport will decline and the vital support from car manufacturers will dry up overnight. As a result, and to counteract this threat, we must create a sustainable business model for motorsport for the future, which does not rely on car manufacturers.

In this model, the critical issue is for motorsport businesses to be close to, and fully understand, the specific consumption segments they serve. They can then offer to "deliver" these segments to their clients. In this consumer-led framework, motorsport competes openly and directly with other sports and media as a brand-communication opportunity. The technology of the race car becomes secondary and is less important in creating revenue streams. Although, even within this model, "winning" is still vital, as the leading car and winner gain a far larger share of media exposure to benefit the sponsor's brand share. It is more likely that marketing skills, rather than technical skills, will be most critical to commercial success.

Motorsport Going Global: Production-Led Business Model

The production-led business model presents a very different scenario to that of the consumer-led model envisaged by David Richards. It is driven by those seeking to develop the motorsport industry through the creation of racing vehicles that promote and develop particular aims. Figure 5.3 summarizes the key stages of the model.

In this model, the process is initiated by the creation of particular motorsport technologies or a series (production), which then leads to participation and subsequent consumption of the ensuing events. In the expert discussions, and from our own reflections, we can distil two different mechanisms for commencing this process—one is OEM/regulation driven and the other entrepreneurial/emerging markets driven.

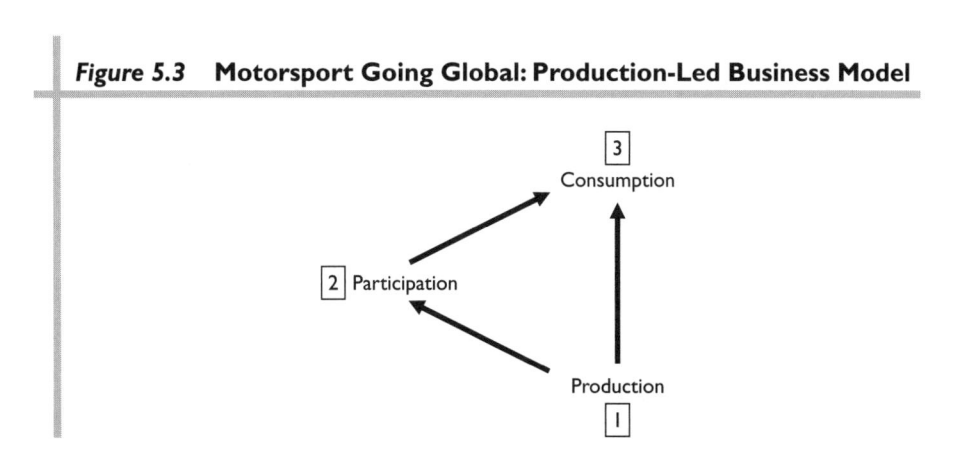

Figure 5.3 **Motorsport Going Global: Production-Led Business Model**

The OEM/Regulation-Driven Production Business Model

This version of the production model is advocated by Herb Fishel, who sees co-operation between the OEMs and motorsport regulators as a huge opportunity for the development of motorsport:

> Consider today how alliances work on an engine or transmission project. Race cars use engines and transmissions, yet there are no race car technical specifications that take full advantage of production components. Hence, the thinking behind technical specifications and sporting regulations will have to change to gain benefit from these new alliances.
>
> The real differentiator will be successfully combining revolutionary race car technical specifications and sporting regulations. This is where established OEMs can be a guiding light, with, for example, their advanced technology and leading-edge systems in electronics and valve train. This is where OEMs have to think ahead and figure out just what their particular advantage from motorsport is going to be.
>
> My point is that, over the next ten years, preferably sooner, there has to be a more tangible and meaningful connection between the race car and the production car to justify ongoing investment by the automotive manufacturers.

At this point, Herb seems to be very close to the position advocated by David Richards in seeking close relevance between the cars raced and those promoted in the showroom. Herb moves on, though, to press home a different case.

> The US domestic motorsport scene is currently one of marketing bliss. It's strictly about delivering TV numbers, about how many people watched the telecast. It's focussed on the personal attraction of the race drivers, not around car manufacturers' brands. Based on fierce competition for brand identity in a global market, automobile manufacturers will soon demand equal billing with the driver and the other consumer sponsors.
>
> The single most important question is whether the future for OEMs in motorsport is more about promoting leading-edge technology or brand awareness.
>
> Remember that reality for the OEM today is all about new products, and that these will have a lower volume and a shorter life cycle. These new products will come through research and the work of innovative and creative designers.
>
> There has never been a greater opportunity for every aspect of the racing industry to change itself, to find new business models and secure new leadership. It has to realize the old system only existed and survived for as long as it did because it was allowed to, not because it was giving so much back to its racing partners and supporters that they just couldn't do without it.

A recent example of this business model in operation is the successful development of the Audi R10 diesel Le Mans Prototype car, which won the 2006

Le Mans event and has gone on to dominate the US ALMS series. From a marketing perspective, Audi were keen to develop their diesel brand and leading technology. They also needed to remove some of the negative perceptions surrounding diesel engines, which included poor performance.

By demonstrating the effectiveness of their diesel race car, Audi have begun to achieve their marketing aims (and we expect further developments incorporating bio-diesel very soon). They did so by working closely with the regulators, in this case the ACO, which owns the Le Mans race, to secure flexibility in the regulations that allowed them to successfully compete with this new technology. In the technology discussion earlier, we noted Pat Symonds's view that F1 should have considered diesel technology more seriously when drawing up their 2008 engine regulations. Furthermore, IRL and the world-famous Indy 500 race, in the USA, will be using ethanol fuel from 2007.

Herb Fishel makes a strong case for this new opportunity to use technical regulations to stimulate OEM demand for motorsport to satisfy their new technical and product requirements, which are a far cry from those of just a decade ago.

Entrepreneurial/Emerging Market-Driven Production Business Model

In addition to the OEM model put forward by Herb, there is a further model recently observed by one of our authors during recent visits to China. It still starts with the production side, but the intention is to initiate and develop the participation and consumerism necessary in the (fast-) emerging motorsport markets in the BRIC countries. These are the four nations that, it is said, will dominate the world economy in the next few decades—Brazil, Russia, India and China (hence BRIC). In most of these countries, with vast populations, there is no motorsport heritage of any size, if any at all.

Stimulus has to be created. This has led to the identification of an entrepreneurial opportunity to develop a business concept around the creation of race events, using funding sources from recently established OEMs and other investors. New entrepreneurs see an opportunity to develop car and consumer goods brand share in these new fast-growing consumer markets by using motorsport.

We must remind ourselves that, at present, there are just four racetracks in mainland China compared to 19 on the small island of the UK or 1,400 in the USA. China has a "middle-class" consumer income group—nearly twice the size of the entire UK population or half of the USA population—which has yet to discover any interest in motorsport. Car ownership is very new to many—they are still first-generation car owners with no heritage in cars, never having been exposed to their use in a sporting capacity. Such a market presents unique challenges to meet the clear opportunities presented.

To draw out this different aspect of the production model we use two contrasting case studies.

Case 1: CF2000

Using a design first developed in the USA, the CF2000 concept involves the production of a series of Formula Ford 2000-equivalent spec cars using components (and engines) entirely produced in China at very low cost, with further models covering 1600 and F3 to follow as demand increases.

The unique approach is to make no charge to drivers, as the local market has yet to appreciate any significant value in motorsport. These drivers will be selected by the series owners, thus delivering a full grid at a series of regional events. The series will find an overall Chinese driver as champion, and then help him or her to move up to higher formulae on an international level.

Funding initially comes from investors, who plan to deliver TV coverage of the series, as the appetite from the public for more TV sport is growing fast in China. The series will gain income from advertisers, who recognize the value of the TV branding opportunity, and from being associated with an internationally successful young Chinese driver.

The approach therefore starts with a production concept, with funding from investors, who seek to create participation and consumption in motorsport as a basis for generating future returns.

Case 2: VW Polo Racing

Close to the Tianma circuit, near Shanghai, sits one of the most impressive race shops in the world. While the buildings and activity may not be as "high-tech" as Western teams, this enterprise is just three years old. What is truly impressive is the sheer scale of this new operation, created to service an under-developed market. We see a fleet of over 40 race-prepared VW Polos (alongside, at least, ten rally VW Polos), using a dedicated FIA-approved circuit on which to train and improve competitors for the national series.

Support provided to the business owner from local industry and OEMs is exceptional but necessary to rapidly create demand in a new market. This whole facility is aimed at serving and developing future demand for motorsport participation in China.

The business model here is encouraged and driven by the cars and spare parts made available by the OEM, together with supplies of tires and fuel, with others paying to advertise their products on the cars. Drivers pay a very low fee (by Western standards) for the whole series, which is televised, and so further income is gained from sponsors, as in the European model.

The objective is to rapidly stimulate participation and, in this case, to make a return through a very low-cost operating base made possible by the OEM support. From the OEM perspective this is a relatively inexpensive promotional mechanism to present the performance aspects of their brand to the valuable and fast-growing Chinese market.

Motorsport Going Global: The Opportunity

What is particularly interesting in both these scenarios is that this huge market is untapped at present, with no existing successful business models as yet created upon which to grow. Both have harnessed entrepreneurial spirit and some advice but adapted this to serve the local market.

We need to consider the substantial potential for the industry in China, Russia and India, where virtually no motorsport of any commercial significance currently exists. These markets will demand true global management skills if they are to deliver any benefit to companies currently based in the developed motorsport world.

In a recent global survey from Deloitte Touche Tohmatsu, we learn that, using purchasing power parity exchange rates, China is the world's second largest economy, behind the USA—with India in fourth place. China and India, for example, are the two fastest-growing cell phone markets. China already sells 350 million cell phones but expects this to reach 600 million in the next three years. India has grown from just over 5 million six years ago to over 55 million cell phones today.

Major companies expect significant sales growth in these markets in the next three years, far more so than in the established Western markets. Why would motorsport not follow this trend? As an example, China is already the world's third largest auto market behind the USA and Japan, yet only produced their first car just 20 years ago.

We are long past the idea that a company can simply seize a sales opportunity in these countries—by doing so they fail to realize anywhere near the full potential. Instead, unconstrained by previous investments in capital equipment, processes and technology, emerging markets can serve as stimulus for innovations across the global marketplace. Customers in these markets are becoming more sophisticated and demanding, expecting products to meet their specific needs.

Companies that vary their product offer to meet these local demands rather than simply trying to sell their European or US models at differing prices are proving to be more successful in gaining greater market share and achieving higher margins. This approach will be a greater challenge, however, for small and medium-sized companies, such as some of those in motorsport, as it requires financial and human resources to achieve success.

In 2004, GDP per capita using purchasing power parity was roughly $39,800 in the USA, $7,940 in Brazil, $5,890 in China and $3,120 in India. Most motorsport products will be beyond the means of all but the most affluent consumers but the number of these is growing fast. In China, there are over 100 million "middle-class" earners already—and Moscow is now the world's most expensive city.

Renault have created their Logan car to be sold at $6,000 and Tata Motors of India has a goal to sell a car at $2,200 to serve India's middle class. These companies have rethought every aspect of the product, manufacturing, sourcing and delivery to reduce costs to attract the market. Tata plans to use a combination of steel and plastic, and industrial adhesives alongside traditional nuts and bolts. Motorsport may have to reconsider its traditional products to make race and rally cars available at acceptable prices.

Motorsport companies will need to decide how they should enter these markets and at what level—perhaps targeting, first of all, the affluent sector, which is eager to consume "Western" products, often at higher prices. Major global manufacturers are conducting R&D in these emerging markets and designing products locally. This trend is bound to affect the motorsport business community in time, as engineering knowledge and skills grow—alongside the increased wealth such work will bring. There is a strong manufacturing tradition in many of these markets, with a highly educated, and growing, technical labor force. In India, 450,000 new students enrolled at engineering schools in 2005—an increase of 200,000 from 2004. It may be possible for motorsport to gain entry to the market by linking to these universities and colleges—and capturing the interest of young engineers early in their careers.

It seems clear that motorsport companies are facing the greatest opportunity in their history, with vast numbers of new consumers buying cars. In the words of Richard Petty, the famous race car driver from NASCAR in the USA, "Racing starts right after you sell the second car!" On this basis, these new markets will soon create eager and willing new customers for the product that is motorsport. Demand will be satisfied either by existing motorsport companies or, failing that, by newly created local ones.

Summary

The motorsport industry is clearly entering a period of unique opportunity with the development of these new, fast-growing markets, from which to buy or in which to sell. This opportunity is coupled with a global requirement for the development of alternative, more efficient and less carbon-intensive automotive technologies.

These two combine to provide an immense opportunity for the industry to pioneer and lead major change in both the automotive and consumer brand areas. The industry is standing on the threshold of an opportunity the like of which it has never encountered before. Can it seize this or will it stumble?

We present here three different business models for how motorsport may develop in the future. As in most cases in business what actually happens will be, in all likelihood, a hybrid of these. However the core essentials have to be there, for without participation, production and consumption there will be no motorsport industry, global or otherwise.

It is this opportunity and challenge that faces constructors, suppliers, regulators, marketers and the myriad of other businesses that makes up the global motorsport industry of today. Time will tell which of these highly competitive companies, and national industries, forces itself to the front of the global starting grid, and gains the checkered winner's flag of *Motorsport Going Global*.

APPENDIX

Global Motorsport Disciplines and Series

Table A1 **Motorsport Disciplines**

Motorsport Discipline	*Description*
Autocross	A circuit is laid out on a grass surface and cars compete individually against the clock.
Autotest	Cars compete alone, against the clock. The driver must negotiate a set route between obstacles, usually plastic pylons or cones. The surface is normally smooth, often tarmac.
Car racing	Cars compete against each other on purpose-built tarmac circuits like Silverstone or Brands Hatch.
Drag racing	The aim of drag racing is to cover a quarter mile (440 yards) as fast as possible from a standing start on tarmac.
Hillclimb and sprint	Two similar branches of motorsport. Each event takes place on a smooth sealed surface over a measured distance against the clock.
Karting	Karting is similar to car racing in that competitors race each other on purpose-built tarmac circuits. Karts are, however, smaller and more basic in appearance than racing cars.
Off road	This category includes a variety of events, including Trials, Competitive Safaris and Team Recovery Competitions, all of which take place over difficult terrain and call for specialist vehicles, normally with four-wheel drive.

(Continued)

Table A1 (Continued)

Motorsport Discipline	Description
Rallycross	Rallycross takes place at permanent venues, using a mixture of surfaced and off-road sections. Cars compete against the clock in qualification heats, then against each other in finals.
Rallying	The most popular form of motorsport in Britain, perhaps because it involves ordinary-looking cars. It involves two people working together: a driver and a co-driver or navigator, and the cars normally run at one-minute intervals, competing against the clock rather than directly against each other.
Trials	The competitive element in a trial is the ability to climb gradients of varying difficulty. Each trial has several observed sections on private ground.

Source: Adapted from: http://www.msauk.org/

Table A2 Motorsport Series Acronyms

Acronym	Meaning
F1	Formula One
WRC	World Rally Championship
A1GP	A1 Grand Prix
NASCAR	National Association of Stock Car Auto Racing
CART	Championship Auto Racing League
IRL	Indy Racing League
GP2	Grand Prix 2
WSR	World Series by Renault
SuperGT	Japanese GT Championship
DTM	Deutsche Tourenwagen Masters
ALMS	American Le Mans Series (American-based)
LMS	Le Mans Series (European-based)
Grand-Am	Grand-American (Sportscar Series)
WTCC	World Touring Car Championship
BTCC	British Touring Car Championship
F3	Formula 3
FR	Formula Renault
F2000	Formula Ford 2000
FF	Formula Ford

Source: MRA (2003)

Bibliography

Accenture (2002) *MSA Strategy Implementation Plan – MSA Board Review and Sign Off*, Accenture, London.

AMRA (2002) *Motorsport Education and Skills Development Strategy*, AMRA, Yorkshire, UK.

Angus, T. (2001a) "Networks of Knowledge: The Case of the Italian Motorsport Industry," unpublished PhD Thesis, University of Birmingham, UK.

Angus, T. (2001b) *The Italian Motorsport Industry and its Relationship to Motorsport Valley: Executive Summary*, MIA, Warwickshire, UK.

Aston, B., and Williams, M. (1996) *Playing to Win: The Success of UK Motorsport Engineering*, Institute of Public Policy Research, London.

Beck-Burridge, M., and Walton, J. (1999) *Britain's Winning Formula: Achieving World Leadership in Motorsport*, Macmillan Business, London.

Competition Commission (2001) *Octagon Motorsport Limited and British Racing Drivers Club Limited: A report on the merger situation*, Competition Commission, London.

DTI (nd) "Harnessing a World Class Industry Cluster to Gain Competitive Advantage for the UK: Motorsport Engineering and Services," DTI, London.

Foreign and Commonwealth Office (2000) *Britain's Motorsport Industry*, FCO, London.

GHK (2003) "The Economic Impact of the British Grand Prix at Silverstone," GHK, London and Birmingham, UK commissioned by EMDA.

Henry, N. (1999) *In Pole Position: Motor Sport Success in Britain and Its Lessons for the World's Motor Industry*, Euromotor Reports, London.

Henry, N., and Pinch, S. (1997) *A Regional Formula for Success? The innovative region of Motor Sport Valley*, ESRC Executive Summary Report, University of Birmingham, UK.

Henry, N., and Pinch, S. (2000) "Spatialising Knowledge: placing the knowledge community of Motor Sport Valley," *Geoforum*, Vol. 31, No. 2, pp. 191–208.

Henry, N., and Pinch, S. (2001) "Neo-Marshallian Nodes, Institutional Thickness and Britain's 'Motorsport Valley': thick or thin?," *Environment and Planning A*, 33, pp. 1169–83.

Henry, N., Pinch, S., and Russell, S. (1996) "In Pole Position? Untraded interdependencies, new industrial spaces and the British Motorsport Industry," *Area*, Vol. 28, pp. 25–36.

InContext Inc (1999a) *The Economic Impact of the Network Q Rally of Great Britain*, InContext Inc, Washington D.C.

InContext Inc (1999b) *The Economic Impact of the European Grand Prix*, InContext Inc, Washington D.C.

MIA (2000) *Promoting the Valley: Motorsport Pathfinder Report* MIA, Warwickshire, UK.

MIA (2001a) *Executive Summary – The National Survey of Motorsport Engineering and Services 2000*, MIA, Warwickshire, UK.

MIA (2001b) *Full Report – The National Survey of Motorsport Engineering and Services 2000* MIA, Warwickshire, UK.

MIA (2002) *Motorsport Valley Cluster Development: Industry Commitment Project*, MIA, Warwickshire, UK.

MIA (2006) *A China Market Overview and Opportunities Study for the Motorsport Industry*, MIA, Warwickshire, UK.

Mintel (2001) *British Motorsport Market Research Report*, Mintel, London.

Monitor Group (2002) *Developing a Winning Strategy for the Motorsport Cluster*, Monitor Group, London.

MRA (Motorsport Research Associates) (2002) *USA Motorsport Market Research Report,* MIA, Warwickshire, UK.

MRA (Motorsport Research Associates) (2003a) *A Study into the UK Motorsport and Performance Engineering Cluster*, DTI, London.

MRA (Motorsport Research Associates) (2003b) *Motorsport Northamptonshire: A Study of the Motorsport Industry in Northamptonshire*, Northamptonshire Partnership, Northampton.

MRA (Motorsport Research Associates) (2004a) *French Motorsport Market Research Report,* MIA, Warwickshire, UK.

MRA (Motorsport Research Associates) (2004b) *Italian Motorsport Market Research Report,* MIA, Warwickshire, UK.

MRA (Motorsport Research Associates) (2004c) *German Motorsport Market Research Report*, MIA, Warwickshire, UK.

MRA (Motorsport Research Associates) (2005) *Motorsport CSW: A Study of the Motorsport Industry in Coventry, Solihull and Warwickshire*, CSW Partnership, Coventry, UK.

MRA (Motorsport Research Associates) (2006) *High Performance Engineering in Northamptonshire,* Invest Northamptonshire, Northampton, UK.

Oxfordshire Motorsport Forum (1999) *Oxfordshire Motorsport Forum 1999*, Heart of England TEC/Oxford Innovation. Oxford.

Performance Racing Industry, various issues, http://www.performanceracing.com/content/?id=2634&MenuID=2634

Bibliography

Pinch, S., and Henry, N. (1999a) "Discursive Aspects of Technological Innovation: the case of the British motor-sport industry," *Environment and Planning A*, Vol. 31, pp. 665–82.

Pinch, S., and Henry, N. (1999b) "Paul Krugman's Geographical Economics, Industrial Clustering and the British Motor Sport Industry," *Regional Studies*, Vol. 33, No. 9, pp. 815–27.

Raven, C., and Pinch, S. (2000) "The British Kit Car Industry," *European Urban and Regional Studies* Vol. 10, No.4, pp. 343–54.

Russell, S. (1994) *In Pole Position: A Study of the British Motor Sport Industry*, unpublished dissertation, University of Southampton, UK.

Trade Partners UK (2000) *Motorsport in Malaysia: A Report by the British High Commission*, British High Commission, Malaysia.

UK Trade and Investment (2005) *The Brazilian Motor Racing Market*, UKTI Automotive Sector Team, Brazil.

In addition a variety of websites and trade press sources were utilized including:

www.autosport.com
www.grandprix.com

Autosport Magazine
Performance Racing Industry Magazine
Race Engine Technology Magazine
Racecar Engineering Magazine
RaceTech Magazine

INDEX

A1GP, 12, 21, 28, 49, 51, 52, 53, 109, 110, 111, 112, 120, 125, 128
Accidents, 36, 64, 144
ADR, 52
Advanced Composites, 52
AER, 26
Aerodynamics, xiii, 4, 27, 34, 52, 67, 76, 79, 82, 86, 146
Aerospace, 52, 84, 85, 86, 89–90
Aerolab, 76, 79
Alcon, 27, 38, 52
Alfa Romeo, 24, 34, 54, 74, 75, 79, 80
Alliances, *see* Collaboration
ALMS, 24, 39, 153
Alonso, 101, 104, 133, 139
Amateurs, 1, 6, 7, 24, 42, 142
AMG, 26, 66, 70, 72
  see also Mercedes Benz
Andretti Green, 4
AP Racing, 27, 52, 79
ARCA, 37
Arden, 52
Argentina, 24, 27
  see also South America
Arrington Manufacturing, 26, 42
ASCAR, 25
Asia, xiv, 23, 54, 62, 126
Asiatech, 85
ASM, 90
Aston Martin, 51, 54, 133
ATR, 78
ATS, 65, 74
Audi, 24, 26, 34, 39, 64, 66, 67, 82, 135, 144, 152–3
  Audi Sport, 26, 67, 69
Audience, 2, 5, 7, 11, 28, 96, 138, 139, 143, 149, 150
  see also Consumption: Spectators
Australia, x, 13, 14, 15, 18, 24, 28, 32, 54, 79, 96–101, 115, 116, 136
Autocross, 42, 157
Autosport International Show, 53
Autotest, 157

B3 Technologies, 4, 52
Bahrain, *see* Gulf Region
BAR, 54–5, 58, 59, 133
BBS, 67
Bedford Aerodrome, 53
Benchmarking, xvi, 10, 13–20, 32, 34, 96, 117, 136
Benetton, 55, 84, 85, 133
Bentley, 47, 51, 66, 67
Berta, 2, 106, 107, 108
Biesse, 79
Birel, 79
BMW, xiii, 21, 23, 25, 34, 54, 57, 64, 65, 66, 67, 69, 70, 87, 103, 128, 129, 133, 142
Bosch, 67
Brabham, 38, 48, 66, 98
Brakes, 27, 42, 51–2, 76, 79, 86, 89
Brand, xi, 7, 18, 28, 34, 95, 106, 149, 150, 151, 152, 153, 154
Brazil, *see* South America
Bridgestone, 61, 86
British Rally Championship, 53
British Touring Car Championship, *see* BTCC
Brembo, 27, 76, 78–9, 83
BTCC, 24, 30, 31, 53, 54, 71, 102, 103, 119
Bugatti, 74, 83, 135
Buick, 36

Canada, 28, 45, 111
Car racing, 157
Carlin, 52
Carbon Industrie, 86, 89
CART, 1, 22, 23, 25, 33, 39, 41, 43, 44, 48, 49, 57
Caterham, 51
CF2000, 154
Champcar, 2, 22, 25, 48, 98, 109, 110, 125
Chambon, 86, 89
Championships, 1
Chas Howe, 39

163

Index

Chase Competition, 39
Chassis, 12, 21–5, 33, 49, 57, 58, 59, 61, 63, 65, 66, 67, 75, 79, 81, 82, 84, 85, 87, 99, 100, 103, 106, 107, 113, 114, 119, 129, 141
Chevrolet, 21
Chevron, 42, 48
China, xi, xiv, 14–15, 18, 20, 32, 98, 117, 124–7, 131, 134, 135, 141, 142, 143, 148, 153–4, 155
Chrysler, 87
Circuit racing, 99, 101, 102, 104, 105, 106, 107, 110, 112, 113, 115, 121, 122, 123, 124, 126, 127, 128, 129–30
Circuits, x, 1, 4, 5, 6, 12, 15–17, 28–30, 32, 34, 36–7, 43, 52–53, 62, 63, 70, 71, 74–5, 90, 91, 92, 94, 97, 98, 105, 106, 108, 118, 120–1, 122, 125, 127–8, 136, 140, 154
    Bahrain International, 120, 121, 124
    Bathurst, 97
    Brands Hatch, 53
    Brno, 127–8, 130
    Brooklands, 47
    Cadwell Park, 53
    Castle Combe, 54
    Daytona, 4, 37; Daytona 500, 28, 134
    Goodwood, 4, 52, 53, 54,
    Hockenheim, xii, 4
    Indianapolis, 4, 36, 37, 43; Indianapolis 500, 28, 36, 38, 44, 134, 153
    Istanbul Park, 123
    Johor Bahru, 117
    Losail, 121
    Maroubra, 97
    Monterrey, 110
    Most, 127
    Oulton Park, 53
    Pau Street Circuit, 91
    Paul Ricard, 86, 92
    Phillip Island, 97
    Sepang, 118
    Shah Alam, 117
    Silverstone, xii, 4, 52, 53, 75
    Snetterton, 53
    suppliers/operators/designers, 43, 52–3, 71
    Suzuka, 62
    Twin Ring, 62
    see also Le Mans; Metrics of global motorsport industry; Oval racing venue
Citroen, 20, 21, 25, 34, 85, 86, 87, 90, 92

Club/Club racing, 6, 7, 9, 24, 27, 31, 49, 52, 54, 71, 80, 81, 92, 104, 118, 120
Cluster, *see* Motorsport Valley®
Clutch, 67, 70
Collaboration, 48, 63, 76, 79, 119, 152
Coloni, 75, 79
Comer, 79
Coming through the field, xi, 14, 18, 32, 116, 117–31
Communication, 135, 137, 138, 140, 143, 150, 151
Competition, 35
Competition licenses, *see* Licenses
Competitors, 27, 28, 37, 38, 106, 113, 115
Competitive racing, 1
Component suppliers, 5, 70, 76, 146
Components, 47, 65, 78, 81, 99, 103, 141, 152
Composites, 22, 52, 67, 78, 113, 114, 141, 142
Conoco, 42
Constructors, x–xi, 2, 4, 6, 21–5, 27, 33, 34, 39, 41, 45–6, 47, 48, 49–51, 57, 59, 69, 73–4, 75, 78, 83, 84, 85, 87, 156
    suppliers, 2, 4, 25–31, 41–2, 51–2, 59, 61, 70, 78–9, 89–90
    see also Global chassis constructor
Consultancy, 4, 52, 79, 81, 82, 90
Consumer-led motorsport, xi, 149–51
Consumption, x–xi, xv, 5, 12, 18–20, 31, 44, 53–4, 62, 72, 81, 91–2, 116, 137–40, 149, 151, 154, 156
    see also Audience; Distribution; Domestic television viewing; Media coverage; Regional television viewing; Spectator
Cooperation, *see* Collaboration
Cooper, 38, 42, 47–8, 98
Cosworth, 4, 25, 26, 36, 38, 41, 51, 66, 133
    DFV, 38, 133
Courage, 24, 85, 86, 87, 90
Crawford, 39
Crespi, 107, 108
CRG, 79
CTG, 52
Czech Republic, xi, 13, 14, 17, 20, 21, 117, 127–30

Daimler Chrysler, xiii
Dale Earnhardt, 22
Dallara, 4, 23, 24, 34, 38, 39, 49, 58, 75, 76, 78, 79, 81–2, 83, 99, 103, 107, 134, 135, 148

Index

DAMS, 4
Danielson Engineering, 87, 90
Darraq, 83
Darrian, 51
Defense industry, 113
Definition, *see* Motorsport, definition of
Delage, 83
Delahaye, 83
Desert raids, 30
DeTomaso, 74, 80
Distribution, xv, 4–5, 30, 39, 43–4, 53, 71, 81, 91, 113
   see also Consumption; Media coverage
Dome, 23, 58, 59, 63
Domestic, 22, 24, 25, 26, 27, 33, 34, 38, 39, 41, 42, 43, 45, 47, 55, 57, 58, 59, 61, 63, 73, 78, 81, 85, 89, 90, 94, 95, 99, 100, 101, 106, 107, 114, 115, 122, 125, 126–7, 128, 129, 136
   see also Local; National
Domestic events/series, 62, 63, 72, 80, 90, 110, 118
   see also Events
Domestic supply chain, 42, 43, 99, 113, 116
   see also Supply chain
Domestic television viewing, 30, 53–4, 62, 91
Doran, 39
DPR, 52
Drag racing, 1, 29, 33, 36, 37, 38, 39, 41, 42, 43, 44, 45, 52, 71, 72, 99, 110, 120, 121, 122, 124, 134, 139, 157
Drivers, 6, 7, 9, 37, 47, 48, 49, 85, 98, 105, 106, 107, 108, 126, 138–9, 144, 152, 154
   see also Supporting service industries (driver management)
Drivetrain component, 27
DTM, 23–4, 26, 67, 70, 71, 72, 80, 128
Dubai, *see* Gulf Region
Duesenberg, 36
Durango, 79

Economics, x, 1, 33, 36
EDL, 26, 52
Eibach, 67
Elan Motorsport Technologies, 23
Electronics, 27, 34, 67, 100, 103
Elf, 90
Engineers, 7, 48, 98, 118, 144

Engineering, 1, 37, 39, 48, 67, 85, 86, 122, 127, 129, 143, 144, 149, 156
Engines, 4, 22, 25, 26, 27, 34, 36, 38, 41–2, 47, 49, 51, 57, 58, 59, 61, 62, 63, 65–6, 67, 69, 70, 72, 79, 82, 83, 87, 89, 92, 99, 103, 106, 107, 119, 145, 146, 152
Enthusiast, *see* Amateur
Entrants (licenced), 4, 6, 27–8, 42, 52, 59, 61, 70–1, 79–80, 102
Entrepreneurs, xi, 48, 73, 112, 147, 151, 153–4, 155
   see also Specialists
ERA, 47
Europe, 23, 24, 25, 27, 32, 35, 36, 37, 38, 39, 41, 42, 43, 45, 51, 52, 53, 54, 58, 61, 70, 71, 76, 78, 80, 91, 100, 105, 106, 107, 110, 113, 134, 135, 136, 139, 140, 150, 154, 155
Events, 1, 4, 6, 7, 10, 12, 15, 27, 28, 29, 31, 42–3, 52–3, 62, 71, 80–1, 90–1, 94, 99, 138
   BMP/SRO, 4
   BRSCC, 4
   Marquee events, 28
   750 Motor club, 48
   see also Domestic events; Events' suppliers; Promoters
Events' suppliers, 4, 28–30, 45, 53, 62, 71, 81, 91
   see also Circuits (suppliers/operators/ designers); Suppliers
Evernham, 22, 26, 42
Experience, 9, 142, 148
Expertise, 26, 27, 34, 49, 66, 95, 113, 114, 116, 146, 147
   see also Specialists

F1, *see* Formula One
F3, *see* Formula 3
FABCAR, 39
Ferrari, xii, 2, 18, 20, 34, 47, 48, 54, 67, 69, 74, 75, 78, 79, 80, 81, 83, 95, 99, 100, 103, 119, 128, 133
Ferrea, 107
FF1600, 24
FIA, *see* Regulation (FIA)
FIA GT, 24, 52, 53, 54, 79, 90, 91, 120, 123, 125, 128
Fiat, 74, 75, 79, 105, 123, 124
Fiks, 129
Fondmetal Technologies, 4, 76, 79, 83
Ford, 21, 25, 36, 38, 49, 54, 97, 98, 101, 110, 112, 133
   Performance Vehicles, 24

Index

Formula 2, 63, 64
Formula 2000, 23,
Formula 3 (500cc formula), 23, 24, 26, 27, 47, 49, 52, 53, 58, 59, 61, 63, 70, 81–2, 87, 90, 99, 101, 103, 105, 106, 123, 126, 141, 154
Formula 3000, 23, 48, 89, 99
Formula 4000, 99, 101
Formula Arabia, 121
Formula Atlantic, 23, 25
Formula BMW, 23, 26, 86, 87, 102, 119, 121
Formula Campus, 87, 126
Formula Ford, 1, 23, 26, 86, 87, 99, 100, 101, 113, 141, 154
Formula Mazda, 23
Formula Nippon, 6, 49, 61, 63, 99
Formula One, 1, 5, 9, 11, 12, 18, 21, 22, 23, 25, 26, 27, 28, 30, 31, 33, 34, 38, 39, 42, 43, 44, 48, 49, 51, 52, 53, 54, 55, 56, 57, 58, 59, 61, 62, 63, 64, 65, 66, 67, 69, 70, 71, 72, 75, 76, 78, 79, 82, 84, 85, 86, 87, 89, 90, 91, 97, 98, 99, 101, 105, 112, 118, 119, 120, 122, 123, 125, 131, 133, 134, 136, 137, 138, 139, 140, 141, 142, 143, 144, 145, 147, 159
Formula Palmer Audi, 4
Formula Renault, 23, 105, 107, 110, 119, 126
Formula Vee, 99, 100, 101, 110, 113
Founders, 21
France, x, 4, 5, 13, 20, 21, 23, 24, 25, 26, 27, 28, 32, 33, 34, 51, 54, 57, 70–1, 80, 83–93, 95, 103, 113, 136, 140, 142, 143
Frontrunners, x, 13, 14, 17, 18, 20, 21, 23, 25, 28, 32, 33–95
Fuel and lubricants, 4, 42, 90, 154
Funding, 7, 9, 112, 119, 153, 154
see also Sponsorship

G-Force, 23
Garagistes, 47, 149
Gearbox, 4, 27, 89–90, 99, 103, 106, 146
Germany, x, xii, 5, 13, 15, 17, 18, 27, 28, 32, 33, 34, 47, 54, 55, 57, 58, 59, 63, 64–73, 78, 80, 83, 87, 91, 92, 95, 103, 128, 129, 136, 139, 140, 142, 143
Ginetta, 51
Global chassis constructor, x–xi, 21–5, 33, 34, 45–6, 48, 55, 63, 93, 94, 95, 96, 101, 115, 127
Global impact/presence, 28, 48, 58, 66, 73–4
Global metrics, *see* Metrics of global motorsport industry
Global motorsport business, 1–32

Global motorsport industry, x, 10–20, 31–2, 52, 66, 96, 108, 111, 113, 133, 137, 156
Global motorsport value chain, *see* Motorsport value chain
Global series/events, 7, 9, 17–18, 33, 34, 46, 49, 55, 63, 81, 94, 95, 96, 101, 112, 117, 120, 122, 123, 125, 127, 130, 131, 137–8
Global starting grid, x–xi, 1, 10, 13, 14, 18, 20, 31, 32, 33, 34, 95, 96, 100, 108, 116, 117, 119, 124, 131, 156
Global supply chain, 24, 34, 48, 70, 113, 114
Globalization, x, 45, 66, 116, 131, 132, 134–7, 145, 147, 148
Gordini, 83
Governance, 20
Governing body, *see* Regulation
Government, 36, 83–4, 85, 92, 100, 106, 118, 119, 124, 130, 142–3, 146
GM, 26, 97, 98, 105, 133–4
Goodyear, 4, 42
GP2, xv, 23, 26, 27, 52, 53, 61, 70, 76, 79, 82, 86, 89, 90, 120, 123, 134
GPC Squadra Corse, 79
Grand-Am, 24, 39, 110
Grand Prix, 28, 31, 37, 38, 42, 43, 47, 48, 62, 66, 71, 74, 80, 81, 83, 84, 90, 91, 98, 101, 105, 112, 118, 119, 123, 125, 131
Grass roots, 7, 9, 31, 45, 52, 73, 80, 81, 106, 107, 108, 122, 124, 127
GT car/series, 1, 51, 53, 54, 80, 90, 91, 99, 100, 101, 102, 103, 113, 125, 128, 129
Gulf Region, xi, 14, 17, 32, 117, 120–2

Hendrick, 4, 22, 26, 39, 42
Hess, 39
Hewland, 27, 51
Hillclimb, 29, 52, 97, 157
Historic car/racing, 1, 43, 53, 54, 71, 80, 91, 109, 110, 113
History, x, 7, 28, 33, 34, 35–6, 46–8, 49, 52, 56–7, 64, 74–5, 83–5, 96–100, 101–3, 105–7, 109–10, 111–14, 117–19, 120–2, 123–4, 127–9, 140
HKS, 58
Holden Special Vehicles, 24, 97, 98, 99, 101
Hollinger, 99, 101
Honda, 2, 21, 24, 25, 34, 38, 41, 54, 55, 56, 57, 58, 59, 61, 62, 144
Hoosier, 42
HPD, 25, 41, 57, 58
HSCC, 54

Index

HSR, 43
Huger, 89
Hybrid car/technology, xii, 144, 145
Hyundai, 21, 102

IAME, 79
IASA, 107
Ilmor Engineering, 25, 26, 38, 41, 51, 58, 66, 67, 70
Illegal street racing, 37
Impact Racing, 42
India, 14, 32, 131, 136, 139, 141, 142, 148, 153, 155
Individuals, 7, 27, 52, 70, 90, 138
Indy Car, 36, 37, 38
  see also IRL
Indy Racing League, see IRL
Infiniti Pro Series, 23, 25, 75, 81
  see also Indy Car
Interdependency, 6, 7
  see also Relationships
Internal combustion engine, xii
International, 24, 25, 26, 27, 33, 34, 59, 63, 64, 66, 76, 78, 79, 80, 83, 91, 98, 99, 100, 101, 102, 103, 106, 107, 109, 112, 116, 118, 119, 121, 122, 124, 127, 129, 142
International Rally Championship, 79, 112
International series, 27, 105, 154
Internationalization, 12, 27
Interrelationships, see Relationships
Investment, see Funding
IRL, 1, 22–3, 25, 33, 39, 41, 43, 44, 51, 53, 57, 58, 62, 81, 82, 134, 141, 153
  see also Indy car
Italsystem, 79
Italy, x, xv, 2, 5, 13, 17, 18, 20, 21, 23, 24, 26, 27, 28, 32, 33, 34, 38, 47, 49, 54, 55, 58, 63, 67, 69, 70–1, 73–83, 92, 95, 99, 103, 106, 107, 134, 135, 136, 139, 140, 143
Isuzu, 103

Jacer, 99, 100
Jaguar, 107
Japan, 13, 14, 22, 23, 25, 26, 32, 33, 34, 42, 55–64, 65, 86, 95, 99, 100, 103, 135–6, 140, 150, 155
Jericho, 27, 42
Joint venture, see Collaboration
Jolly Kart, 79
JPX, 89

Karting, x, 1, 12, 28, 29, 30, 34, 42, 52, 62, 76, 79, 80, 81, 83, 99, 102, 105, 106, 107, 108, 118, 119, 122, 124, 126, 157

Knowledge, xv, 7, 9, 101, 119, 127, 135, 142, 143, 156
Kurtis, 37

Labor, 111, 116, 141, 143, 156
Lamborghini, 74, 80
Lancia, 34, 74, 75, 80
Le Mans, 24, 28, 54, 58, 64, 66, 85, 86, 87, 90, 91, 92, 134, 139, 144, 152–3
Le Mans Company, 58, 59
Legislation, 25
  see also Regulation
Licenses, x, 10, 12, 21, 27, 52, 70, 80, 90, 105
  see also Entrants (licenced)
Ligier, 84, 85, 87
Lister, 51, 52
LMS, 52, 53, 79, 90, 123
Local, 7, 9, 24, 25, 81, 99, 124, 138, 143
  see also Domestic; National
Local governing body, 39
Lola, 2, 21, 22, 23, 24, 37, 38, 39, 48, 49, 51, 57, 58
Long Beach Champcar, 28
Lotus, 38, 48, 51, 57, 84, 113, 119, 126
LRP, 41

Mader, 26, 86, 89
Magneti Marelli, 76
Mahle, 67
Malaysia, xi, 14, 18, 117–20
Mallock, 48
Management, 144–5
Management of globalizing motorsport, 137, 146–8, 155
Manor Motorsport, 4, 52
Mapping the motorsport industry, 10, 31–2
March, 48
Marenello Kart, 79
Market penetration, 33, 41
Market share, 37, 79, 95, 138, 155
Marketing, see Supporting service industries (marketing)
Maserati, 34, 74, 75, 80
Matra, 84
McLaren, 21, 48, 57, 66, 67, 134
Mechanics, 7
Mecachrome, 26, 85–6, 89
Media coverage, 4–5, 6, 7, 30
  internet, 4
  press/print, 4, 30, 44, 71, 81, 91, 139;
    Haymarket, 4, 30, 53
  radio, 4
  television, 4, 6, 30, 31, 43–4, 53–4, 71, 72, 81, 91–2, 137, 138, 139, 154
  see also Consumption; Distribution

Index

MEL, 25, 26
Menard, 33
Mercedes Benz, 24, 25, 26, 34, 64, 66, 67, 70, 72, 128
   Mercedes High Performance Engineering, 51, 67, 70
Merchandise, 44, 45, 137
Metrics of global motorsport industry, x, 10–12, 13–20, 31, 32, 34–5, 47, 55, 57, 63, 65, 73–4, 83, 84, 94, 96, 97, 101, 102, 104, 108–9, 111–12, 114, 117, 118, 120, 121, 122, 123, 124, 125, 127, 128, 130
   chassis constructors, 17–18
   circuits as indicators, 11, 12, 15–17
   Gross Domestic Product (GDP), 10, 12, 14–15
   participation indicators, 10
   spectators, 10, 15
   viewing figures, 18–20
Mexico, x–xi, 14, 15, 28, 45, 108–11, 115
MG–Rover, 24, 54
Michelin, 86, 89
Midfield, x–xi, 14, 17, 18, 32, 95, 96–116
Miller, 36
Minardi, 75, 79, 83
Minister, 26
MIRA, 4, 52
Mitsubishi, 2, 21, 25, 34, 57, 58, 59, 87, 99, 103, 105, 106, 107, 110, 113, 121, 129
MMSP, 103
Motec, 100, 101
Moto-cross, 1
Motorcycles, 1, 56, 62, 63, 81, 101, 104, 118, 119
Motorsport, definition of, 1–2, 6, 10, 31
Motorsport going global, xvi, 132–156
Motorsport management, *see* Management of globalizing motorsport
Motorsport value chain, xv, 2–6, 7, 10, 12, 20–5, 32, 34, 38–44, 49–54, 59–62, 67–72, 76–81, 86–92, 131, 137
   key drivers of, 7–9
Motorsport Valley®, xiii, 34, 48–9, 55, 57, 58, 74, 85, 98, 134, 140–1, 146
Motul, 90
M-Sport, 25, 49
Mugen, 26, 58, 61, 62–63
Mygale, 23, 51, 86, 87, 113

NASCAR, xiii, xv, 2, 5, 6, 12, 22, 26, 27, 28, 30, 31, 34, 37, 38, 39, 41, 42, 43, 44–5, 51, 52, 53, 57, 58, 106, 109–10, 111, 113, 134, 139, 150, 156

Busch Series, 28, 42, 44, 110
Craftman Truck, 28, 41, 42, 44, 110
Nextel Cup, 28, 41, 42, 43, 44, 58
National, 23, 24, 32, 33, 62, 73, 78, 96, 101, 102, 103, 105, 106, 107, 116, 129, 131, 137, 142
see also Domestic; Local
National events/series, 7, 9, 27, 31, 53, 58, 66, 71, 81, 90, 99, 103, 105, 106, 110, 111, 112, 113, 115, 123, 124, 128, 154
National media coverage, 30
National motorsport industries, 10
National sport authority, 39
Neil Brown, 26
Network, 2, 47, 48, 65, 73, 78, 92, 95
NHRA, 37, 38, 39, 43
Niche, 32, 45, 51, 113, 114, 116, 131
NISMO, 58
Nissan, 24, 57, 58, 103, 107, 112, 113
   World Series, 79
Nogaro Technologies, 90
Non-regulated, *see* Supporting services industry (driver experiences)
NTechnology, 79, 83

OEM, xi, 2, 7, 21, 23, 24, 25, 34, 36, 38, 49, 54, 57, 58, 59, 61, 62, 63, 64, 73, 80, 82, 83, 84, 85, 86, 91, 92, 94–5, 97, 98, 99, 102, 103, 105, 106, 110, 112, 113, 126–7, 129, 135, 144, 145, 151–3, 154
Off-roading, 28, 30, 41, 42, 69, 90, 99, 101, 102, 103, 104, 105, 106, 107, 109, 110, 111, 112, 113, 114, 115, 120, 157
Offenhauser engine, 36, 38
Ombra, 78
One-make, xiv, 6, 21, 22, 23, 25, 63, 70, 75, 81, 86, 89, 91, 99, 102, 103, 105, 106, 107, 110, 113, 121, 123, 124, 126, 128–9
Opel, 24, 26, 66, 67, 70
Open wheel car, 1
ORAL Engineering, 26
ORECA, 4, 87
OSCA, 74
Osella, 76, 79
Oval racing/venue, 11, 15, 30, 33, 35, 36–8, 39, 41, 42, 43, 44, 45, 99, 100, 110, 115
see also Circuits
Owners, 21, 24, 48

Panhard, 83
Panoz, 4, 22–23, 33, 39, 49
Paris–Dakar, 28, 69, 87, 90, 91, 92

Index

Participant/participation, xi, xiv, xv, 10, 31, 32, 44, 45, 52, 55, 58, 63, 91–2, 94, 99,118, 119, 121, 126, 131, 135, 138, 149, 151, 153, 154, 156
Partnerships, 57, 58, 63, 95
Paul Belmondo, 90
Pavesi, 79
PCR, 79
Penske–Jaspar, 26, 42
Performance engineering, 79, 114, 119, 129, 130
Performance Friction, 42
Pescarolo, 24, 90
Petronas, 118, 119
Peugeot, 20, 21, 24, 25, 34, 83, 84–5, 86, 87, 89, 90, 92, 105, 110, 129
PFC, 33
Pi Research, 38
Picchio, 24, 76, 79
Pipo Moteur, 25, 89
Pirelli, 4, 83
Pistons, 67
PMIA, 33
Porsche, 34, 37, 54, 65, 66, 67, 69, 70, 78, 99, 100, 103, 119, 126, 128, 135, 144
Pratt & Miller, 39
Prema Powerteam, 79
Price, 135, 144, 155
Prodrive, 2, 21, 24, 25, 26, 51, 52, 54–5, 58, 59, 90, 98, 103, 133, 135, 136
Production, xv, 31, 32, 47, 149, 156
Production-based sportscar/racing, 24, 36–7, 41
Production-led business, xi, 151–4
Professional, 42, 66, 105
Promoters, 1, 53, 71, 81, 91, 135
 see also Events
Prost, 85, 87
Proton, 118, 119
PSA, 129
Purpose-built/designed, 41, 83

Qatar, *see* Gulf Region

Race track, *see* Circuits
Racers, *see* Drivers
Racing, 1, 27, 28, 80
Racing teams, 4, 6, 27, 138, 139
Radical, 51
Raikkonen Robertson Racing, 52
Rallying (rallycross), 1, 4, 27, 30, 42, 43, 52, 54, 57, 58, 65, 66, 78, 80, 83, 84, 85, 86, 90, 92, 99, 101, 102, 103, 104, 105, 106, 107, 109, 110, 112, 113, 114, 115, 118, 120, 121, 122, 123, 124, 126, 127, 128, 129, 133, 158
 see also World Rally Championship

Ralt, 81, 98
Ray, 23, 51
RCR, 22
Rear engine car, 47–8
Reggiani, 79
Regional, 22, 23–4, 32, 38, 96, 102, 115, 129
Regional series, 27, 28, 31, 53, 105, 111, 112, 113, 119, 137–8, 154
Regional sporting authority, 39
Regional television viewing, 30
Regulation, xv, 5, 11, 20, 24, 27, 38–9, 41, 45, 49, 51, 67, 78, 87, 106, 107, 113, 135, 139, 143, 151–3, 156
 ACCUS, 5, 20, 39
 ACO, 5
 CBA, 105
 CIK, 5
 CSAI, 5, 20, 78, 80
 DMSB, 67
 FFSA, 87, 90, 91–92
 FIA, 5, 12, 20, 25, 28, 39, 49, 59, 67, 78, 87, 144, 154
 FIM, 5
 JAF, 59
 MSA, 20, 49, 52
 safety regulation, 5
 SCCA, 5
 see also Legislation
Relationships, 2, 6, 72
Renault, xiii, 4, 23, 24, 25, 34, 57, 65, 70, 83, 84, 85, 86, 87, 89, 90, 91, 102, 105, 106, 110, 133, 136, 142, 145, 155
 World Series, 75, 82, 90
Reputation, 28
Reynard, 23, 81, 98
Rial, 65
Ricardo, 4, 27, 51, 52, 90, 129
Riley, 23, 39
RML, 21, 24, 51, 52
Road racing, 35–6, 37, 39, 42, 61, 70, 97, 106, 109, 127
Rondeau, 85
Roush, 2, 22, 33, 41
Russia, 14, 32, 131, 135, 136, 153, 155

Sabelt, 79, 83
Sachs, 67, 70
SADEV, 4, 27, 89
Safety, *see* Regulation
Safety equipment, 42, 70, 79, 144
Sainz Performance, 107
Saloon championship/car/series, 23, 24, 27, 34, 39, 41, 42, 58, 62, 66, 72, 78, 80, 89, 97, 99, 101, 102, 103, 105, 106, 107, 108, 110, 113, 121, 123–4, 128–9

Sanctioning, *see* Regulation
SARD, 59
Sardou Group, 90
Sauber, 17, 66, 67, 70, 119, 142
Saulnier, 90
Scale, 10, 12, 78
SCCA, 37, 39
Schnitzer, 26
Schubel, 103
Schumacher, xii, 69, 71, 72, 133, 139
Scope, 10, 12, 20, 78
Scott, 23
SCSA, 27
Scuderia Italia, 79
SEAT, 21, 24, 102, 103, 104, 123, 124
Semi-professional, 42
Simpson, 42
Single-seat, 1, 2, 21, 22, 23, 24, 25, 26, 33, 34, 36, 37, 38, 39, 43, 48, 49, 51, 52, 58, 61, 62, 64, 65, 70, 75, 78, 79, 81–2, 86, 87, 89, 90, 98, 99, 100, 101, 103, 105, 106, 107, 108, 110, 113, 114, 119, 121, 123, 126, 128, 129
Skills, 7, 9, 111, 142, 144, 151, 156
Skoda, 21, 128–30
SLC, 23
SNBE, 87
SODEMO, 89
Solution F, 87, 89, 90
South Africa, x–xi, 14, 32, 111–15, 116, 136
South America, x–xi, 14, 15, 23, 32, 104–8, 115, 136, 153, 155
  see also Argentina
SPA composites, 52
Spain, x–xi, 14, 17, 18, 21, 27, 54, 101–4, 136, 139
Sparco, 79, 83
Specialists, 21, 48, 61, 64, 65, 66, 73, 75, 76, 83, 84, 85, 92, 103, 106, 113, 119, 120, 127, 129, 136, 142, 146
  see also Expertise
Spectators, x, 6, 10, 31, 36, 38, 39, 44, 45, 54, 62, 72, 90, 99, 104, 105, 106, 137, 139, 140, 146
  see also Audience; Consumption; Metrics of global motorsport industry
Spectrum, 99, 100, 101
Spiess, 26
Sponsorship, xv, 5, 6, 11, 20, 27, 36, 38, 39, 42, 45, 49, 59, 69, 79, 80, 87, 119, 138, 149, 151, 152, 154
  tobacco, 5, 7, 85, 150
  see also Funding
Sports Compact, 1

Sportscar, 1, 34, 51, 52, 58, 59, 62, 64, 65, 66, 67, 69, 70, 72, 75, 78, 80, 83, 84, 85, 86, 90, 91, 114
Sprint cars, 39, 41, 99, 121, 158
Staircase of talent, 7
Stockcar, 25, 26–7, 38, 39, 105, 106
Stanguellini, 74
Stewart Grand Prix, 133
Subaru, 21, 25, 34, 54, 57, 58, 59, 62, 99, 103, 105, 106, 107, 113, 129, 133
Super Aguri, 21, 59
SuperGT series, 59, 61, 62, 63
Superperformance/Hi-tech Automotive Group, 113
Supertourisme, 24, 89, 90, 91
Suppliers/supply, 2, 4, 6, 22, 23, 78, 83, 106, 107, 113, 135, 136, 137, 140–3, 156
Supply chain, 1, 5, 6, 27, 31, 48, 51, 70, 71, 73, 78, 85, 86, 87, 89, 90, 92, 99, 103, 106, 107, 110, 111, 113, 142
Supporting services industry, 5, 6, 20–1, 39, 49, 59, 69, 78, 87
  catering, 4, 30
  driver experiences, 39, 52
  driver management, 6, 20, 49, 69, 78, 87; CSS Stellar, 21; IMG, 21, 39
  finance, 5, 49
  freight, 5
  hospitality, 4, 21, 30
  insurance, 5, 6, 20, 49
  legal, 5, 20
  logistics, 5, 20, 34, 78
  market research, 5
  marketing, 5, 20, 37, 38, 39, 45, 49, 69, 78, 87, 101, 151, 153, 156
  media, 20
  personnel management/HR, 5, 49
  racing schools, 5, 20, 39, 49, 59, 87, 120
  see also Sponsorship
Surtees, 48
Suspension, 67, 70
Sustainability of business systems, 6
Suzuki, 21, 56, 59, 61, 86, 99
SVRA, 43
Swift, 25
Switzerland, 17, 66, 67, 70, 86, 89, 142
SWOT analysis, 34, 45, 46, 55, 56, 63, 64, 72–3, 82, 92, 93, 96, 100, 103, 107, 108, 110–1, 114, 117, 119, 120, 122, 124, 126, 127, 129

Talbot, 83
Tatuus, 2, 34, 49, 75, 79, 83
Tauranac, 98
TC2000/TC3000, 24, 106, 107

Index

Technology/technological, xi, xiv, xv, 6, 33, 38, 45, 54, 55, 85, 86, 99, 100, 106, 118, 119, 127, 134, 137, 140, 142, 143–6, 151, 152, 153, 154, 155, 156
Team Ghinzani, 79
Teams, *see* Racing teams
Tex, 27, 42
Tires, 4, 42, 61, 79, 86, 154
TOMS, 58
Tony Kart, 79
Torro Rosso, 79
Total, 90
Touring cars, 1, 2, 54, 110, 119, 126
Toyota, 22, 24, 25, 34, 38, 41, 57, 58, 59, 61, 62, 65, 66, 67, 69, 70, 82, 86, 95, 99, 103, 112, 113, 141
Tracks, *see* Circuits
Training, 48, 78, 105, 118, 148, 154
Trans Am, 113
Transmissions, 22, 34, 42, 51, 89–90, 134, 152
TRD, 25, 26, 57, 58
Trials, 158
Triple 8, 24, 98
Trophee Andros Ice Racing Series, 90, 91
Truck racing, 105–6
Trulli, 79
Turkey, xi, 14, 18, 27, 117, 122–4, 143
TVR, 51
TWR, 24
Tyrrell, 48, 84

UK, x, xv, 2, 4, 13, 14, 15, 17, 20, 21, 22, 23, 24, 25, 26, 27, 28, 30, 31, 32, 33–4, 36, 38, 39, 41, 45, 45–56, 57, 58, 59, 61, 63, 65, 66, 67, 70–1, 73, 75, 78, 80, 81, 84, 85, 87, 90, 91, 92, 94, 95, 97–8, 99, 100, 101, 103, 105, 113, 114, 119, 135, 136, 140, 141, 142–3, 146, 148, 149, 150, 153
Universities, 52, 129, 156
    Cranfield, 52, 133
USA, x, xv, 2, 4, 13, 14, 15, 17, 18, 20, 22, 23, 24, 25, 26, 27, 28, 29, 30, 31, 32, 33, 34–6, 49, 51, 54, 55, 57, 58, 62, 63, 67, 75, 76, 80, 86, 94, 95, 99, 100, 106, 107, 109, 110, 111, 113, 114, 134, 135, 136, 137, 138, 139, 140, 141, 142, 148, 150, 153, 155, 156
USAC, 39

V8 engine, 26–7, 42, 113
V8 Supercar, 24, 27, 53, 54, 97, 98, 99, 101, 112, 120, 122, 125
    Bathurst 1000, 28, 97
VAG, 66, 67, 104, 129, 144
Value chain, *see* Motorsport value chain
Value creation, 9
Value for money, 38, 43
Valvoline, 42
Van Diemen, 23, 24, 38, 51, 99, 113, 129
Vanwall, 48
VARA, 43
Vauxhall, 24
Vega, 79
Venue, *see* Circuits
Viper, 87, 99
Visions of the future, xi, 137, 148–56
Volvo, 24
Vortex, 79
VW, 69, 105, 106, 110, 112, 113, 122, 124, 126, 129, 154

Watson, 37
Wheels, 67
Westfield, 51
Williams, 21, 48, 57, 59, 84, 98, 133
Willwood, 42
Wind tunnel, xiii, 76, 79, 107
World Rally Championship, 6, 9, 11, 12, 18, 21, 25, 27, 28, 30, 31, 33, 34, 39, 43, 48, 49, 51, 52, 53, 54, 58, 59, 62, 69, 70, 71, 79, 80, 85, 86, 87, 89, 90, 92, 98, 101, 105, 109, 111, 123, 124, 126, 128, 134, 129
    see also Rallying
World Touring Car Championship, xv, 12, 21, 28, 49, 52, 53, 75, 80, 81, 86, 102, 103, 109, 111, 123, 128
World Wars I and II, 36, 37, 38, 46–7, 64, 66, 74, 83, 97
WRC, *see* World Rally Championship
WTTC, *see* World Touring Car Championship

Xtrac, 4, 27, 38, 51, 134, 146, 148

Zakspeed, 65
Zytek, 21, 24, 26, 51